Mental Lives

B

Mental Lives

Case Studies in Cognition

Edited by

Ruth Campbell

BLACKWELL
Oxford UK & Cambridge USA

Copyright © Basil Blackwell Ltd 1992

First published 1992

Blackwell Publishers
108 Cowley Road
Oxford OX4 1JF
UK

Three Cambridge Center
Cambridge, Massachusetts 02142
USA

British Library Cataloguing in Publication Data
A CIP catalogue record for this book is available from the British Library.

Library of Congress Cataloging-in-Publication Data
Mental lives: case studies in cognition/edited by Ruth Campbell.
    p. cm.
Includes bibliographical references and index.
ISBN 0–631–17504–0 (alk. paper). — ISBN 0–631–17505–9 (pbk.: alk. pbk.)
1. Cognition disorders—Case studies. I. Campbell, Ruth, 1944–
[DNLM: 1. Cognition Disorders—case studies. WM 40 M5492]
RC394.C64M46 1992
616.8—dc20
DNLM/DLC
for Library of Congress   91–33162
                                                                                      CIP

Typeset in 10 on 12pt Sabon by TecSet Ltd, Wallington, Surrey
Printed in Great Britain by T. J. Press Ltd, Padstow, Cornwall

This book is printed on acid-free paper

Contents

Contributors   vii

Introduction: *Ruth Campbell*   1

1 The girl who liked to shout in church: *Simon Baron-Cohen*   11

2 More than meets the eye: *Linda Pring*   24

3 Visual thoughts: *Barbara Dodd and Judith Murphy*   47

4 When language is a problem: *M. Gopnik*   61

5 Developmental verbal dyspraxia: a longitudinal case study: 84
   Joy Stackhouse

6 Developmental reading and writing impairment: *Maggie*   99
   Snowling and Nata Goulandris

7 Deaf to the meaning of words: *Sue Franklin and David*   118
   Howard

8 The write stuff: a case of acquired spelling disorder: 134
   Janice Kay

9 The two-legged apple: *Jennie Powell and Jules Davidoff*   150

10 The smiling giraffe: an illustration of a visual memory dis- 161
   order: *M. Jane Riddoch and Glyn W. Humphreys*

vi *Contents*

11 Drawing without meaning?: dissociations in the graphic per- 178
    formance of an agnosic artist: *Sue Franklin, Peter van
    Sommers and David Howard*

12 Developmental memory impairment: faces and patterns: 199
    Christine M. Temple

13 Face to face: interpreting a case of developmental proso- 216
    pagnosia: *Ruth Campbell*

14 Transient global amnesia: *John R. Hodges* 237

15 Adult commissurotomy: separating the left from the right 255
    side of the brain: *Dahlia W. Zaidel*

Glossary 276

Author index 281

Patient index 286

Subject index 288

Contributors

Simon Baron-Cohen studied human sciences at New College, Oxford, before working as a teacher in a special unit for children with autism. Following this, he carried out his doctoral research at the MRC Cognitive Development Unit in London. He has held lectureships in psychology at University College London and is currently a lecturer at the Institute of Psychiatry, London.

Ruth Campbell's PhD thesis (1979) was on cerebral lateralization and faces. She is particularly interested in the distinctions between linguistic and non-linguistic cognitive processes and for this reason has made a special study of lip reading in neurological patients with and without speech problems. She is Professor of Psychology at Goldsmiths' College, London University.

Jules Davidoff is Senior Lecturer in Psychology at the National Hospital's College of Speech Sciences, London. Previously, he taught and conducted research at the universities of Edinburgh, London, Oxford and Wales. His research aims to provide theoretical descriptions of perception by analysing its impairment after brain damage.

Barbara Dodd is Professor of Speech Pathology at the Department of Hearing at the University of Queensland. She initially trained as a speech pathologist in Sydney, then worked at the MRC Developmental Psychology Unit in London, gaining a PhD in linguistics. Her research focuses on disordered phonology.

Sue Franklin originally qualified as a speech therapist and worked for many years with neurological patients. She now works as a lecturer in the Psychology Department at the University of York. Her research focuses particularly on the types of auditory comprehension impairments which may follow brain damage.

Myrna Gopnik is Professor in the Department of Linguistics at McGill University, Montreal, Canada. Her interests in psycholinguistics are wide, but recently the focus of discussion and debate has been her work on child language disorders.

Nata Goulandris is a research psychologist at the National Hospital's College of Speech Sciences, London. She is also a course tutor for teachers of children with specific learning difficulties.

John R. Hodges qualified in general medicine and psychiatry at the London Hospital in 1975. He then entered neurology and held the posts of registrar and clinical lecturer in Oxford. He obtained an MD for work on transient global amnesia in 1988 and was awarded an MRC Travelling Fellowship in neuropsychology, which he spent at the University of California at San Diego, 1988–89. Since his appointment as University Lecturer/Consultant Neurologist at Cambridge University he has continued to pursue research into memory, language and dementia.

David Howard lectures in neuropsychology at Birkbeck College, London University. He is a qualified speech therapist, and his research has centred on applying models from cognitive psychology to the understanding of acquired disorders of language, reading and short-term memory.

Glyn W. Humphreys is Professor of Cognitive Psychology at the University of Birmingham, having formerly been Professor of Psychology at Birkbeck College, London University. He is interested in visual cognition, cognitive neuropsychology and neural network modelling. He has written/edited six books, and published papers on a range of topics, from aspects of skilled reading to neural network models of cognition and the effects of brain damage on vision and action. He is editor of the *Quarterly Journal of Experimental Psychology*, and sits on the board of three other major journals.

Janice Kay studied at the Applied Psychology Unit, Cambridge. She has developed a battery for the diagnosis of language deficits in aphasia funded by the MRC and has lectured in cognitive neuropsychology at York University. She moved recently to Exeter, where she holds a Wellcome University Award.

Judith Murphy has a Masters degree in Speech Therapy and currently works as a speech pathologist with hearing impaired children for the Queensland Education Department, and as a part-time lecturer at the Department of Speech and Hearing.

Jennie Powell is a speech and language therapist specializing in adult neurological impairment. She obtained an MSc in Human Communication from the City University, London and is currently undertaking postgraduate research in the field of cognitive neuropsychology at the University College of Swansea.

Linda Pring studied at the University of Newcastle and later at Birkbeck College, London University. She has worked for the Medical Research Council, and in 1984 joined the Psychology Department at Goldsmiths' College, London University, where she is now a senior lecturer.

M. Jane Riddoch is a lecturer in psychology at Birmingham University. Her main research interests concern the study of the processes involved in normal visual perception and cognition. This includes the detailed study of individuals in whom the normal processes of perception and cognition have broken down resulting in disorders such as agnosia, attentional problems, apraxia and working memory problems.

Maggie Snowling is Principal of the National Hospital's College of Speech Sciences, London, and Honorary Research Fellow in the Department of Psychology, University College London. She has been actively involved in research on specific reading difficulties for more than ten years and, as a clinical psychologist, has been involved with their assessment and educational management. She is the author of *Dyslexia: a Cognitive Development Perspective* and the editor of *Children's Written Language Difficulties*.

Peter van Sommers is currently Associate Professor in the School of Behavioural Sciences at Macquarie University, Sydney, Australia. He has an MA from the University of Melbourne and a PhD from Harvard. His research monograph *Drawing and Cognition* appeared in 1984. He has published on the history of writing systems as well as on artists and brain impairment. He is about to take up a visiting appointment in the School of Design at the University of Technology, Sydney, to work on visual aesthetics.

Joy Stackhouse, after qualifying as a speech therapist, studied psychology at Birkbeck College, London University, and was then awarded a PhD from University College London for research into children's speech, reading and spelling difficulties. Formerly Head of the School of Speech Therapy at Birmingham Polytechnic, she is now a senior lecturer at the National Hospital's College of Speech Sciences, London.

Christine M. Temple has degrees from the universities of St Andrews, California, and Oxford. Her doctoral thesis was on developmental dyslexia. Following a research fellowship at University College, Oxford, she was appointed lecturer in psychology at the University of London in 1985. In 1990 she became Professor of Psychology at the University of Essex and is Director of the Developmental Neuropsychology Unit there. In 1989 she was the youngest scientist in the UK to receive a Wolfson Foundation Research award.

Dahlia W. Zaidel is a neuropsychologist who obtained her BA degree in psychology from Queen's College in New York, and her PhD in cognitive psychology from the University of California, Los Angeles (UCLA). Her scientific introduction to brain–behaviour relations came from working with Roger W. Sperry at Caltech, Pasadena, California, on the first group of split-brain patients with complete surgical section of the commissures connecting the left and right hemispheres of the brain.

Introduction

Ruth Campbell

This book is concerned with particular aspects of the minds and behaviour of particular people. They are exceptional people in one way or another; usually they are exceptional in the sense that they lack a faculty that most of the rest of us have – sight or hearing, reading skill or the ability to recognize faces. But in this context of inability, some show surprising abilities.

The primary aim of the book is to gain a clear picture of what *exactly* might be amiss in the mind of, say, the child who cannot learn to read, or the man who cannot understand speech but can read. There are all sorts of professional answers to the question 'what is wrong here?' The educationist might say 'poor teaching', the neurologist 'a lesion in the region of the left angular gyrus', but here are the answers that psychologists have given. Some of them are detailed exhaustive explorations, some are much less detailed. This is largely a realistic reflection of the relationship between the investigator and the case subject. Some of these people have been seen only once or twice for psychological study, others a great deal more often.

Psychological explanations can sometimes exasperate a reader. Often they seem nothing other than re-labellings (just as medical explanations can seem to be). The writers of the chapters you read here have tried as far as possible to drive their explanations with some force. It might be important for a professional neuropsychologist to know that Mr X has 'surface dyslexia' and 'short-term memory loss' but what does such labelling tell us? Where psychological explanations work best is where they can give a clear, precise picture of the nature of the disturbed function and its implications for other aspects of mental life. In addition, in considering brain function, such explanations need to fit or extend what is known about how particular brain systems work at the physiological and the anatomical level.

One thing that these sorts of explanation cannot do directly is suggest how best to improve impaired function. Where someone has very impaired vision, which is the best move: to increase the power of visual aids to support the impaired function, or to try to find ways around the deficit, by looking for alternative ways to achieve the goal of relatively normal life? Exactly the same problem presents itself when brain damage or functional damage, like dyslexia, is identified. The answer may not be particularly clear and the theory and practice of remediation is a goal which this book has in mind in many places but which is not actively engaged except in one or two cases. But hints are dropped throughout: in general, where it is clear that a function is well and truly absent there seems little point in restoring it or trying to put a 'normal' function in its place. Instead, particular idiosyncratic, 'sideways' strategies might do the trick. But such absolute evidence is rare; far more often we see some function more or less compromised, or delayed in development, or transient in its appearance. Here, the deficit or cognitive oddness must be placed in the wider frame of a description of all the other cognitive abilities, strategies, skills that the person shows in order to make a best guess concerning the next step.

Single case studies

Every one of the chapters presented here describes a particular individual (occasionally more than one) with something 'abnormal' in the way they think, perceive, read, speak or remember. Normality is a concept experimental psychologists apply to the relationship between an individual and the comparison population. We are each unique and every reader will, I am sure, find some aspects of each of the cases described here to fit their own experience. You might be 'bad with faces' or perhaps had 'glue ear' as a child and remember problems at school associated with it. Perhaps you have a relative who had a stroke, or know from your own experience how head injury can change mental function. Why should the particular cases reported here be more important? What do they tell us about *normal cognitive function*?

If you came to psychology through reading any of Freud's accounts of various psychopathologies you will be aware of at least one reason for single case study. This is that it can give a clearly focused, prototypical account of a particular dynamic development in mental life. This is one of the weaknesses of Freud's approach in the eyes of many experimental psychologists; the generality of such insights is problematic without any concomitant knowledge of the range of 'normal' behaviour. The experimental psychological approach is concerned in part with defining *statistical* abnormality; that is, behaviour that is out of range of that of a group of matched control subjects. So one aspect of these reports is that they set their descriptions in the context of the usual, general, way of doing things. They emphasize the specificity of the problem, the identification of a precise component in the mental machine which is not working, in the context of how most people usually do things. This means the focus in these chapters is different from that, for instance, of Sacks's series of neurological case studies *The Man who Mistook his Wife for a Hat* (1986). The writers of the chapters in this book have one eye on the case they are describing, the other on its implications for the normal range of behaviour.

Implications for normal function

How can this two-eyed technique avoid double vision? There is a set of assumptions and inferences that underlie the use of case-study techniques in relation to the understanding of normal cognitive processes. These serve to focus the investigator's vision closely and to give a depth to these studies that can go beyond general insights into human frailty and diversity. The most important assumption is that mental faculties are componential. That is, the mind is conceived of as a *set* of separate, independent 'modules' (Fodor, 1983) rather than a general purpose machine. Thus, localized brain damage need not cause a diminution of general mental capacity, and generally does not do so. Even some apparently general aspects of mental life such as attention, memory and control of the task in hand are not particularly sensitive indicators of the degree or extent of brain damage. That is, these aspects themselves may be considered part of the mental machinery and can be *independently* impaired by lesions in different cortical regions.

So, when something goes wrong and a faculty formerly present is lost or derailed, the simplest assumption is often the most useful: this is that the faculty has been damaged or become isolated from the rest of the mental machine. The diagnosis applied is akin to that of the motor mechanic, who will quickly point to a faulty transmission system by systematic tests of different functions, or an electrical failure by locating the blown fuse (note that in this latter case the electrical component can still work, but has become isolated from the machine because of the break in the electrical circuit).

What skills does such a diagnostician apply? Dissociation of function is one of the most important. When a patient loses a specific skill, while others are intact, this suggests that brain damage has damaged or isolated that function. The most compelling sort of dissociation is a double dissociation: that is, where one patient tests intact on A, impaired on B, while another patient shows just the opposite pattern. This tells us that the two tests are truly of functionally isolable mental factors (but even this deduction can be fraught with problems; see Shallice, 1988). Where a series of patients can be demonstrated with such dissociable impairments in a particular domain, for instance in different aspects of the ability to recognize objects, then we can start to see how that particular cognitive skill might be composed of the different components isolated by neuropsychological investigation. Many of the chapters in this book follow this line of reasoning (the faulty transmission in the car analogy); they include, for instance, those of Kay (chapter 8), of Franklin and Howard (chapter 7) and Riddoch and Humphreys (chapter 10). Zaidel (chapter 15) uses the inference of isolation, rather than destruction of a function, to show how it might work (more like the blown fuse analogy).

Developmental disorders

What of developmental disorders? Sometimes a similar, componential approach seems appropriate (e.g. Temple, chapter 12, and Campbell, chaper 13). That is, one can start from an adult model of a set of mental operations and indicate an isolated impairment within such a scheme. But developmental disorders often have a different character than acquired ones. A problem in mental function at an early, possibly critical, stage of development can either delay or derail the normal development of that function. In chapter 3 by Dodd and Murphy we see how two girls born deaf can show very different patterns of language development; in one case there is no evidence of delayed or disturbed language, in the other somewhat more abnormal development. It is stunted, rather than slowed, language that emerges here. Gopnik's description (chapter 4) of a child who seems to lack the ability to use morphological and grammatical structures in understanding or producing language shows us someone who is not qualitatively like the adult who becomes insensitive to grammatical structures following a stroke. Stackhouse (chapter 5) traces the development of a child with problems in producing speech sounds fluently (though with relatively good speech comprehension). All these children lead what most of us would consider to be 'normal lives'. But the oddness of the autistic child (Baron-Cohen, chapter 1), while it can be described in terms of isolated abnormalities of cognitive function, shows a more general picture of 'skewed' intellectual life; one where some aspects have come to dominate or sustain mental life which we do not see in most people; not even in the children with language or perceptual problems. This 'skewedness' is not necessarily confined to developmental cases. For instance, one of the problematic aspects of the split-brain patients (see Zaidel, chapter 15) concerns the extent to which their behaviour indicates the normal functions of the hemispheres, clarified by their isolation, and to what extent they show us something different. The 'something different' for the split-brain patient has sometimes been thought to be a combination of the effects of epileptic seizures in early life before the operation on the corpus callosum, which may have led to atypical development of faculties in each hemisphere, and also a direct effect of the lesion on the development or 'release' of atypical function in the newly un-yoked cerebral hemispheres.

So the 'subtractive', motor-mechanical inferences which we might tend to use in interpreting many cases of adult, acquired impairment suggest that functional loss leaves a simple 'hole', the shape of which characterizes the lost component. But this can be too simple, even within a modular and componential view of mental processes. In particular, such inferences cannot take easy account of the way that the organism changes with time – how compensating strategies might come into play, for instance – nor can they encompass the development of immature processes into mature ones when a component may be missing, or just not working too well, at one or another stage.

Here are some more examples. In chapter 2 by Pring we find out that being born blind can have implications for cognitive development which are a long way from what we might believe to be the direct implications of such debility. Lack of sight need not mean just that certain cognitive structures fail to develop, but rather that well-developed processes may tend to be deployed in an unusual way because of the essentially strategic limitations set on some mental operations by lack of sight.

In chapter 6 (Snowling and Goulandris) we can see how two subtly different problems might have contributed to rather *similar* seeming reading difficulties in two brothers, and we can also see how these resolved over several years. The pattern that they describe suggests neither simple derailment nor simple delay of reading, but rather a somewhat spluttering progress in literacy, with rather different 'malfunctions' for each brother at the source of their faulty start. These boys seem to be developing normally in respects other than reading and writing progress; their problems have not distorted their general cognitive growth, at least not as far as we can tell from these studies.

What is normal?

One problem that occurs quite often in these reports is that it can be hard to have a reliable and reasonable idea of what could be 'normal'. Even in reading and writing, where we have schooled skills and have clear goals at different levels of learning, it is not always clear what constitutes 'bad spelling' or 'poor reading'. Here, good comparisons are needed that show us that the impaired skills are really that and are not problems due directly to poor schooling nor to motivational or general intellectual difficulties. These contrasts can be implicit; for instance, we read between the lines of Snowling and Goulandris' case description that the brothers who were dyslexic were so despite living in a book-rich home. We can rule out (at least on the face of it) the possibility that these boys failed to learn to read and write because their environment as well as their nature failed to provide the necessary resources. Comparisons can be explicit; they can be made between similar family members or with other 'matched' groups. In some ways, the best sort of control is that shown in Hodges's description of a transient global amnesic (chapter 14). The precise characteristics of the patient's memory loss could be directly compared with his own performance, before and after his attacks of transient loss of memory. Similarly for EST, the patient who, in addition to his known naming disorder, has profound writing problems (Kay, chapter 8) in the context of well-attested good reading and writing before his illness. But the picture can become confused, too. Who would be the best controls for the people described by Campbell (chapter 13) and by Temple (chapter 12)? Both these women did not recognize faces with anything like the same accuracy as their peers, yet for one of them at least, the problem seems to be shared with her (only) parent. This raises the possibility that what is normal 'on the outside' is actually rather abnormal seen from a perspective within the family, where no one relied on face recognition too much. In the case described by Gopnik (chapter 4) this problem could be faced more clearly. While one of the boys she describes is one of many members of his family who have a specific language problem, other close family members do not, and they have developed strategies for communicating with their relatives as well as showing normal language development. This strongly suggests that his language problems are not primarily a response to social/environmental pressures, but that they might have a genetic basis. The same hint is dropped in Stackhouse's (chapter 5) description of Keith: his verbal dyspraxia might be connected with language difficulties in other members of his family. But it is worth noting just how different these two cases of abnormal language development are: Paul has a defect in his grammar which affects speaking and understanding speech; Keith is affected only in his own speaking abilities, but not in understanding speech.

A quite different picture is painted by Dodd and Murphy's description of two deaf girls (chapter 3). Surely their similar backgrounds and hearing loss should have led them both to similar levels of language competence? But no, here it does seem as if subtle motivational and intellectual differences in the girls' own ideas about language and its uses set them forth on very different roads; one indistinguishable in her speech and writing from any hearing child; one clearly not using language at an age-appropriate level. Deafness here has magnified differences between individuals rather than diminished them. What is the 'normal' baseline here?

Visual knowledge is one area which can give rise to some real problems of matching and control. Norms for tasks are hard to obtain and must, by their very nature, involve just a few probes in a single domain, on a particular task. Here, the reader may suspend judgement concerning interpretation until fuller details – from a range of control subjects as well as internal evidence from the patient – are considered. But it is worth trying to follow the graded assessment tasks of Powell and Davidoff (chapter 9) until you really grasp the point that sometimes what appears to be a real dissociation of abilities might just reflect the fact that one task is harder than the other and that brain damage might have led to a general sensitivity to differences in difficulty between tasks, not necessarily to 'dissociated functional impairment' (and see Shallice, 1988).

One thing that is important is to determine precisely the particular patterns of ability and impairment shown by these people and whether your intuitions concerning which processes go together are confirmed or refuted by them. For example, Stackhouse (chapter 5) suggests why Keith who has problems in speaking should also be expected to have problems in spelling (he has!); but other studies (Bishop, 1985; Bishop and Robson, 1989) show that other youngsters with very poor speech, born with cerebral palsy, and in many ways far less able to produce articulated speech than Keith, can nevertheless do a number of things Keith cannot do (e.g. spell, repeat non-words and make up spoonerisms). Keith's speech and spelling problems may have a common cause, but it need not necessarily be one which is conceived best as 'speech always supports spelling'. Sometimes it does, sometimes it does not. Keith's spelling and speech problems might lie 'farther back', in a functional system that *plans* the segmented structure of both an utterance and of a spelling. By contrast, cerebral palsied children's speech problems may be more peripheral and leave the underlying speech-planning mechanism intact.

Another example: why should occipital damage, causing nearly complete cortical blindness (Powell and Davidoff's patient NB in chapter 9), ruin the ability to comment sensibly from memory on what things look like in this patient but not in others (for instance, HJA, described by Humphreys and Riddoch, 1987)? It cannot just be due to greater severity of 'visual loss' in NB. Dennis (Riddoch and Humphreys, chapter 10), like HJA, sees well enough to be able to copy drawings, but he too has odd ideas about what things look like. In fact, both Riddoch and Humphreys and Powell and Davidoff leave you some interesting clues suggesting that in both these patients there was a deeper problem with *knowledge* of visual aspects of things in the world. The graphic artist described by Franklin, van Sommers and Howard (chapter 11) seems to tell a complementary story; in that case it seems to be that *access* to knowledge of what things look like and how to depict them is limited to just one type of input: the real life object that is being drawn or a detailed pictorial representation. How these rather different problems (which dissociate from simple visual loss) might relate functionally to each other is an area of current concern which is well reflected in these chapters.

Mental lives

All of these cases are those of real people. Some of them have not been written about before, and in each report there is new information about these individuals and how they function. This book is intended to stand alone, rather than open the door to more detailed case studies. Nevertheless, detailed references to further work are given by several authors. You will also find it useful to read the works recommended by some of the authors at the ends of their chapters. These are intended to give context and round out the issues raised.

These cases have been chosen to sample and highlight just some interesting aspects of cognition. This is not the first book to take such an approach; for instance, Obler and Fein's *The Exceptional Brain* (1988) is a showcase of a range of exceptional case studies. In the present volume the emphasis is on exceptional language (speech, reading, writing) and non-linguistic visual function and on how these can illuminate our knowledge of the normal acquisition and use of these faculties. But this focus is not exclusive and as well as chapters on developmental aspects of rather different abilities (Baron-Cohen, chapter 1), there are cases of acquired lesions that have effects that go beyond the verbal/non-verbal distinction: these are the transient amnesia (Hodges, chapter 14) and the split-brain (Zaidel, chapter 15) studies. For these chapters, particularly, you may need to have an impression of the brain structures implicated in the people with suspected cortical damage. Kolb and Whishaw's *Fundamentals of Human Neuropsychology*, 3rd edition (1990) presents material in a way well suited to the needs of the student whose concerns are psychological rather than clinical.

Here are some 'mental lives'. I believe they can contribute to our knowledge of normal mental processes by helping to answer such questions as these: what is the relationship between the modality of input (sight, hearing) and the development of a mental faculty (vision, language)? How might the loss of one mental component affect the function of another? How is learned knowledge organized in complex information-handling systems, including the brain? What processes are involved in normal mental development? This introduction may alert you to the ways in which these individuals might help answer these important general questions.

References

Bishop, D. V. M. (1985) Spelling ability in congenital dysarthria: evidence against articulatory coding in translating between graphemes and phonemes. *Cognitive Neuropsychology*, 2, 229–51.

Bishop, D. V. M. and Robson, J. (1989) Unimpaired short-term memory and rhyme judgement in congenitally speechless individuals: implications for the notion of 'articulatory coding'. *Quarterly Journal of Experimental Psychology*, 41, 123–41.

Fodor, J. (1983) *The Modularity of Mind*. Cambridge, Mass.: MIT Press.

Humphreys, G. W. and Riddoch, M. J. (1987) *To See but not to See: a Case Study of Visual Agnosia*. London: Lawrence Erlbaum.

Kolb, B. and Whishaw, I, Q. (eds) (1990) *Fundamentals of Human Neuropsychology*, 3rd edn. New York: W. H. Freeman.

Obler, L. K. and Fein, D. (eds) (1988) *The Exceptional Brain*. New York: Guilford.

Sacks, O. (1986) *The Man who Mistook his Wife for a Hat*. London: Duckworth.

Shallice, T. (1988) *From Neuropsychology to Mental Structure*. Cambridge: Cambridge University Press.

1

The girl who liked to shout in church

Simon Baron-Cohen

I first met Jane when she was six years old. She was a pupil in a small school for children with autism, and I was a teacher there. She had perfectly upright posture, like a dancer, and walked everywhere on tip-toes, as if gliding through life and wishing to have minimum contact with the earth. She was standing by the window by herself, and her eyes seemed transfixed on the shadows cast by the swaying branches of a tree outside. She was talking in an eloquent voice, to herself. 'I mustn't shout in church, must I? Dodecahedrons have 12 sides, decagons have ten sides, octagons have eight sides, and hexagons have six sides. It's rude to say frontbottom in church, isn't it?'

Upon entering the room, Jane glanced briefly across to me, and asked me my name. I told her. She touched my sweater, and said 'Soft wool, beige and brown'. I asked her if she liked my sweater. She said 'Smooth, my blanket is smooth and soft.' Then, without looking at me, she took my hand and lifted it towards a shelf. I guessed she was trying to get me to pass her one of the toys out of her reach. I handed one to her and still without looking at me, she took it and sat down in the middle of the floor, playing with it by herself.

Suddenly, she asked, 'Simon, I mustn't shout in church, must I?' Staring at her toy, she waited for me to reply. 'Well, no', I said, rather taken aback at the oddness of the question. It struck me that for children with autism many social conventions might be rather hard to see the point of.

'It's rude to say frontbottom in church, isn't it Simon?' 'Yes', I said. 'I mustn't whisper frontbottom noisily in church, must I Simon?' 'No', I said, feeling that this conversation was getting rather predictable.

I wondered if these questions reflected Jane's inability to understand the meaning of the term 'rude'. She could certainly say the word, but did she really understand it? She glanced at me, but then turned her eyes back to a shiny red-and-silver milk bottle-top which she rotated at high speed near one eye.

She started again 'It's rude to shout in church, isn't it Simon?' I felt her set of repeating questions was leading nowhere, so I decided to take control of the conversation. 'Come on, Jane, let's do some reading', I said, leading her gently over to the table and picking out a story book. She sat down next to me, and before I could begin she asked 'Dodeca-hedrons are 12 pentagons, aren't they Simon?' I confessed that I wasn't sure, but she immediately followed this up with 'I mustn't shout in church, must I, Simon?'

I abandoned the book and decided to explore Jane's interest in geometry. After all, how many normal six-year-olds knew that 12 pentagons made up a dodecahedron? (She was right, by the way. I checked later.) We started our lesson by drawing as many geometric shapes as she knew. She was remarkably skilled at producing a large range of such shapes, and knew all of their names. It soon became clear that my efforts at using this educationally was simply providing her with an opportunity to indulge in a favourite ritual, namely reciting geometric terms. Once she was onto this, there was no shifting her. For example, I asked her to describe her house, and she brought this back to geometry. 'My bedroom window is a rectangle, an oblong, and it has little triangle window-catches. What shape are your bedroom windows, Simon? Are they rectangular or round?'

I soon learnt that whatever educational progress Jane was going to make, it was going to be in tandem with her own interests in geometry, churches, and other favourite topics. Any attempts to repress these repetitive themes proved unsuccessful. As she learnt to read and write, she chattered away to herself about such obscure things as quindecagons and tetrahedrons, or shouting in church, and as the months passed, her reading, writing and arithmetic all developed.

Her parents interpreted this progress as a sign that she was emerging from her autism, but socially she was really as one-sided as ever, talking with others only about her own restricted topics, and often simply talking to herself. She was also still quite oblivious of other people *as* people. For example, one day we were having lunch with the other teachers and children. I was seated next to her. Before I could stop her, Jane suddenly climbed up on the table, putting one hand on my head to steady herself, then, quick as anything, crawled over (with no regard for where her knees and feet were going) to grab a piece of cake on the far side of the table. Miraculously, only one person's meal got a foot in it, although a cup of orange juice got knocked over in her single-minded pursuit of the cake. The idea that she could have used words, or gestures, or even eye-contact, to request a piece of cake did not seem to have even entered her mind. And the idea that I might be more than just a useful object to hold on to, and that both I and the others might have thoughts and feelings about her walking in our food, did not seem to concern her at all. I was reminded of a description of another child with autism, by Leo Kanner, the psychiatrist who first described the condition:

> on a crowded beach he would walk straight toward his goal irrespective of whether this involved walking over newpapers, hands, feet, or torsos, much to the discomfiture of their owners. His mother was careful to point out that he did not intentionally deviate from his course in order to walk on others, but neither did he make the slightest attempt to avoid them. It was as if he did not distinguish people from things, or at least did not concern himself about the distinction. *(Kanner, 1973, p. 95)*

Jane interacted, in her bizarre way, with adults only, making fleeting eye-contact with them. Occasionally, she stared long and deep into my eyes, but it never felt like any connection was being made between her and me. With children she acted as if no one was there, instead taking one of her bottle-tops out of a pocket, and twidding it close to the corner of her eye, rotating it at tremendous speed and giggling quietly to herself.

During the next year, I got to know Jane well. Each morning she arrived in school with the same of kind of greeting. 'Hello, Simon. It's rude to hiss loudly in church, isn't? Diamonds aren't decagons, are they Simon?' She was almost always in a good mood, usually smiling (but mostly to herself), and always trying to extend her interest in geometry to new objects, such as the design of buildings. Her play rarely included any make-believe. On one occasion I attempted to introduce this, taking her into the playhouse and setting up a 'tea-party' with the teddies. This just led to a series of confused questions from her: 'Are we pretending now? This isn't a real house, is it? Why are we pretending, Simon?' I was struck by how odd it was to have to explain what pretence was, or what it was for, given how naturally this seemed to be a part of other children's play. Without my direction in this, her play soon reverted to endless drawing and cutting out of geometric shapes.

At the end of the year, Jane moved to a new school, and I also left to return to university. I wondered what would become of her. Imagine my surprise when, ten years later while working as a research psychologist in another school for children with autism, I encountered a rather graceless adolescent, but with a shrill, eloquent voice, standing beside a window, reciting to herself 'I mustn't shout in church, must I? Dodecahedrons have 12 sides, decagons have ten sides, octagons have eight sides, and hexagons have six sides.'

'Jane?' I said gently. She turned round, glancing at me briefly, and then turned back to her earlier position of staring down into the garden from the classroom window. 'Do you remember me, Jane?' I asked. Without looking at me she said, 'Yes, your name is Simon, and your birthday is on August the 15th.' She was right, and I suddenly had a flash-back to a day ten years earlier when I had told her the date of my birthday, when she was asking everyone this question. Her memory was impressive. I said to her 'Do you remember when I used to teach you, when you were just a child?' She replied with characteristic accuracy. 'Yes. You had a beard then, and different shoes.' As usual, she was right about these details. But what obscure details to remember! I smiled, and asked her how she was. She replied with a question. 'It's rude to shout frontbottom in church, isn't it, Simon?'

What might be causing Jane's social and communication abnormalities?

Since the pioneering studies by Hermelin and O'Connor, working in the Medical Research Council's Developmental Psychology Unit in London in the 1960s and 1970s, evidence has been accumulating that there are cognitive deficits in people with autism. Perhaps the clearest evidence comes from standard intelligence tests which shows that some two-thirds of people with autism have IQs below the average range, and even among those whose IQ is in the normal range, verbal IQ is usually significantly lower than visuospatial IQ.

Could Jane's unusual social behaviour and odd style of communication also be the result of a specific cognitive deficit? It seemed plausible that some aspect of her understanding of people might be impaired, and that this might underlie her social difficulties. When she was 16 years old I examined her using a variety of psychological tests, in order to clarify this question. Behind each test lay a specific hypothesis.

Did Jane recognize faces?

Faces are an important part of people. They contain information relevant to recognizing a person's age, gender, emotional state and, of course, their identity. Imagine how confusing the social world would appear if faces were unrecognizable. To check if this was any part of Jane's problem, I tested her understanding of each aspect of face recognition in turn.

To test age recognition, I gave her a set of photographs of young and old people, and asked her to put them into two piles accordingly. She did this with no difficulty at all. She did the same with gender recognition, sorting the pictures into piles of male and female faces without any hesitation. What of emotion recognition? Here, I gave her pictures of four kinds of facial emotional expression: happy, sad, angry and afraid. Again, she performed without error on this task. Finally, I presented her with a set of photographs of faces of other children in her class, and asked her to name them. She had no difficulty at all in recognizing their identities from their faces alone. Her understanding of faces and at least these aspects of the information they contain seemed to be unimpaired, and thus could not be causing her social and communication problems.

Did Jane recognize different people's perspectives?

Since much of Jane's behaviour appeared to be profoundly 'egocentric', it seemed reasonable to consider whether this might be due to an inability to appreciate that people have different perspectives on the world. Jean Piaget, the Swiss child psychologist, suggested that in normal develop-ment there was a stage of extreme egocentrism, and that this could be measured using tests of 'visual perspective-taking'. This idea has been disproved by newer tests, in that normal children who fail Piaget's tests turn out to be quite competent at passing other, purer tests of visual perspective taking, and in this sense do not shown any egocentrism. But perhaps Jane would fail such tests.

The visual perspective-taking task I used to check this possibility was modelled on one developed by the American child psychologist, John Flavell. He had shown that even normal two to three-year-old children could pass such tests. I positioned six toys around the room, and then sat opposite Jane, and said to her 'Now, I am going to look at each of these toys, and I want you to tell me which toy I am looking at.'

I then closed my eyes, keeping my head facing straight ahead, and then opened my eyes so that I was looking at one of the toys to the left. I said to her 'What am I looking at now, Jane?' She identified the toy in my visual field immediately. Then I closed my eyes again, and without moving my head, opened my eyes again so that I was now looking at a different toy, this time on the right. Jane again named the correct toy without any hesitation.

By the time I had looked at all six toys, in random order, and had heard her name them correctly as I looked at each of them in turn, I was in no doubt that she understood my visual perspective, and appreciated that it was different from hers. Indeed, given that three of the toys were positioned behind her, so that she could not see them but I could, there was no doubt that she was distinguishing her own perception from mine. In this sense, she did not demonstrate any egocentrism. A sketch of the experimental set-up is shown in figure 1.1.

Did Jane recognize that someone else could have different thoughts?

Although she was clearly not egocentric when it came to understanding *visual* perspectives of different people, it remained possible that she might be egocentric on a different level, that of appreciating people's thoughts. When I was with her, it certainly felt as if Jane was oblivious to what I and others might be thinking. I set out to check this possibility.

I decided to examine her using a test of 'conceptual perspective-taking', and chose a test that had been developed for use with normal four-year-old children by Josef Perner at the University of Sussex, and Heinz Wimmer at the University of Salzburg, Austria. This test was designed to check if a child can appreciate that people have different beliefs about the same situation, depending on the information to which they have access. Normal children of less than three and a half years tend to fail this test, revealing their egocentrism after all. Would Jane, despite being 16 years old, also fail such a test?

The test went like this. I showed her two dolls, Sally and Anne. I then checked that she could distinguish the two characters (which she could), and then told her a short story about the two dolls. 'Sally has a marble, and she puts it into her basket.' I placed a marble into Sally's basket. Then I continued. 'Now Sally goes for a walk. (Exit Sally.) Now look. Naughty Anne takes Sally's marble, and puts it into her own box.' Jane watched all of this being enacted by the two dolls. Then I said to Jane 'Oh look! Here comes Sally, back from her walk.' I brought Sally back into full view. Then I asked Jane 'Where will Sally look for her marble?'

The correct answer, of course, is that Sally will look in her basket, where she still *believes* it is, since that was where she left it. However, Jane failed this test, saying that Sally would look for the marble in Anne's box. I asked her why she would look there, and Jane said 'Because that's where the marble is.' I was astonished, since most people with a *mental age* above three to four years old never make this mistake, and there was

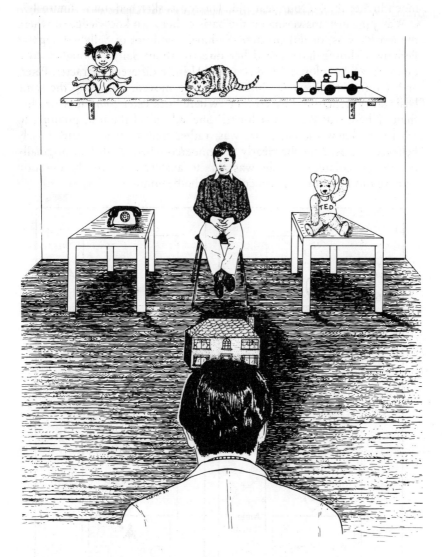

Figure 1.1 Visual perspective-taking test.
(Reproduced with permission from S. Baron-Cohen, *British Journal of Developmental Psychology*, 1989, vol. 7, pp. 113–27.)

no doubt that on all other measures of intelligence, Jane had a mental age much higher than a four-year-old. The test is sketched out in figure 1.2.

   Was Jane just answering on the basis of her own knowledge of where the marble was, or did she actually have a concept of Sally's thoughts? Perhaps I should have asked her directly about Sally's thoughts. In a quick retest, I explored this possibility. Using a different character, Peter, and a different object (a chocolate) being moved, but using the same basic story structure, I asked Jane 'Where does Peter *think* it is?' rather than 'Where will Peter look for it?' She still failed the test, pointing to where she knew the chocolate was, rather than to where Peter falsely believed it was. And she clearly remembered where Peter had originally put the chocolate, since she was able to answer correctly the question 'Where did Peter put the chocolate in the beginning?'

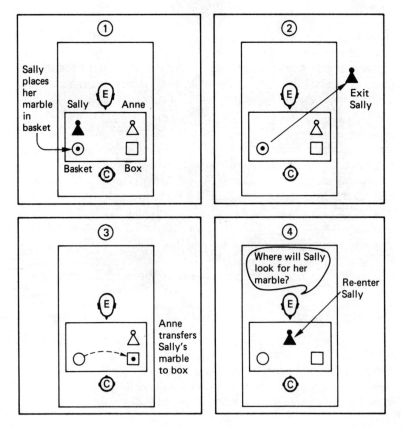

Figure 1.2 Conceptual perspective-taking test.
(Reproduced with permission from S. Baron-Cohen, A. M. Leslie and U. Frith, *Cognition*, 1985, vol. 21, pp. 37–46.)

Here, then, was clear evidence that Jane was actually functioning at below a three-year-old level in her understanding of other people's thoughts, despite her high ability in many other areas. She seemed very egocentric in this key area.

Testing this deficit further

Although the puppet story method suggested a specific deficit in Jane's understanding of other people's thoughts, there remained a niggling suspicion on my part that this could still simply be a by-product of some feature of this particular test. I therefore retested her, but this time using a different technique altogether, a picture sequencing task. In this task, I showed Jane a set of four pictures, told her which one to start with, and then asked her to put the other three pictures together to make a story with them. One set of stories involved a character who, like Sally in the first puppet experiment, was tricked, and therefore held a false belief.

For example, in the first picture a girl was depicted putting her teddy down on the ground. In the second and third pictures she was depicted picking a flower, whilst behind her back a naughty boy sneaked in and took her teddy. In the final picture, the girl turned back again, only to discover her teddy was gone. The girl looked astonished. This story is shown in figure 1.3.

Jane could not sequence any of these stories correctly, although she did attempt to put them into a story. When I asked her to tell me the story she had created, she simply described each picture in terms of the physical objects and actions depicted: 'Here's a girl. Here's a boy picking up the teddy. Now the girl is picking a flower.' There was no mention of the characters' *mental states*, their thoughts, desires, intentions, etc.

This strengthened the conclusion from the Sally–Anne experiment that Jane really was unable to appreciate other people's thoughts. But I still

Figure 1.3   Picture sequencing test of a mental-state story.
(Adapted from S. Baron-Cohen, A. M. Leslie and U. Frith, *British Journal of Developmental Psychology*, 1986, vol. 4, pp. 113–25.)

needed to check some other possibilities. For example, could the problem on the picture-sequencing test simply reflect an inability to *sequence*, and be nothing to do with understanding thoughts?

I checked for this by giving Jane a different set of stories which were simply about physical objects interacting, and which could therefore be sequenced by simply using a concept of physical causality. Understanding mental states was not necessary for this set, although of course sequencing ability was. In one such story, for example, a girl was walking along, and tripped over a brick. Jane had no difficulty with stories of this sort. This story is shown in figure 1.4.

Nor did she have any problems sequencing stories where people were involved, but where the story could be understood simply in terms of their *behaviour*, not their mental states. For example, she had no difficulty putting together a picture story showing a boy eating an ice cream, and a girl grabbing it for herself (figure 1.5). This strongly suggested that what Jane specifically failed to understand was human action in which the person's mental states had to be considered for the action to be understood. It was not just people that confused her. It was their mental states.

Figure 1.4   Picture sequencing test of a physical-causal story.
(Adapted from S. Baron-Cohen, A. M. Leslie and U. Frith, *British Journal of Developmental Psychology*, 1986, vol. 4, pp. 113–25.)

Figure 1.5   Picture sequencing test of a behavioural story.
(Adapted from S. Baron-Cohen, A. M. Leslie and U. Frith, *British Journal of Developmental Psychology*, 1986, vol. 4, pp. 113–25.)

Was Jane's world a purely physical one?

This prompted me to explore what her view of the world must be like. Imagine being in a world in which there was no such thing as a mental state. What would this mean? Would this mean that one was simply restricted to understanding everything in terms of physical events and physical causes?

I decided that a clear test of this would be if I explored Jane's concept of the *brain*. Supposing she knew that the brain existed. What would she understand of its function? Would she, like normal adults and even like normal four-year-old children, and indeed like people with learning difficulties, understand that the brain has a range of *mental* functions, like thinking, dreaming, hoping, pretending, wishing, etc.? Or would she, as we might predict given her performance on the earlier tests of understanding other people's thoughts, simply be oblivious of the mental, and conceive of the brain only in terms of its *physical* functions?

To find out, I asked her, first, to tell me where her brain was. She pointed to her head. Clearly, she was aware of the existence of this organ. I then asked her 'What is your brain for?' She replied 'It makes me move. It makes me do things. It makes me walk and run.' I asked her if it was for anything else. She said no.

Matching her failure on the tests of understanding beliefs, she seemed to view the world purely in terms of physical events and objects with physical functions alone. She seemed blind to the existence of mind. Indeed, I was drawn to the conclusion that autism was a cognitive disorder which could be thought of as a case of *mind-blindness*.

How might mind-blindness relate to Jane's behaviour?

Relating cognition to behaviour requires a degree of speculation. Nevertheless, it seems plausible to regard Jane's odd social approaches and her strange use of language as directly related to her mind-blindness. For example, Jane did not avoid people. She tried to interact with them, yet seemed to relate only to their physical aspects. She noted their clothes, their hair-style, their date of birth, etc., but seemed unaware of what they might be thinking, either of her, or of things that could be shared.

She was clearly confused by social conventions, conventions like sitting quietly in church, which depend upon appreciating other people's thoughts, beliefs, desires and intentions. She treated people, in one sense, like any other physical object in the room. Thus, she pushed my hand up towards an object out of reach, treating me like a physical object that could get things for her, or that could be used to climb on in order to reach things.

In another sense, she was very aware of people being animate, complicated objects. Most of the things they did or said she did not understand, and so she tended to withdraw from them. It is plausible that this was because she could not understand them in terms of their mental states. Instead, she seemed to attempt to control them in much the same way as one might try to control a complex machine that one does not understand. Thus, she asked highly repetitive questions which elicited highly predictable replies. She would ask 'I mustn't shout in church, must I?', and listeners tended to reply 'No'. Thus her language, although technically normal, seemed inflexible and insensitive to the thoughts or intentions of her listener. She would stick to factual questions with predictable answers: 'Hexagons have six sides, don't they?' Her repetitive questions allowed her to participate in a sort of conversation, and to avoid the confusion of a more normal, flexible conversation which would require an understanding of communicating intentions and beliefs.

Her play, focused as it was on the visual aspects of objects, their geometry, colour, size, etc., also allowed her to exercise her clear intelligence, without entering into the activity of sharing the mental state of *pretending*. And the final clue to her mind-blindness could be seen in her odd use of eye-contact: she seemed unaware of how this is normally used to communicate thoughts to other people.

Was Jane's mind-blindness total?

Although Jane was particularly poor at understanding other people's beliefs, it was not the case that she was completely unaware of all mental states. For example, she was certainly aware of people's *desires*, in that she could identify what people liked or disliked. She was also aware of simple emotions (like happiness and sadness) that occur when desires are fulfulled or unfulfilled. Another mental state she certainly understood was *perception*, this was evident in the case with which she passed the visual perspective-taking test, described earlier.

Since both desire and perception are mental states that are understood very early in normal development, this suggested that Jane had developed a little way in her appreciation of mental states, but obviously not as far as understanding pretence or beliefs. This raised the possibility that what was wrong in her case was not a complete absence of an understanding of mind, but a *delay* in the full development of it. It also suggested that, with time, or with the right intervention, this ability might develop further. Certainly, there were some other teenagers with autism who had eventually reached the stage of being able to pass the Sally–Anne test, and who even showed some pretending. But in these few cases, such developments were *years* after their normal appearance in other children.

Jane seemed suspended in a twilight of awareness: her world was not totally devoid of the notion of people's mental states, but almost so. Would she emerge from this state with time? Or could some form of treatment free her from the confines of her largely physical worldview? And if she could be liberated in this way, would her social and communication problems diminish? Frustatingly, there were as yet no answers to these questions.

Acknowledgements

This work was written while the author was in receipt of grants from the Medical Research Council, the British Council, the Royal Society and the Mental Health Foundation.

Further Reading

Baron-Cohen, S. (1988) Social and pragmatic deficits in autism: cognitive or affective? *Journal of Autism and Developmental Disorders*, 18, 379–402.

Baron-Cohen, S. (1990) Autism: a specific cognitive disorder of 'mind-blindness'. *International Review of Psychiatry*, 2, 79–88.

Baron-Cohen, S. Leslie, A. M. and Frith, U. (1985) Does the autistic child have a 'theory of mind'? *Cognition*, 21, 37–46.

Baron-Cohen, S. Tager-Flusberg, H. and Cohen, D. (eds) (1991) *Understanding Other Minds: Perspectives from Autism*. Oxford: Oxford University Press.

Frith, U. (1989) *Autism: Explaining the Enigma*. Oxford: Blackwell.

Kanner, L. (1943) Autistic disturbance of affective contact. *Nervous Child*, 2, 217–50.

Kanner, L. (1973) *Childhood Psychosis: Initial Studies and New Insights*. New York: John Wiley and Sons. (Contains reprint of Kanner, 1943, above.)

2

More than meets the eye

Linda Pring

Sight is probably the most important sense with which we explore the world around us. So important is sight that the lack of it not only affects our perception of the world but also the way we come to think about it. It is hard to characterize the problems of the visually handicapped in general terms since the individuals concerned differ so very much. Certainly, children born blind have many more difficulties than those who lost their sight in later life. Their appalling problems in the early years of blindness may seem insurmountable; those of cognitive, social and personality development can, however, often be alleviated by compensatory strategies.[1] Visual information plays a significant role in nearly all mental activities, and models of learning and memory, reading and cognition have all been developed with vision often playing an implicit but crucial role. The question arises as to how well such models serve as the basis from which to interpret data drawn from those without vision. The answer needs to assure us that the models are indeed general and that data from the visually handicapped can be used to modify the models and engineer a robust framework from which we can learn and interpret new data as they arise. It is therefore very important to find out in what ways blind children's thinking and learning differs qualitatively from that of sighted children. In addition, and not least, the results of such studies may allow us to devise the most effective teaching methods for the visually handicapped and thus help such children to realize their full potential.

This chapter describes work with two blind children. One is a girl, who is now 12 years old, who became totally blind very suddenly at the age of 16 months. She is exceptionally intelligent and imaginative. I have chosen therefore to take a close look at her drawings, which are produced by making raised outlines on special paper, because this might tell us something about how she represents the world in her head. The other is also a girl, she is six years old and was totally blind from birth with no light or pattern perception. She has begun to read Braille and it is mainly this learning process that is described here.

Portrait of Sally

As a baby her development had been entirely normal. She was an amiable, bright child, who had walked before her first birthday and was active and curious in most things. Her language development was, in fact, rather precocious. She was speaking many single words, two- and, indeed, three-word sentences at 15 months when she lost her vision very suddenly over a period of a couple of weeks. Her interest in books waned, she no longer wanted to name her farm animals and the last straw came when she continued to try to stroke the family cat after it had left the room; bilateral optic atrophy with an unknown cause was diagnosed. She was left totally blind. Yet, surprisingly, this did not halt her normal development. Indeed, she adapted to the new situation with great ease and a startling ability to cope. For example, Sally immediately began to compensate for her loss of vision by humming to get 'echo location' and room discrimination. The trauma was for Sally's parents. Looking back at those early days they report that the insecurity expressed by Sally then was no more than that expected for any child in the course of adapting to a new situation. She went to a local nursery and from there to a school for the visually handicapped. Her parents have always been supportive and tried their best to make Sally's life as close to any other child's as possible, helping all the time to bring the visual world to Sally through language and touch.

I met Sally at her school when she was 11 years old, a very bright, self-possessed and pretty girl. She has a happy disposition and lively personality, and, as it transpired, a good deal of charm. She is extrovert yet thoughtful, and can also be quite assertive. I do not think Sally would regard herself as handicapped. She has succeeded in doing everything that she has attempted, up until now at least. Sally wants to become a writer and she may well achieve this as she is ambitious, highly intelligent and has a healthy amount of egotism. Her teachers think she has an outstanding sense of language and phraseology and also an excellent spatial sense. Sally cannot remember a time when she could see, but that early experience of sight may have allowed her to form a useful internal spatial reference framework.

As she enters adolescence she has become somewhat self-opinionated and tends to try to get her own way in a rather determined fashion. She is very close to her best friend whom she met in the early days of primary school. This friend, who is partially sighted, happens also to be very bright. The two girls make a delightful duo: they have a well-developed sense of humour, though it may well be that Sally sees herself as the dominant player in this partnership. Though totally blind, Sally can use her friend's eyesight, and this is surely an important component in the development of their relationship.

Sally was tested on the Williams intelligence test for children with defective vision and obtained an IQ score of about 140. She was equally able at the verbal and performance components of the intelligence test. This would put her in the top range of university students. She has achieved scholastic success commensurate with her high intelligence level and she is certainly comparable, in marks attained for school exams, with her sighted counterparts. Sally exercises her own judgement on what to make an effort for, a trait not always appreciated by her teachers!

Drawing without sight

My attention was first drawn to Sally by two independent reports made by her teachers. They both remarked on the fact that Sally was worthy of study as she had such an unusually well-developed imagination, in stark contrast to many other totally blind children. One aspect of this imagination showed itself in her outstanding ability, when compared with other blind chidren, to produce drawings. Sally had quite recently been given a present of a rubber mat with several sheets of thin plastic-like paper. This 'German film', as it is known, can be placed on the mat and raised lines are produced when drawing with a biro or pencil. The thickness of the point determines the width of the raised line and the force used to press down defines the height of the raised line. To the touch it feels as if a thin plastic string has been glued to the page: there are no grooves only the ridge is felt. For almost the first time Sally had a very effective means of producing a tangible form of her own internal representations through the production of drawings.

There are many problems for a blind child in drawing: some of these will be experienced by a sighted, blindfolded drawer. For instance, without immediate visual feedback one forgets what has been drawn and where it is on the page and feeling it is not the easiest way to localize it within a spatial framework. But, in addition, blind children have to try to reconstruct their own mental images with little guidance from their everyday experience and thus the drawings of a blind child pose real problems of interpretation. Kennedy (1980, 1982) has conducted a careful analysis of the drawings of the visually handicapped and he is convinced that the blind do understand the art of image depiction on two-dimensional surfaces. He notes that picture recognition and production by the visually handicapped has been almost entirely overlooked. This is ironic since the benefit blind children might derive from dealing with pictures is, if anything, greater than that for the sighted (Pring and Rusted, 1985; Pathak and Pring, 1989; Pring, 1987).

Models of picture and object recognition are being developed all the time. Recently, there has been an upsurge of interest caused partly by the computational approach exemplified by Marr (1982) and partly by the cognitive neuropsychologists who have attempted to re-examine the models, by trying to place the performance of brain-damaged patients, with selective impairments in picture and object recognition, within the same framework (see Riddoch and Humphreys, chapter 10; also Campbell, chapter 13, and Temple, chapter 12, in this volume). This has consisted of attempts to isolate those cognitive operations or structures which play a necessary part in the identification of perceived objects.

Humphreys and Riddoch (1987) have identified three crucial forms of knowledge for the recognition and comprehension of objects. First, we need to be able to gain access to the name of the object from memory and this means we have to select the appropriate phonological representation. Secondly, we need to be able to locate the appropriate part of semantic memory in order to address the correct semantic knowledge about an object. Thus, through this representation function and meaning are made available. Thirdly, we need to have access to that part of memory which has object form knowledge. In this component we have the spatial descriptions of objects we have seen in the past or for which we have been able to develop prototypical examples. Any one of these three components may be impaired without necessarily affecting appropriate functions of the other two. For instance, the semantic component can be selectively impaired through brain damage, but a patient can still have access to the object form knowledge and thus sort real objects from nonsense objects in a reliable way (Riddoch and Humphreys, 1988).

Humphreys and Riddoch have argued that for *visual* object recognition, cascade processing of information is likely to take place from one component to another. This means that there can be interactive feedback between the relevant components, serving to 'home-in' on the target object, and eventually identify it for certain.

There really is no reason to suppose that the central cognitive components outlined as important for vision will not be equally valid for tactual object recognition, though of course the processing of the target may well invite different procedures. Nevertheless, because there is such a paucity of research on tactual picture recognition, even some of its basic components are worth considering.

To investigate Sally's system of pictorial representations, I first presented her with 15 raised outline drawings of common objects, such as a hat, hairbrush, drum and gun (figure 2.1). These were drawn to be simple, and have as little internal detail or features as possible, while at the same time presenting a clear outline. Sally was given each drawing and I moved her finger around the outline. Then she traced the drawing on her own. I asked her to tell me the name of the pictured object. Sally proved to be poor at this. She could only name the gun and the comb. She really had little idea of what the other 13 drawings depicted. This confirmed results that I had previously obtained with other groups of children. Jenny Rusted and I looked at congenitally blind, late blind children and sighted, blindfolded children and found that in all these groups the majority of children failed to recognize a single picture (Pring and Rusted, 1985).

Why should recognition by sight be successful and by touch a failure? If we take a look at the mistakes children make, an answer becomes apparent. Most of their errors, and also Sally's, fall into two categories. The first is characterized by a complete inability even to guess. The child indicates that the drawing could be of almost anything, even a guess would be impossible. The second, less frequent, category of errors is misidentifications. These substitute the target for another object that

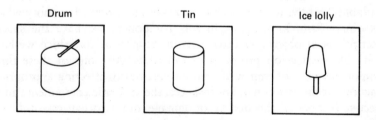

Figure 2.1 Drawings given to Sally for identification.

shares some prominent perceptual feature. For example, Sally guessed that a picture of a flower was a toothbrush because it has a stalk and a head. It seems that tactual recognition proceeds by trying to identify the drawings of objects solely through their form. So object form knowledge is a crucial first port of call for correct recognition. From there the connections with meaning can begin to be made. Thus, sharp objects often have piercing functions, objects with handles suggest that they can be grasped and four legs may mean an animal. This sort of information, which clearly can be picked up by touch, is, however, almost always insufficient for full identification. Spatial descriptions operate at a rather superficial level and, as a result, structural descriptions cannot disambiguate objects which broadly share the same form.

How could I restrict the number of possibilities from which Sally had to choose? We do not normally see drawings only as single isolated items. We know them to be members of a category of things. Thus a cat is an animal, a table a piece of furniture, and a hammer is a tool. Such categorical learning occurs very early in life. Perhaps by giving a clue as to the category to which the pictured object belongs one might give the child a chance to restrict the choice. What may then be possible for the child is to use a kind of *guess and check* procedure for a limited number of instances. In other words, given the category 'furniture', the child could check if the raised drawing was of a chair or a table.

In the next test, therefore, I gave Sally another set of drawings with clues as to the class of objects to which the drawing belonged. She was told, for instance, that the picture of a frying pan was a drawing of an object which belonged in a kitchen. She was therefore very unlikely to confuse it with a tennis racquet. Sally's performance improved dramatically and became almost completely accurate, though she took several minutes to feel each picture before offering a name. This result has been repeated with other congenitally blind children, where cued object recognition significantly improves performance (Pring, 1987).

So it became apparent that Sally really could use pictorial information, provided that she was given some idea to guide her towards the appropriate location in memory, where the representation of the object was likely to be stored. This must mean that Sally not only has a structural description of a table or a drum, but can use tactually derived images to access or match the internal memory or knowledge of those objects. Could Sally also recognize pictures of things that she could never have felt in their entirety? I gave her two classes of drawings, one of which was again of common objects with which I felt she was bound to have had 'first-hand' experience, the other group of objects consisted of items such as a crescent moon, a tree and a mountain which I expected and later confirmed she had not *felt* before. I tested her recognition ability on these two classes of pictures. I did this in two ways: either I presented her with the target drawing and asked her to say which of three words was the correct label or I gave her three pictures and asked her to identify the one I named. To make it harder, at least one of the choices was structurally confusable with the correct target. For example, a picture of a banana was presented together with a crescent moon and a non-confusable picture like a knife. Sally's task was to pick out the picture of the moon when I named it.

The results were perhaps rather surprising. I certainly expected that Sally would recognize pictured objects that she had handled before with more ease than objects, like a mountain, which she might have encountered, but obviously had no chance to feel around. Nevertheless, Sally recognized both classes of picture equally well. When she did make mistakes, however, she always chose the featurally similar object instead of the target itself. This was so for both classes of pictures. How then did Sally manage to identify pictures of things she had never felt? Clearly she must be able, just like all of us, to imagine things she has not experienced but has learnt about in other ways, either through reading, or being told and no doubt by relating her own experience in an analogical way to those instances she has not come across. That this is so is also evident from Sally's own drawings. She is exceptional in this, as most blind children have real difficulty in drawing pictures.

Figure 2.2 shows a glass drawn by an early totally blind adult next to Sally's drawing of the same object.[2] Sally can keep in mind what she has drawn and does not lose her place, so her drawings do not repeat lines. Also the pictures seem to look more like the drawings of a sighted person. This point is taken up later. On another occasion, Sally was asked to draw things she was likely to have felt before and others where this was more unlikely. Some of her illustrations are given in figure 2.3. As in the recognition test, it seems to make little difference to the quality of the drawing whether or not she had previous tactual experience of the object. This reinforces the idea that object form knowledge is acquired in many different ways other than direct experience, but also that such knowledge can be used to generate images.

Of course, I was aware as time went on that Sally was getting lots of experience of raised pictures that had been drawn for her by her sighted friends, and that this might gradually have improved her own drawing ability. But it was quite surprising to me that her very first drawings and the ones she produced nearly two years later were very similar in quality. The first drawing I asked her to do was a picture of the sun and she produced the drawing shown in figure 2.4. I then asked her what were the lines coming out of the circle and she replied 'well, I might have drawn the sun as round but I was told that lines came out when the sun

Figure 2.2 Wine glasses drawn by an early totally blind adult (left) and Sally (right).

Mountain

Cat

Woman

Train

Figure 2.3 Sally's drawings of objects.

Figure 2.4   Sally's first drawing.

was usually drawn.' I pressed her to tell me what the lines were and she said 'I think they are the light or heat from the sun.' This shows Sally's excellent verbal and spatial memory. She does not only remember what she is told about things and their characteristics, her drawings also show that she remembers with precision her own motor movements. Her lines join up, and detailed features are placed at the correct location on the drawing.

I also asked Sally to describe her other drawings. The exact question I put was 'If somebody came from outerspace and didn't know the word (for example) "spider" how would you describe your drawing to him?' Although it is really quite impossible to find a reasonable control sighted child to compare with Sally, in this instance I thought it might be worth showing a comparison with a sighted child, Ellie, who was two years younger and was also drawing on German film. Ellie was also asked to describe the drawings (not the object themselves) as if to a man from outerspace. Examples of both children's drawings are given in figure 2.5. In all Sally's descriptions the aspects of form dominated. For instance, when asked to describe a tree she had drawn (figure 2.5), her response was 'a shortish round cylinder, with triangles getting shorter as it goes up, like a pyramid'. A wine glass she described as being a flat, round

Telephone   Spider   Tree

Figure 2.5 Examples of Sally's (above) and Ellie's (below) drawings.

base, with a cylinder stick going up from the bottom, curving out and up, ending in a slightly rounded box. These descriptions indicate that Sally finds it easy to give access to the spatial structure of objects and gives this priority over their function. In contrast, Ellie tended to describe her drawings in terms of function and often also included colour descriptions of them. For her, the tree was 'bushy, green leaves with lots of sticks and twigs and branches inside' and the wine glass was described as 'a U-shaped cup with wine in it, probably red, and a long stem to hold and a round base'.

Thus, what Ellie appeared to do in her descriptions of her own drawings was to use her knowledge of the objects themselves. This included structural descriptions, but also the rich, compound representation which contains meaning, function and colour, as well as form. In contrast, Sally tended to isolate and emphasize the structural properties of the object she had drawn. However, one should keep in mind that Sally, of course, knew about the items very well. The point here is that the blind child when asked to draw and describe objects appears to approach object knowledge by first providing a structural description.

A comparison of this kind must reflect the different amount and kind of information one obtains from vision or from facts. For a sighted child a picture, or for that matter an object, is immediately and unequivocally connected with a semantic description. That is, the object's meaning and identity are almost simultaneously evoked. As we have seen, blind children have to be given cues about the meaning to help them with both object and picture identification. Consequently, it makes sense that Sally stressed the perceptual features in terms of shapes and patterns completely separately from their semantic representation. It was rare that Sally gave us an insight into the mental image, though an exception was the 'ice-cream tops' of the mountains.

In summary, what does Sally's ability to deal with pictures contribute to our understanding of blind children? She presents a somewhat contradictory pattern. On the one hand, she is exceptionally intelligent, has imagination and an excellent memory. This set of abilities allows her to use the spatial knowledge she has to the full and, together with what she has learnt, also allows her to depict a more accurate, tangible reflection of what she herself has never seen since she was 16 months old. According to her, she has no visual memory at all. She has to rely on touch and spatial relation to produce the competent drawings illustrated here. But, on the other hand, her blindness has set limitations. There are suggestions that the accuracy of her conceptual knowledge derived from perceptual details remains limited and many misconceptions are present.

The necessity of relying on touch makes the match between percepts and concepts less congruent. She therefore refers to pattern and shape with ease, since this intermediary step is a far more crucial component to her understanding of pictorial representation. For the sighted, this intermediate step is largely redundant. Sally's drawings and her descriptions of them are specially fascinating because they illustrate and support these conclusions.

I shall postpone discussion of the conclusions we can draw from Sally's drawings and picture recognition processes until I have presented the case of a second blind child called Becky and considered her progess in learning to read and write Braille. Words and pictures are both symbolic representations, but children from most cultures recognize pictures very easily, and early in their development. Indeed, most children also draw pictures spontaneously. This is in contrast to reading. Literacy is artificial in the sense that it needs to be taught, and written language had to be invented (Diringer, 1962). It may therefore provide some rather different insights from the ones obtained hitherto.

Portrait of Becky

Becky was four years old when I first met her, and just entering full-time education. Becky was diagnosed as having retinopathy of prematurity, a condition often arising as a consequence of high oxygen levels given to premature babies. The condition damages the retina of the eyes, and visual information cannot therefore pass to the brain leaving the infant congenitally and totally blind. In terms of development there seems to be no general mould into which blind children such as Becky fit. Blindness can have very different consequences for the development of the individual child (see Fraiberg, 1987). In general terms, though, developmental milestones are somewhat delayed in the blind and cognitive development may lag behind that of the sighted, in some cases up to two years or so. Language development may be an exception to this in that some components may emerge either at the same time or on occasion even earlier than in the sighted (see Mills, 1983) but this was not true in Becky's case. Her language development was very slow but steady and she had the disconcerting pattern of often repeating back exactly the same words she had heard, commonly known as echolalia. As Becky's language improved, for example, Mum might say 'Do you want to take off your coat?' and Becky would make the reply 'do you want to take off your coat.' Talking to Becky you become aware of her echolalia when she repeats back your own phrases or sentences verbatim. She can cleverly imitate tone of voice, intonation and even accents, but without humour.

A deep concern of Becky's parents was her failure to respond to kisses or hugs or any kind of physical contact. In many ways her behaviour in the preschool years seemed one of isolation and had much in common with that found in autism (see Fraiberg, 1978; Hobson, 1990). Lately, Becky has been more forthcoming as her confidence in the school environment has increased. She will now spontaneously talk across the classroom or dinner table to other children, where earlier she tended not to initiate conversations. Becky is certainly becoming more sociable in other ways too. At first she tended to be remote from her playmates and teachers, not seeking to give or readily accepting a cuddle or a hug. She has now made a 'best friend' and, for the first time, has begun to play imaginatively, a crucial component for the normal development of cognition (see Hinde, 1987; Baron-Cohen, this volume, chapter 1). Before this, most of her play was restricted to repetitive and ritualistic behaviour. Now all this seems to be changing. Becky is playing with dolls, putting them to bed, and pretending they are real babies. So there is a startling change; Becky is using her imagination in a play context.

At present Becky is a pleasant, if rather shy and withdrawn, six-year-old girl. Like so many young blind children, she seems on first impression to be colourless and tends to have rather blank facial expressions. She has a very good vocabulary, tending to use a wide range of words and expressing herself quite clearly. In this respect her performance is one or two years ahead of her age group. However, she does seem to use language less as a means of communication, and more as a reflective device. She tries to make events and occurrences in her life explicit to herself. She is likely to utter her exact statements again and again, rather as if she is rehearsing them. As an example Becky may repeat, 'I can't go home this weekend because Mummy is busy' or 'I am having my birthday at school now because we are moving house but I will have it again at the weekend at home.'

Becky is intelligent and her mental development is ahead of her chronological age. On the Williams intelligence test for children with defective vision she obtained an IQ score of 111. In tests of memory, learning ability and number it was clear that Becky was competent and performing on average about 18 months ahead of her age group.

In summary, the able young child whose reading progress is the main focus for investigation here is a six-year-old girl born totally blind. Becky's early emotional disturbance, not least reflected in head-banging in the nursery school and lack of social competence, has almost disappeared. She is rapidly maturing in all areas of development and shows the first signs of becoming more sociable and imaginative.

Learning to read Braille

It is going to be crucial for Becky that her potential assets are maximized to compensate as far as possible for her restricted visual experience of the world. Apart from learning about the world through our own first-hand experience, or being told, we also read about it. Writing presents a permanent record of accumulated knowledge, as well as being able to represent a world created by the imagination. It can be used as a vehicle for disseminating thoughts, ideas and arguments. It is therefore important for Becky that she is not cut off from the written word.

Letters and symbols in Braile reading material for the blind consist of different numerical and spatial permutations of six embossed dots, arranged in two columns and three rows. Figure 2.6(a) shows the 2 × 3 dot matrix. For example, the letter F looks like this ⠆, the letter R looks like this ⠗. All the letters in the alphabet have a different configuration. In many circumstances letter clusters like 'ed' or 'tion' are presented as

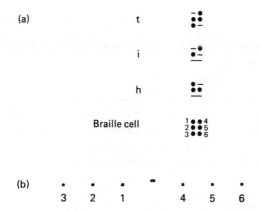

Figure 2.6 (a) Braille cell with dot numbers and example Braille letters. (b) Layout of the dot position keys on a Perkins Brailler.

just one or, at the most, two symbols. These cut across phonological boundaries so that, for example, in the word paint it is the two letters 'in' which are depicted as one symbol. Such contractions are often taught right from the beginning and exist to help increase the speed of reading, which is the most obvious disadvantage of Braille as a reading medium. There is a wide range in reading speed; some readers are quite fast, averaging about 150 words per minute (half the speed of skilled silent visual reading in English), but many readers are much slower than this, managing only 40 words per minute. Often writing in Braille is introduced at almost the same time as reading. A writing machine known as the Perkins Brailler is the one adopted by the vast majority. Figure 2.6(b) illustrates seven of the keys available on the register. Each character is formed by depressing the keys (at the same time) that correspond to the dots in each position. Thus writing in Braille involves rather different action sequences from writing in English.

There are other differences too. Touch is not so accurate in its 'information uptake' as vision. There is evidence that Braille reading by touch may be rather like 'blurred vision' (Apkarian-Stielan and Loomis, 1975; Pring, 1984). Also, of course, touch is characterized as a sequential processing modality, with consequences dependent on that (O'Connor and Hermelin, 1978). Braille has almost no redundancy. Each Braille character carries maximal information; a dot in one position and not a few millimetres to the left or right allows for the discrimination between individual letters. This can be illustrated by showing how, if one of the three dots in the letter F (⠿) is misplaced, then the letter becomes a D (⠿) instead! This, of course, is not at all true for print. Huey (1908) showed how well we can read a letter, word or page of print even if much of the display is missing (~~for example the bottom half of words~~). So the blind must pay full attention to the fine perceptual distinctions while dealing with Braille.

Given the very marked differences that exist between Braille and written English as orthographies, can the models of reading and the development of reading acquisition skills, drawn from our knowledge of the sighted child, adequately predict the likely paths that Becky will take on her journey to efficient Braille reading and writing?

There is a certain amount of research on Braille reading (Lowenfeld et al., 1974). For example, areas such as perception (Millar, 1977, 1986) and memory processing of Braille, as well as hemispheric dominance in Braille (O'Connor and Hermelin, 1978; Mousty and Bertelson, 1985) have attracted interest. Many Braille readers use two hands to read, often the right hand locates the ends and beginnings of lines on the page, while the left hand deals with the words (see Millar, 1988). Methods for increasing speed of reading, along with dot discrimination techniques and the influence of complexity and redundancy, have also been studied (Foulke, 1982; Hall and Newman, 1987). However, there are few studies which try to place the early stages of Braille reading within the current cognitive development framework.

In recent years there has been some agreement about the early stages in reading development (Marsh et al., 1981; Frith, 1985; Seymour, 1986). Visible language, as Frith terms it, provides for the infant as well as the young child early experience with letters; even before reading materials are introduced explicitly. Cornflakes packets have lots of written information and logos, as do advertisements on billboards in the street, traffic signs, not to mention the frieze in the child's room presenting the written label along with the picture. In learning how to read, one early goal is to develop a sight vocabulary, a visual/orthographic word recognition system. Frith (1985) has termed the acquisition of words on this basis (i.e. without the use of letter-sound knowledge) a *logographic* phase of development. A second stage in development which can be sparked off from the knowledge a child draws from spelling and writing has been called an *alphabetic* phase. This phase relies for development on the child's phonological expertise and refines and extends the knowledge of the ways the letters and sounds go together as well as the ability to segment spoken words into individual sounds or phonemes. Bradley and Bryant (1983), for example, have shown that there is a crucial relationship between reading success and early phonological segmentation skills. Finally, a third phase has been identified, where spelling pattern information is amalgamated within the child's lexical system, reorganizing the knowledge a child has and allowing analogies between words and letter strings to drive at least part of the word recognition process. This has been called the *orthographic* phase.

Thus, changing phases have been identified and it was our aim to see how well Becky's progress would slot into such a description. Becky's teacher had imagined that Becky would pick up the mechanics of reading and letter recognition relatively easily as she was articulate and able, her touch-based skills were good and her fingers were sensitive to minor changes in materials. Thus it came as some surprise to find that it took Becky a long time to learn to discriminate all the Braille letters. This seemed to be neither a memory problem nor a tactual insensitivity problem but rather a motivational one. Becky did not seem to see the sense in learning Braille letters. Nevertheless, with perseverance by teacher and pupil, by the end of the first year and a quarter at school, Becky was well able to recognize all the letter in the alphabet with very few errors.

Becky showed no evidence of going through a logographic phase in the way that Frith had described it. Few, if any, sighted children spend their first year of reading instruction concentrating only on learning single letters of the alphabet, but in Braille this is necessary. Becky, of course, really had had no exposure to 'visible language' except that which was involved in her reading scheme. There, most of the effort went into teaching letter recognition processes and words were simply not intro-duced until at least some letters were known. The implicit knowledge of written words, which visible language helps to build up, seems to be a necessary component for the logographic phase to develop. Sighted children learn to connect visual patterns containing letters with the meaning of the pattern. They see that the stop sign means 'stop'. They are developing a mechanism which allows input from the environment to address already learnt and stored internal representations of words; where both the 'look' of the word, as well as its 'meaning', are connected. A direct route from sight to meaning is evolved and what is more, word knowledge has letter knowledge built in. It is *not* the case that a child only remembers a 'picture' of the word, the letters are a salient component too (Seymour and Elder, 1986). For a blind child such as Becky there is no mechanism for her to take in written language in any other way than explicitly, and probably quite abruptly, at school age. Her lack of visual experience does not only lead to conceptual restric-tions but also to perceptual ones too.

Another consequence of blindness is the absence of the ability to read at the outset a small set of idiosyncratic words. It would be extremely unusual for a blind child to have any Braille books at home to explore. Thus Becky's vocabulary depended entirely on her teacher and what she chose to give to Becky to read. The sighted child's sight vocabulary usually contains words that reflect his/her visual experience and interests (or her parents' interests!). Words like Goldilocks or Harrods, drum, apple and cat are likely to figure. Such words were not found in Becky's early corpus of words in her Braille vocabulary. Indeed, even the word Becky, which approximates closest to a word that might be learnt implicitly and be read via direct 'touch to meaning' strategy was very easily misread or not identifed at all in the early days.

The first letters that Becky learnt were *a*, *b*, *l* and *g*, which have one, two, three and four dots respectively. She learnt to give them sounds as well as their names and the emphasis was on the sounds. She progressed systematically to include others in the set which differed in discriminability. Her first words were Becky, ball, bag, bat, bib.

Although the logographic phase seems to have been completely bypassed, the mechanics of reading and remembering letters is clearly similar for the blind as well as the sighted child. Children often fail to respect the specific nature of a letter's orientation. Reversals are common in early reading; a sighted child may mistake, *p* for *b* or *m* for *w*. Similarly, Becky mistakes *d* for *f* or *h* •⁝, ⁝•, ⁝••. Unfortunately, there is far more room for reversal or orientation errors in Braille than in print and these certainly make up nearly all of Becky's reading errors at this stage.

Becky is a bright girl, her syllable-segmentation skills are good and she can make up rhymes very easily. Her phonological awareness is certainly developing since she could segment the sounds of words quite well when tested on a set of phonological awareness tests (Bradley, 1980), although she had had no experience of the letters in written form. She could identify 'miss' as the odd-one-out from the set 'lick, lid, miss, lip', for example, scoring 7/10 on this test and could segment /m/ and /a/ in the word 'mat', although she failed to segment the final /t/ sound. Clearly, experience with written letter forms is not a prerequisite for the ability to divide words into their constituent sounds. It took Becky the whole first year at school to master fully the letter recognition process. By the first term of her second year at school Becky was gaining in confidence; nearly all letters would, with some effort at times, be identified. She is taught letter-sound decoding, blending, letter recognition. At the same time the Perkins Brailler machine is introduced and she is beginning to write Braille for the first time.

So, for Becky, reading is only just now beginning; she can transform graphemes to phonemes rather well and the alphabetic stage of development emerges quite clearly. Becky sounds out each letter of a word, and, so long as the right letter has been identified she then blends the sounds together well and reads aloud. She has few problems with decoding or blending, the accuracy of the process seems only to be dependent on her letter discrimination ability. Thus the alphabetic phase of development follows a very similar path in Becky as it does with sighted children. Words are read aloud via a letter-sound decoding and blending strategy. In the beginning, the use of this strategy is revealed quite nicely, since it leads children to 'regularize' on the basis of the general rules. English is not known for its regularity. Funny mispronunciations can occur. Becky's errors at this time reflected this; pronouncing 'post' as if it rhymed with 'lost', and reading 'late' as /lat/. When asked to read a set of regular English words (e.g. run, bed and think) and a set of irregular ones (e.g. who, said and could), matched on familiarity, the discrepancy between the two lists was marked. She read correctly 8/10 regular words but only 3/10 irregular words. Her reading of made-up words like 'slint' or 'mil' were nearly perfect, reflecting her facility with the letter-sound conversion process. What she had not yet learnt, was context dependent rules, such as 'soft *g*' or 'final *e*', but those were coming with teaching and practice.

Becky knows a lot about written language. She has not experienced a wide variety of words, but the ones she knows, she knows well. She is unlikely to recognize the word 'television', though a sighted counterpart might, because 'it is long and has two *i*'s in it.' The idea of a word representation which is only partially specified (as with the example above, or 'begins th' or 'has double *l* in it') does not really make sense where Becky is concerned. All her training and experience has been carefully structured. The words experienced by her have been learnt, 'hard' words have simply not been made available. For sighted children reading is often easier than spelling because of the partial specification of the representation. If you like, a sighted child makes 'educated guesses'. We know this because when they are faced with the task of spelling irregular words, which cannot rely on the 'sound-to-letter rules', they will then need to have a full specification to succeed and they often fail. However, this is not so for Becky. Her spelling is surprisingly good; if anything it is better than her reading because it lacks the difficult identification process in its early stages. Given 30 words to read and spell, Becky accurately read 19 and accurately spelled 22 (naming the letters out loud). This is certainly an unexpected pattern for a six-year-old.

Becky's reading towards the end of her second year at school remains in the alphabetic phase, although she is beginning to build up a 'touch' vocabulary, a lexicon where the feel of the word is familiar and addresses an internal representation stored in its entirety. However, the crucial problem identified for Becky, making her performance distinguishable from a sighted child, is the role that word meanings play. Sighted children will as their reading expertise develops, address more and more their own spoken language system (Pring and Snowling, 1987). The meanings of words can help them decode new letter strings, the meanings of words can help them guess (Marsh et al., 1981). Not so for Becky. She continues to decode words rather well but seems unaware of their meaning. Given semantic cues like 'chair' as an aid for the recognition of the word 'table', does not speed up the recognition process. Decoding is mechanically applied in all situations.

Reading is a task for Becky that she has been asked to master so for her it is like gaining an expertise without any very significant reinforcement. She is gaining a skill. No one said anything about semantics to Becky. No one told her that her own speech was important in the process. Once she had mastered the letter discrimination process her word reading vocabulary exploded. Before Christmas she could read only ten or fifteen words, after Christmas she could read almost any three- or four-letter word provided it was regularly spelt. She does not bring an interest in words and meanings to the reading lessons. She reads in spite of the message. Perhaps it goes deeper than this. Her language may only now be beginning to be used in an effective, communicative form where ideas and feelings can be expressed. As awareness of this increases and the value of 'the message' in learning to read becomes more apparent, then this should be reflected in her skill and in her motivation to read. On the basis of previous research we could predict that by about the age of 12 Becky's reading ought to have little to distinguish it from that of competent sighted readers of a similar age (Pring, 1982, 1984).

Conclusions

What are the main conclusions that can be drawn from the study of Sally's picture processing and Becky's reading acquisition? Are there some common features which these activities share?

Sally seemed to process pictures primarily according to their structural features. When these were not precise enough to allow her picture identification, she was quite lost. Her conceptual knowledge cannot compensate fully for the limitations of the perceptual input. Becky similarly needs structural knowledge, in her case perceptual letter recognition, in order to succeed in reading. She will not guess what a word could be. She has to use a letter-by-letter strategy. Visual handicap can be characterized, perhaps, as leading to a qualitatively different 'interface' between sensory and semantic information processing. It is not just a question of limitations in either sphere, but the need to adopt different cognitive strategies.

Vision provides a great deal of information about the world, yet this can often be compensated for. What cannot so easily be overcome is the direct and nearly simultaneous connection between visual and conceptual knowledge. Getting data from touch is truly a difficult task. The information which is obtained is not precise enough to provide knowledge without some guided search within the appropriate context. Otherwise the margin of error is likely to be too great, particularly for children who yet lack extensive experience. In consequence, children have to allocate a great deal of their attention to the perceptual aspects of the tasks at hand. This is, unfortunately, not done without a cost. It may lead to a temporary neglect of semantic and contextual processing. Thus the whole mental activity tends to become far more fractionated than it does for the sighted. The coherence for the different levels of processing were reduced for Becky and Sally because feedback from continued perceptual analysis was less available. Nevertheless, both these girls will, I am sure, succeed. Sally has prodigious talent and imagination and her teachers predict that she will go far. We also know that Becky will read, and when she is older written information will be as important for her as it is for any sighted individual.

Acknowledgements

Some of the research mentioned here was supported by a grant from London University central research fund. I am most grateful to Sally and Becky for their willing and good natured cooperation. I would also like to thank their teachers for their very generous help and advice, as well as the children's parents for the information and discussions we had. Sally Freestone did some of the testing and B. H. Hermelin helped me in writing the chapter. Helpful comments came also from Chris French, Slater Newman and Ruth Campbell.

Notes

1. The reader is advised to refer to Fraiberg (1978) for detailed accounts of the development of blind children or Lewis (1987) for an excellent brief review of the visually handicapped child.
2. The pictures are reproduced here by photocopying the original raised line drawing and using a felt tip pen to bring out the outline.

Further Reading

Mention was made in the chapter of interactive models in visual object recognition. Good insight into these and a more general understanding of connectionist models can be found in Biederman (1990) on higher-level vision. In addition, Chapman and Stone (1988) provide an informed and detailed appraisal of the needs of visually handicapped children. Although the book is focused on the impact of such children in ordinary schools, many of the issues it raises go beyond this to a more general level of interest. A current US perspective on reading and its development which stresses the componential approach can be found in a recent edited volume by Carr and Levy (1990). This can provide a useful source text.

References

Apkarian-Stielan, P. and Loomis, J. M. A. (1975) A comparison of tactile and blurred visual form perception. *Perception and Psychophysics*, 18, 362–8.

Bradley, L. (1980) *Assessing Reading Difficulties: a Diagnostic Remedial Approach*. London: Macmillan.

Bradley, L. and Bryant, P. E. (1983) Categorizing sounds and learning to read: a casual connection. *Nature*, 301, 419–21.

Biederman, I. (1990) Higher level vision. In D. N. Osherson, S. M. Kosslyn and J. M. Hollerbach (eds) *Visual Cognition and Action*, vol. II. Cambridge, Mass.: MIT Press.

Carr, T. H. and Levy, B. A. (1990) (eds) *Reading and its Development*. London: Academic Press.

Chapman, E. K. and Stone, J. M. (1988) *The Visually Handicapped Child in your Classroom*. London: Cassell.

Diringer, D. (1962) *Writing*. London: Thames and Hudson.

Foulke, E. (1982) Reading braille. In W. Schiff and E. Foulke (eds) *Tactual Perception: a Source Book*. Cambridge: Cambridge University Press.

Fraiberg, S. (1978) *Insights from the Blind*. London: Souvenir Press.

Frith, U. (1985) Beneath the surface of developmental dyslexia. In K. E. Patterson, J. C. Marshall and M. Coltheart (eds) *Surface Dyslexia*. London: Lawrence Erlbaum.

Hall, A. D. and Newman, S. E. (1987) Braille learning: relative importance of seven variables. *Applied Cognitive Psychology*, 1, 133–41.

Hinde, R. A. (1987) *Individuals, Relationships and Culture*. Cambridge: Cambridge University Press.

Hobson, R. P. (1990) On acquiring knowledge about people and the capacity to pretend: response to Leslie (1987). *Psychological Review*, 97, 114–21.

Huey, E. B. (1908) *The Psychology and Pedagogy of Reading*. Cambridge, Mass.: MIT Press, 1968 edn.

Humphreys, G. W. and Riddoch, M. J. (1987) (eds) *Visual Object Processing*. London: Lawrence Erlbaum.

Humphreys, G. W., Riddoch, M. J. and Quinlan, P. T. (1988) Cascade processes in picture identification. *Cognitive Neuropsychology*, 5, 81–95.

Kennedy, J. M. (1980) Blind people recognizing and making haptic pictures. In M. A. Hagen (ed.) *The Perception of Pictures*, Vol. 2. New York: Academic Press.

Kennedy, J. M. (1982) Haptic pictures. In W. Schiff and E. Foulke (eds) *Tactual Perception: a Sourcebook*. Cambridge: Cambridge University Press.

Lewis, V. (1987) *Development and Handicap*. Oxford: Basil Blackwell.

Lowenfeld, B., Abel, G. L. and Hatlen, P. H. (1974) *Blind Children Learn to Read*. Springfield, Ill.: Charles C. Thomas.

Marr, D. (1982) *Vision*. San Francisco: Freeman.

Marsh, G., Friedman, M., Welch, V. and Desberg, P. (1981) A cognitive-developmental theory of reading acquisition. In G. E. Mackinnon and T. G. Wall (eds) *Reading Research: Advances in Theory and Practice*. New York: Academic Press.

Millar, S. (1977) Tactual and name matching by blind children. *British Journal of Psychology*, 68, 377–87.

Millar, S. (1986) Aspects of size, shape and texture in touch: redundancy and interference in children's discrimination of raised dot patterns. *Journal of Child Psychology and Psychiatry*, 27, 367–81.

Millar, S. (1988) Prose reading by touch: the role of stimulus quality, orthography and context. *British Journal of Psychology*, 79, 87–103.

Mills, A. E. (1983) (ed) *Language Acquisition in the Blind Child*. London: Croom Helm.

Mousty, P. and Bertelson, P. (1985) A study of Braille reading: 1. Reading speed as a function of hand usage and context. *Quarterly Journal of Experimental Psychology*, 37A, 217–34.

O'Connor and Hermelin, B. (1978) *Seeing and Hearing and Space and Time*. New York: Academic Press.

Pathak, K. and Pring, L. (1989) Tactual picture recognition in blind and sighted children. *Applied Cognitive Psychology*, 3, 337–50.

Pring, L. (1982) Phonological and tactual coding of Braille by blind children. *British Journal of Psychology*, 73, 351–9.

Pring, L. (1984) A comparison of the word recognition processes of blind and sighted children. *Child Development*, 55, 1865–77.

Pring, L. (1987) Picture processing by the blind. *British Journal of Educational Psychology*, 57, 38–44.

Pring, L. and Rusted, J. (1985) Picture for the blind. The influence of pictures on the recall of text by blind children. *British Journal of Developmental Psychology*, 3, 41–5.

Pring, L. and Snowling, M. J. (1987) Developmental changes in word recognition: an information processing account. *Quarterly Journal of Experimental Psychology*, 38A, 395–418.

Riddoch, M. J. and Humphreys, G. W. (1988) Visual object processing in optic aphasia: a case of semantic access agnosia. *Cognitive Neuropsychology*, 5, 26–34.

Seymour, P. H. K. (1986) *Cognitive Analysis of Dyslexia*. London: Routledge and Kegan Paul.

Seymour, P. H. K. and Elder, L. (1986) Beginning reading without phonology. *Cognitive Neuropsychology*, 1, 43–82.

3

Visual thoughts

Barbara Dodd and Judith Murphy

For parents of young profoundly deaf children, choice of communication mode is the most important and controversial decision to be made, and it must be made quickly. All experts are agreed that intervention must begin as soon after diagnosis as possible. The choice is no longer just between spoken or signed language. Spoken language can be accompanied by signed speech sound cues (cued speech). If a sign language alone is chosen then there is the problem of which sign language to adopt: a version of signed English or the sign language preferred by the local deaf community. A third possibility is 'total communication' where children are exposed to a signed language accompanied by speech.

Spoken and sign systems approach each other along the language continuum. Signed exact English is just that, a manual representation of spoken English where word order conveys meaning (e.g. 'Mary hit John' is different from 'John hit Mary'). Signed English follows the same word order as English but omits function or 'little' words like pronouns (e.g. 'my'), articles (e.g. 'the') and grammatical morphemes (e.g. plural 's', 'ed' verb endings). The structure of Pidgin sign language resembles that of sign language, but includes some conventions derived from signed exact English. Sign language does not rely on the order of words in a surface string, being more economical. Space, time and memory are basic to sign language. For example, a word can be signed and then shifted to another space outside the usual signing frame. Any subsequent signs made in that new space refer back to the original word which does not need to be signed again. The relationship between the languages can be shown as follows:–

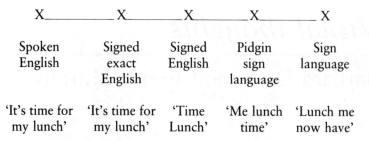

Spoken English	Signed exact English	Signed English	Pidgin sign language	Sign language
'It's time for my lunch'	'It's time for my lunch'	'Time Lunch'	'Me lunch time'	'Lunch me now have'

The history of education for the deaf is 500 years old. Every now and then there is a new *right* choice of communication mode, teaching approach and educational environment (e.g. signing/speaking, cueing; integration/special units). However, hearing impaired children, like hearing children, have their own individual talents, difficulties and style.

Ann and Margaret were both born in 1976 in Queensland, Australia. That year there had been a rubella epidemic, and as a result of maternal infection both girls were born profoundly deaf to hearing families. Margaret's mean hearing loss is 97 dB for the better ear, and Ann's is 100 dB. The families live close to each other and were advised similarly. They went to the same early intervention programme and schools where the communication choice was total communication: the sign language taught was Australian Signed Exact English. Through social interaction with deaf children of deaf parents they also acquired Auslan (the sign language used by the deaf community). Both girls escaped other sequelae of rubella infection. Their only difficulty is profound hearing impairment. They are, then, a closely matched pair: same sex, age, cause and degree of hearing impairment, non-verbal intellect, socioeconomic group, family support (both mothers became fluent in signed English), educational experience and provision of speech therapy. However, at 14 years Margaret has exceptional spoken and written language ability while Ann relies on sign language.

Margaret

Margaret has no problem making herself understood when talking to strangers, although they would be aware that her intonation was odd. She can produce all speech sounds and, when concentrating, makes no errors. However, when not focusing on speech production she may develop a nasal tone, substitute some sounds, delete some word final consonants and reduce some consonant clusters, e.g. firt for first. Margaret's language is age appropriate for a hearing person; she makes few errors of grammar which she often spontaneously corrects. She occasionally misuses a colloquialism or an unfamiliar word, but these errors show her willingness to experiment with spoken language. At school, Margaret attends all academic subject classes (maths, science, English, history, geography) with hearing children. She has a teacher-interpreter who signs what she does not understand in class and provides tutorial support. In examinations, Margaret performs better than most of her hearing peers in all subjects, coming 'in the top ten'. Margaret reads age-appropriate books (e.g. *The Diary of Adrian Mole*); she also rides a bike and plays organized sport. She was sports captain in her final year at primary school, elected by her hearing peers. Her teachers report that she is shy with strangers and lacks confidence away from the unit for hearing impaired students. She is afraid of shining in front of other children and gets embarrassed when praised. Margaret's closest friends are hearing impaired (with whom she communicates in Auslan) but she also has hearing friends.

Margaret wrote the following story:

On a warm afternoon, I was doing my homework when an extraordinary creature popped into my bedroom window. I was scared until he said 'Hi, I'm from Mars.' He gave me a Marsbar. and he was orange. He did my big heap of homework in about 1 and a half minutes. He had green stringy hair, bulging eyes, three fingers on each hand. He told me he went to school at the age of 2 years and graduated High School at the age of 12. He had always been a hard worker and he was extremely clever. He had the same cleverness as the ingenious human being ever invented on Earth. He invited me for a ride in his flying saucer to his special hiding place located at an isolated island in the Pacific Ocean. When we arrived to the isolated island named Marsee. (Marsee was named by the creature I met.) I asked him if he had a name. 'Oh yes. My name is Mark Martian. What is your name.' 'Oh my name is Margaret. What do you do here?' I asked curiously as there were nothing surrounded by us except for sand and clear water. Mark got a pink crystal out of his pocket of his shirt and put it down into the sand. Gradually a smooth surface was coming up. 'What is it' I asked 'It's a fun house, You can paint, ride, watch movies, fly and give your wishes which will be granted.' He said all that as proud as he could be. 'Wow' I whispered. When it was up, Mark and I ran into it and we painted pictures, went on 15 thrilling rides, watched happy and sad movies, Mark put some gold glitter on top of my head until I started to float way around the fun house. Mark met me up in the very top ceiling. It was as big as the Logan Hyperdome! 'Lets get down Mark' I demanded. (I was sick of flying around for 5 hours.) 'I'd better get home before my Mum arrives from work.' 'Yeah OK' and he free walked to a green cupboard on the wall and got some purple ointment. He scooped out a full teaspoon and smeared it over my nose as if it was zinc. 'Time for your wish Margie' He took me to a colourful machine. It took me a long time to think of a wish. 5 minutes passed. An idea popped into my head. 'I know' I exclaimed. 'I wish I could go to Mars one day!' The colourful machine gave me a card which read *your wish is granted. When do you want to go.* 'On the weekend would be ok.' I said truthfully. Mark Martian took me home in his flying saucer; When we landed in our backyard, he gave me 5 Marsbar to share with my family. 'Good bye Margaret. See you on Saturday.' 'Thanks Mark See ya!' I stood on the backyard stairs and waved him good bye until the flying saucer was no where to be seen. Mum has just drove into the driveway. Wow what a great evening I had!

Ann

Ann is understood only by those familiar with the speech of hearing impaired children. Her voice has a harsh tone and she substitutes, omits and distorts speech sounds. Ann relies on the use of signs although her speech is understood by her family. Her spoken language is characterized by omission of verbs, subject predominance, repetition, and 'setting the stage', e.g. 'My big bike, do you know where it is?' Ann uses signed English in class, but Auslan when chatting with friends. At school Ann follows the Hearing Impaired Unit programme that focuses on life skills rather than academic skills. Ann is integrated with hearing children only for craft work. It is likely that she will leave school at 16 and her employment options will be limited. Ann reads comics (Ken and Barbie, Superman), loves bike riding and playing netball. Her teachers describe her as 'chatty', happy go lucky with a great sense of humour. Ann is an extrovert.

Ann was first asked to tell a story in sign. The story she told was creative and followed a proper narrative sequence. The story (adult paraphrase) told how some boys and Ann (the heroine) went rowing to an island for an adventure. It was a very long way to the island, and on the way they found some killer whales. They were splashing about having fun. Everybody on the boat was very frightened. One of the whales saw them and came over and broke the boat. The boys couldn't swim and they drowned. Only Ann could swim. She was a very good swimmer, and she swam as fast as she could back to the shore. She told everybody what happened and one strong boy said he would help her find the dangerous whales. He went out by himself and speared the whale and frightened the others away. Ann was sad that the boys had died but she was very happy that the whale was killed.

When asked to write the same story she produced:

on the Boat 5 boys 1 girl find island.
Long way row and find island.
But saw a whales splash and Broke Boat.
5 Boy died and then girl fast swimming Back home.
Ask everyBoDy HelP whales.
1 Boy Kill the whales dies.
girl happy now.

The contrast between Ann and Margaret's ability to use spoken and written language is striking. Such wide variation in ability is often ascribed to differences in cause, degree and onset age of hearing loss and social and educational experience. Yet Ann and Margaret share a common history. The primary aim of our investigation was to discover in what ways the girls' thinking might differ. To this end we selected tasks from the Muma Assessment Program (MAP, Muma and Muma, 1979), a test battery devised to describe ways of thinking (cognitive strategies), and a task from Goodglass and Baker (1976) that assessed semantic fields. However, we first needed to establish Ann and Margaret's ability to comprehend language since all tasks were to be presented by the girls' speech-language pathologist, using total communication (signed exact English plus speech).

Assessment

The MAP language comprehension screening test consists of 105 items. The girls were asked to point to one of four or more pictures to comply with each test item. Examples include: point to the yellow triangle; point to a large red triangle and small blue circle; point to standing and walking; point to strong; point to in; point to her dog; point to those butterflies. Margaret made only two errors. Ann made 15, having particular difficulty with those items where she had to carry out instructions like 'Point to the blue circle *and* the red square.' Ann's poorer performance on these items is puzzling because she responded correctly when presented with more linguistically complex and longer items (e.g. 'Point to the large red triangle and the small yellow square'). Her comprehension of signed English was, by any standards, adequate for comprehension of the test instructions.

Our first choice of assessment was to compare the girls' ability to abstract (discover) the rules that govern how the environment functions and how language is structured. This is a basic cognitive skill because it allows experience to be mentally represented so that productive action can be planned. For example, when acquiring grammar children discover that plurality can be marked by adding /s/ to nouns (car, cars). Initially, they overgeneralize the rule to all nouns, producing examples like sheeps and mouses. So children also have to maintain flexibility – a willingness to modify rules they have abstracted. Although sign languages are rule governed, the linguistic rules governing spoken English (e.g. which speech sounds can be legally combined) seem particularly difficult. Perhaps Ann's poorer spoken English could be attributed to difficulty in *abstracting rules*.

The MAP examines rule learning and rule flexibility using 50 cards presented one at a time. There are two pictures on each card (e.g. a large red house and a small blue house). The instruction is: 'Try to guess what picture I'm thinking of. Point to it.' The examiner chooses a dimension (size or colour) and gives the child feedback. For example if the examiner has chosen 'red' as the dimension and the child points to the large red house then examiner indicates that the choice was correct. If, when the next card is presented (say a large blue fish and a small red fish) the child points to the large blue fish, the examiner would indicate that the choice was wrong. The score is the number of cards presented till the child makes eight consecutive correct choices. Then the examiner reverses the colour that has to be chosen (i.e. blue shapes now become the 'correct' choice). When the child has discovered the changed rule by choosing correctly on eight consecutive trials, the examiner shifts the correct choice to the other dimension: size. The child must learn that small (or large) is the dimension the examiner is 'thinking of', irrespective of colour. Again, the score derived is the number of cards presented until the child makes eight consecutive correct responses.

Children usually take up to 15 cards to abstract the rules. Learning the last rule (changing dimension) is harder and often takes more cards than the first two rules. Ann was adept at this task, the first rule taking 12 card presentations, the second, 10 cards and the third rule 22 cards. Margaret abstracted the first two rules easily (needing 12 and 9 card presentations respectively). However, she had real difficulty discovering the third rule, needing 40 presentations. That is, Margaret showed less flexibility in rule abstraction than Ann.

We then turned to the question of whether knowing sign languages influences how the world is perceived. The MAP perceptual salience task detects preference for a particular perceptual domain: colour, size or shape. The test stimuli are 36 cards, each with three pictures of geometric shapes that vary in size and colour (e.g. large red circle, small red square, large white square). The instruction is to 'Point to the two things that you like'. The test criteria quoted as showing preoccupation with one perceptual variable is 67 per cent. Margaret chose shape on 58 per cent of trials, and Ann shape on 61 per cent of trials. While not reaching the criteria indicating preoccupation with one perceptual variable, both girls showed a strong preference for shape. This may be a reflection of their everyday use of sign languages where hand shape carries meaning. If so, does the preference for shape dominate perception of what is most similar about objects?

Iconic thinking is dominated by attending to perceptual patterns of objects, whereas *symbolic thinking* is dominated by their functional properties. To assess whether their thinking was predominantly symbolic or iconic, the girls were shown 18 cards one at a time. Each card had three pictures (e.g. lamp, torch and umbrella). Two of the pictures share the same colour, two look the same pictorially (lamp and umbrella), and two are semantically related (torch and lamp). The instruction given was: 'Point to the two things that go together.' The results were very clear cut. Ann chose to pair pictures according to their iconic relationship (colour or shape) on 88 per cent of trials. Margaret chose to pair pictures according to their symbolic relationship on 83 per cent of trials. The finding cannot be simply accounted for by Margaret having a better knowledge of object names and their functions. Rather, it raises the question of whether the girls' organize their information about the world differently, e.g. how are their semantic networks organized?

To assess the girls' knowledge of *semantic relationships* they were shown 14 pictures, one at a time (e.g. cactus). For each picture twelve words were signed/spoken, and the girls had to indicate whether each word was related to the picture by saying yes or no. Six words were related to the picture (e.g. desert, prickly) and six were not (e.g. key, teeth). Margaret's performance did not differ from that of hearing adults. Ann's performance was judged by a researcher who uses the task with communication disordered people as reflecting 'mild–moderate semantic disorder'. She had some difficulty recognizing superordinate relationships (name of the class of which the picture is a member, e.g. plant) and functional relationships (situation in which the object occurs, e.g. desert). However, she recognized other relationships like attribute (prickly) and contrast coordinates (another member of the same class, e.g. tree). However, this latter semantic link was weak for Margaret, as it is for most hearing people. Ann's semantic network should not be considered disordered, but it does seem different. Perhaps using sign language as a primary means of gaining information about the world influences the development of semantic associations. If so, would this lead to other differences in ways of thinking?

One well-identified example of 'thinking style' is the difference between *analytic* and *synthetic* cognitive strategies. Synthetic thinking involves putting things together to make a whole, whereas analytic thinking reflects the ability to analyse component parts or to deduce alternative exemplars of a category. The task has 21 cards, with three pictures on each card, e.g. ring, hand, glove. The girls were asked which two pictures they preferred on each card. Pairing ring and hand or glove and hand shows synthetic thinking whereas pairing ring and glove suggests analytic thinking. Both Ann and Margaret showed a strong preference for analytic choices (18/21). Muma and Muma (1979) claim that such a performance shows an inordinate orientation to one thinking style since most children show no strong preference for part/whole pairs versus alternatives. This task then, while not differentiating the girls, set them apart from hearing children. Another possible way of assessing thinking style is by testing *divergent thinking*.

We presented Ann and Margaret with the task of turning drawn squares and circles into as many objects as possible in five minutes. Ann changed the circles into a face, perfume spray, a spinning top, a cone, a ceiling fan, a clock and a tadpole (7); Margaret drew a face, sun, orange, coins, cake, spoon and ball (8). Margaret changed the squares into a book, hardball court, swimming pool, window, poster, bedroom plan, and clock (7); Ann made the squares into a sound speaker, book, Coke dispenser, house and handbag (5). Neither had difficulty understanding or performing the task. While Margaret produced more drawings she was, perhaps, less imaginative (e.g. clock appeared twice, and she drew not only a 2 cent coin but coins of other denominations). So, again we found little difference.

In a third task assessing cognitive styles we assessed impulsivity versus reflectivity. There are 20 paired cards. In each pair one card has one picture (e.g. clock) and the other card has four pictures (e.g. four clocks: one identical to the one on the first, and three slightly different). The instruction is 'Point to the picture below that is just like the picture on top.' Many errors and short response time shows impulsivity, whereas few errors and long response time suggest reflectivity. The average number of errors in this task is five, and average response time is 2.5 seconds. Both girls performed extremely well on this task, Margaret making only two errors with response time well under 2.5 seconds, and Ann, making four errors, also having a short decision time. That is, both girls were accurate and fast. Perhaps their need to make high speed discriminations when sign-reading and lip-reading accounts for their superior performance.

Finally, we turned to two speech tasks to discover whether Ann's poor spoken language was a fair reflection of her linguistic knowledge. The first task focused on phonology (the speech sound system) and asked the questions: do Ann and Margaret have a concept of rhyme? And, do the girls differ in their ability to derive how written words might sound when spoken?

In the *rhyming* task Ann and Margaret were presented with 24 pairs of written words. There were six pairs of each of the following four types: rhyme, graphically similar (pair/hair); rhyme, graphically dissimilar (night/kite); non-rhyme, graphically similar (most/lost); and non-rhyme, graphically dissimilar (shoe/sheep). They were told to write R next to pairs that rhymed and N next to the pairs that did not rhyme. Margaret made four errors, identifying four pairs that did not rhyme but looked similar (most/lost) as rhyming. So, she was somewhat misled by the orthographic form of words. Nevertheless, she was not misled by pairs that look dissimilar but rhyme (night/kite, rough/fluff). Her pattern of errors on this task is unusual. The task is part of a test battery designed for testing the phonological abilities of children with speech, spelling and/or reading difficulties. None of these children (and over 100 have been tested) has presented with this asymmetry of performance.

Ann made 10 errors, which is close to chance performance. However, her pattern of errors showed the use of a strategy that led to a high error score. All six pairs that did not rhyme but looked similar (most/lost) were identified as rhyming. Her four other errors were distributed across the other three types of pairs. Her poorer performance probably reflects her smaller reading vocabulary. However, like Margaret, Ann was aware that words that are spelled similarly also tend to sound the same when spoken; or perhaps, more accurately, look the same when they are lip-read. Do the girls' lip-reading skills differ?

We expected to find that Margaret's *lip-reading* ability was superior because of her excellent expressive spoken and written ability. Lip-reading depends only partly on the ability visually to discriminate the articulatory movements associated with the production of speech. Lip-reading cannot provide information about some important aspects of speech, e.g. pairs of sounds like p/b, t/d, s/z look identical because they are made at the same place and manner of articulation, differing only in their level of voicing. Thus, successful lip-reading involves the use of additional information such as the context and subject matter, and linguistic cues like whether the word is likely to be a verb or a noun, whether a 'missed' word can be adduced from what was understood.

Margaret's superior spoken language should, then, enhance her ability to lip-read sentences. Each of the 20 sentences were spoken by a familiar speaker (e.g. 'Every weekend it pours with rain'). As predicted, Margaret performed better making only two errors. Ann successfully lip-read only seven sentences. This task is very hard, and probably not a fair reflection of Ann's ability to understand conversation in context. However, it is likely that her poor performance can be attributed to her poorer general knowledge of spoken English rather than to her ability to discriminate lip movement patterns visually.

Interpretations

Comparison of Ann and Margaret's spoken and written language shows a marked difference. Ann relies primarily on signing; Margaret relies increasingly on speaking. This difference in primary communication mode is reflected in their ways of thinking. Ann's thought patterns show some evidence of being visually based (e.g. preference for iconic over symbolic relationships). Margaret's thought patterns predominantly resembled those of hearing people (e.g. semantic fields). Nevertheless, the girls performed similarly on a number of tasks: preference for shape as a perceptually salient variable; analytic rather than synthetic thinking; and, rapid accurate visual discrimination matching. Further, when presented with the written word rhyme judgement task, Ann showed the same pattern of response as Margaret, even though she made more errors. That is, despite her poor speech and lip-reading she had a concept of rhyme that was not totally governed by orthography.

Oliver Sacks (1989) argues that the natural mode of communication for those born deaf is the deaf community's sign language. He writes that teaching spoken and signed English wastes time that should be spent providing knowledge about the world. Yet, Margaret communicates so well in spoken and written English that her academic performance is better than most of her hearing peers. Her poem (see below) is ample evidence that Margaret does not find using spoken language 'unnatural'. Sacks also writes that deaf children's poor functional literacy is a direct result of not learning sign language early in life. They cannot acquire information about the world, and this deprives them of the knowledge base necessary for literacy. But is this the sole reason for many deaf children's functional illiteracy? Ann acquired signed English (which she uses with her family and teachers) and Auslan (learned from familiarly deaf schoolmates) at an early age. She should, therefore, have no literacy problems. The example we have given of her story writing demonstrates that she does.

Recent research into hearing children's poor reading and spelling suggests that many have phonological coding problems, e.g. problems in abstracting the rules governing the relationship between speech sounds/syllables and letters; difficulty recognizing rhyme; and segmenting words into sounds and syllables. Acquiring literacy would seem to be largely dependent upon the ability mentally to manipulate speech units. Hearing impaired children are, then, at a distinct disadvantage when it comes to learning to read and write, irrespective of their competence in any sign language.

Perhaps the most important implication of our study is that individual deaf children's abilities vary enormously. There is an assumption in the neuropsychological literature that observation of the developing language of children who have never heard provides evidence concerning the role of audition in language acquisition. This assumption has driven a great deal of research. Profoundly prelingually hearing impaired children have acted as control groups for 'normality'. If their performance was found to be similar to that of hearing children then audition could be excluded as a necessary source of information for developing the mental processes for performing the task. If the deaf children differ from hearing children then the difference can be attributed to the task being crucially dependent on audition. That is, hearing impaired children have been investigated to assess the influence of sensory modality on cognition. There are four major problems with the basic assumption.

1 Hearing impaired children are not an homogeneous group. Deficit specific factors, like degree, cause and age of onset of the hearing loss vary widely. Other influential factors – type of early intervention, education, associated disabilities, communication mode, culture, family attitude and socioeconomic circumstances – make each child's language learning experience unique. Even when two children, like Margaret and Ann, have very similar sensory deficits and experience, they exhibit very different abilities.

2 Most hearing impaired people are not totally deprived of auditory information; it is just different. It is rarely true that deaf people 'live in a world of utter, unbroken, soundlessness and silence' (Sacks, 1989, p. 6).

3 Speech perception is not specific to the auditory modality. Hearing people make extensive use of lip-read information in sensing speech particularly, though not only, in noisy situations. Further, the brain processes speech information in the same way, irrespective of whether it is heard or lip-read. Even profoundly prelingually hearing impaired

people mentally process lip-read speech as if it had been heard not seen (see Dodd and Campbell, 1987). From a neuropsychological perspective it is therefore possible and natural for profoundly prelingually hearing impaired people to perceive speech visually.

4   Audition is the major contributing source of information for the development of language concepts by hearing people. Profound, prelingual hearing impairment means that development of language concepts is dependent upon visual information: signs, lip-read speech, reading. The type of information perceived is thought to influence conceptual development. However, the type of information perceived may be less important than the mental schemas developed for the organization of experience and planning of action.

Since both signed and spoken languages were available to Ann and Margaret from a tender age, their different language mode might not reflect inherent ability or special experiences (unknown to us). Ann and Margaret's thinking is remarkably similar, despite their contrasting approach to communication and their different semantic organization and ways of perceiving relationships. Why, then, given their common history do Ann and Margaret differ? Perhaps individual choice plays a part. Ann views language as a tool for social communication, which she enjoys. Her language is concrete and situation bound. Her signed language is rich in visual drama rather than linguistic form. In contrast, Margaret finds language itself fascinating. She asks questions that demonstrates deep metalinguistic awareness, and is unafraid to experiment with language.

Perhaps asking why Ann and Margaret's communication skills differ is like asking why one hearing child pursues music and another art. Inherent talent is not enough; curiosity, willingness to attack difficulties and practice is crucial. To understand the differences between Ann and Margaret, we need to look beyond their audiograms, communication modes, and academic and social experience. Behind the results of the standard tests are two individuals – two girls who are developing their own style, personality and interests. They are two very normal teenagers who just happen to be deaf.

Ann: on Being Deaf

I hate being deaf because people can't sign. People sign to me at high school, but I have one hearing friend that talks to me, not in sign, about school work. Hearing people talk to me and I can understand them. If I had a wish I would wish for Superman to fly me off to a restaurant, I would talk to him and he would understand me because he can do everything. I would not wish to be hearing because I wouldn't have my deaf friends. I would feel sad.

Margaret: I Cannot Hear

I go to school during the day
I sit and add and take away
In class the others talk all year
But I don't mind cause I can't hear

At lunch time I like to play ball
With my friends or against the wall
I run and jump and have no fear
They don't mind that I cannot hear

On weekends I try to stay cool
My brother and I often go to the pool
This is the best time of the year
It makes no difference that I cannot hear

I like to ride my bike around the house
I try to be as quiet as a mouse
So as not to annoy Mum, who is such a dear
She doesn't mind that I can't hear

I play netball in a team
When the times comes my eyes really gleam
I dress up in all my netball gear
None of them mind that I cannot hear

I can see through my eyes
My sense of smell survives
I sign with my hands and speak very clear
Its no problem to me that I cannot hear

So those are my feelings on hearing impaired
I am happy and for life prepared
For it gets exciting year after year
Because no-one really cares that I cannot hear

Acknowledgements

Ann and Margaret have our gratitude and admiration for their patience and cooperation. Colleagues were invaluable: Gail Woodyatt, Anne Ozanne, Meredith Kennedy, Helen Chenery and Faye Jordan.

References

Dodd, B. and Campbell, R. (1987) *Hearing by Eye*. London: Erlbaum.
Goodglass, H. and Baker, E. (1976) Semantic field, naming and auditory comprehension in aphasia. *Brain and Language*, 3, 359–74.
Muma, J. and Muma, D. (1979) *Muma Assessment Program. Descriptive Assessment Procedures: Cognitive-Linguistic-Communicative Systems*. Lubbock, Texas: Natural Child Publishing Company.
Myklebust, H. (1964) *The Psychology of Deafness*. New York: Grune and Stratton.
Sacks, O. (1989) *Seeing Voices*. London: Picador.

4

When language is a problem

M. Gopnik

When I first met Paul he was only eight years old. In many ways he was a perfectly normal child. This did not mean that he always did what he was supposed to do. He teased and joked and fooled around when I wanted him to be serious. Once when we were in a break between tests he hid behind a door and jumped out to scare me. He was very successful – I jumped a mile! He was fond of sports of all kinds, but especially hockey. He was the goalkeeper on his hockey team and whenever you gave him a chance he would tell you all about their last game.

In some ways Paul was even outstanding. At school he was by far the best in his class at maths. He was not that good at calculation; what was really impressive about him was the ease with which he understood new mathematical concepts. His teacher said he always caught on long before any of the other students and was bored waiting for the others to catch up. His second passion, after hockey, was his computer. He was a junior hacker and, for his age, was a real whizz kid. When I told him that I would be giving him some tests on the computer, he asked me detailed questions about the language the system was programmed in and what its logical structure was. I had to admit that I did not know; that I had left all the details up to my programmer. He rolled his eyes as if to say what could you do with these computer illiterates.

But when it came to language it was quite another story. Words tumbled out and he was glad to tell you stories about his hockey team, about going swimming with his cousin, about getting lost in the underground. But, though he was speaking fluently and with emotion and expression, it was very hard for an outsider to understand him. And even after you knew him well, there were still times when you did not understand what he was saying at first. But he was very patient with the uncomprehending listener. He would repeat what he said until the listener either understood or gave up. Usually he was patient, but sometimes he would protest, 'Repeat, repeat. It's boring repeating.'

I first met Paul in the children's hospital at a clinic that specializes in cognitive problems. I am a linguist and I had been invited by the pediatrician in charge of the clinic to have a look at Paul because he was such an interesting case and to assess his language. I went for an afternoon and have been working on the problem ever since. I am still trying to understand exactly what is wrong with Paul's language and the language of other children like him.

Several things were clear from the very first. He did not have any physical problems which interfered with his language. His hearing was fine and he could move his lips and tongue normally. He was not mentally retarded. He scored at least in the normal range on all of the standard IQ tests, except those which involved language. He did not have any particular emotional problems, except the perfectly normal frustration at not being understood.

There was no suggestion that the language in the family was particularly unusual in any way. He had an older sister and a younger brother, David, whose language was absolutely normal. Well, not precisely. David was really quite exceptional at language. He wrote long stories and loved literature and poetry. But things evened out. He was not nearly as good at maths as his older brother. So Paul helped David with his maths and David, in turn, tried to help Paul with language, but without notable success.

Paul's mother reported that his language development had been odd from the start. She had already had a child and so she knew what to expect. She was quite surprised when Paul was three and not talking at all. But she was not particularly concerned because he seemed bright in every other way, and besides boys were reputed to speak later than girls. By the time he was four he was talking or, more precisely, he was producing strings of sounds which were clearly intended to be language, but they were mostly unintelligible, even to her. When he started school at five his language problem was obvious and debilitating, so he started to receive speech therapy. By the time he came to the clinic he had been receiving therapy for three years, but he was still very hard to understand. He is 15 now, and though his language is much better, it is still far from normal.

Paul is not the only child with this problem. There are lots of them, children who seem to be fine in every other way. They are not deaf; they are not mentally retarded; they are not psychotic; they just cannot learn language. As they get older their language improves, but they almost always have some remaining problems with language. There are no standardized language tests for this problem. Clinicians do not even agree on what to call them. Some like the term 'specific language impairment' because it is descriptive of the problem; others prefer 'developmental dysphasia' because it relates this problem to the problem referred to by the term 'aphasia': specific language problems which result from some trauma to the brain later in life.

But the name really does not matter. No matter what it is called, the children still have the same problem. The question is what exactly is their problem and what causes it. It was clear from the start that there were two different kinds of problem which all of these children shared. They all had problems producing the right sounds to form the words of English and they also had problems using these words in sentences. To begin with, we decided to concentrate on the grammatical problems and leave the questions about the sound system till later. (We are just now looking at the sound system, but that is a story for another time.)

Finding out just what was wrong was rather like being a sleuth. The first thing was to discover where to look for the evidence and how to gather it. The second, and much harder, job was to take all the bits and pieces of evidence and put them together to tell a coherent story. As with any mystery, the clues and the answer which seem obvious once they have been discovered, were elusive to start with. The first and most obvious place to look for evidence was in Paul's spontaneous speech. So I taped conversations with him in which he told stories, answered questions and had conversations. He told me about the time he got lost:

> Last time I lost my Mommy in the metro. And last time I'm waiting in the Berri d'Montonigny [the name of a metro stop] and there's another trains coming.

I showed him a picture-book about a king and a queen and this is how he described what happened in the pictures:

> Once upon a time there's a dragon and they help on the Christmas time and the king decorate the Christmas tree and now there they put present under the Christmas trees. And then after everybody is going to bed except the dragon. He's looking to peek in the gifts. And now there the dragon's start to take one and the trees just fall down.

It is not hard to see that something is wrong with his story. But when Paul was asked questions about what happened he showed that he understood what was going on as well as any normal child. He had no problem understanding the story which the pictures told. He just had problems putting what he knew into language. If we look closer we can see some of the problems that he had. For one picture he said: 'they put present under the Christmas trees.' Now it was perfectly clear from the picture that there was only one tree and there were lots of presents and it was perfectly clear that Paul knew this. He has no problems with numeration. He obviously understands the difference between one and many or he could not do so well in maths. Yet he gets something simple like singular and plural wrong in language.

But everybody makes a mistake now and then. What had to be shown was that this was a systematic error. One which reflected something deep about the nature of his language. And now we had a problem about where to look and what to look for. The first and easiest situation was when we knew what he was talking about. In the picture stories we knew for certain what he was referring to and we could tell when he made a mistake and referred to a single thing with a plural word or to more than one thing with a singular. But when he was talking about things in the world it was harder to tell. Sometimes we could tell, however. We know that there is only one Montreal Forum, the mecca of hockey enthusiasts, and we know that he knows this. Yet he says: 'Can watch them at the Montreal Forums.'

So, instead of just worrying about matching the number of objects being referred to with the plural marking of the word, we looked at the nouns which occurred after the determiner 'a', because plurals may never occur in that context. And sure enough, in a sample chosen at random, he got about half wrong: 'You got a tape recorders.' 'I find a cops.' Then we looked at the opposite case, after numbers where only plurals should occur: 'I was make 140 box.' 'He only got two arena.' Could an eight-year-old not know what every normal three-year-old knows? Maybe he really knew about singulars and plurals in language and how to mark them, but perhaps he was just careless in speaking.

To test this we gave him sentences, some of which had mistakes in singulars and plurals, and asked him to tell us which ones sounded right and which ones sounded wrong, e.g. 'I can cut a trees.' 'I have two puck.' And then we gave him the same sorts of sentences and asked him just to repeat them. He could not reliably judge which sentences were right and which were wrong and when he repeated the sentences sometimes he put in an 's' and sometimes he did not. Then we tried him on another test. All of the previous tests had used whole sentences. Perhaps that was too hard, suppose we looked at just single words. Would he have the same problem? We turned to an old test of nonsense plurals, the 'wug' test. We drew pictures of silly animals (figure 4.1). We pointed to the single one and said, 'This is a wug.' Then we pointed to the group of these animals and said 'These are ____?' He said 'wug'. We were now getting confident that he really did not have any rule in his grammar for using an 's' to distinguish plural from singular. But all of the evidence so far involved speaking and hearing. If he really did not know how to use 's', then it should show up in other facets of language, like writing. So we studied the spelling and sentence dictation tests which he had taken over the past year and we saw the same pattern. In the dictation test he left out the 's' on almost all of the dictated plural words. It was possible that he just could not hear or did not pay attention to the little sounds. But he did get a few of the plurals right, so he must have heard the 's'. When we checked further we discovered that the plurals which he got right were all in the spelling list. He could learn that a particular word that meant there were more than one of the items was spelled with an 's'. But what he could not do was learn the general rule that, generally speaking in English, if a word refers to more than one object it ends with an 's'. It looked as if Paul was treating all words as if they were like 'child' and 'children', irregular forms which you had to learn one by one.

The question now was did he just have problems with 's' marked plurals or was his problem a more general one with number marking in language? If the problem really was with the grammatical feature *number* then he should also get pronouns wrong because they are marked for number too, though not by an 's'. *He* can only refer to singular items and

Figure 4.1 A test of nonsense plurals.

they to plural. In looking at his language we found that he often confused pronouns. In response to a picture of a child dropping a bowl, he said: 'They drop the bowl on the floor', even though the picture clearly showed only one child. He made the same sort of mistake in repeating simple phrases: 'when it rains' was repeated as 'when they rain.' It became clear that Paul had trouble with the grammatical category *number* wherever it was used in language.

But he was bright in mathematics and he clearly understood the concept of number, so that even though he could not understand the rules in the grammar which mark number he worked out his own way to indicate it when he needed to. When it was important to indicate something about the number of items he simply used a real number. For example, when he was describing the rules of a game he said: 'You make one points.' He also told us very proudly that he had: 'two bicycle'. Sometimes the number that he used was not intended to be precisely accurate, but rather to indicate a general quantity: '140 doughnut'.

One of the important things to discover was whether this problem just applied to speaking and hearing or to his language in general. To check this we looked at the spelling and dictation tests which he was routinely given in school. They were the standard kind that we all have taken: a spelling list with 20 words which were studied over the week and some dictated sentences to see if you could spell the words correctly in sentences. On the back of the paper each of the sentences which had mistakes had to be written over correctly. When he was writing these tests he could see what he was writing and could correct it if he wanted. If the errors which he was making in speaking were the result of his simply not hearing the differences or of speech going by too quickly to be fixed, then his performance in writing should have been better because he could see and correct his errors in writing. He did quite well on the dictated spelling words when they were given in a list, but he failed dismally at the dictated sentences. Of the 24 plural nouns in the dictated sentences he left off the 's' in 19 of them. It is possible that perhaps he could not hear the 's' in the dictation and that even though his hearing seemed to be normal it might be impaired in some more subtle way. But he did get five right. This was puzzling at first but when we looked at the spelling lists it all became clear. The words that he got right were all in the spelling list in the plural. He could write *apples* correctly because the word was in the spelling list. He could learn that a particular word with a plural meaning was spelled with an 's' and if he knew the word then he could very well hear the 's' in the dictation. So what might have been taken as evidence for a subtle hearing disability evaporated when we looked at the data more closely. What we knew now was that it was not just that he was missing the 's' on plural words, he was missing the whole abstract category of *plural* in the grammar.

But that was not all that was wrong with his language. It was also clear that he had problems with tense. In all of the many conversations that we had he had never used a regular past tense word marked with 'ed'. He did have some past tense verbs, e.g. 'I was about eight years old', but they were always irregular forms which were very frequent in the language. Was this absence in his speech just a result of inattention or did it reflect a real gap in his knowledge of language?

We again designed several tests to answer this question. We tried to see if he could simply fill in the blanks in sentences like: 'Everyday he walks five miles. Yesterday he _____ ?' He answered: 'Yesterday he walk.' He never filled in the blank with a regular past tense verb. Of the 12 sentences which we gave him he got none right. Not surprisingly he had the same trouble in repetition and in writing tests. Out of 12 regular 'ed' marked past tense verbs he got only five right. And all of those were in the spelling list. The picture for tense looked exactly like the picture for number. Though he did not use tense in his grammar, he clearly knew the difference between past events, present events and future events. But he could not mark this difference in the grammar. When it was important to tell the hearer when the event took place he used explicit words, just as he did for number. If he wanted to make sure that you understood that something took place in the past he simply prefixed the sentence with *last time*: 'Last time we arrive.' In the same way he used *now there* to indicate present and *and after* for future: 'And now there he's dry hisself.' 'And after it fall down.'

It was clear that he simply did not have the feature *tense* in his grammar. He simply had one form of the verb in his mental dictionary. He had the word 'arrive' which meant 'to get to a designated location' but which did not indicate when the event took place. The meaning of some words did include the meaning of when the event took place. For example, he knew that 'was' meant existence in the past and 'is' meant existence in the present, but from his point of view these words just had a different meaning. He had no systematic way within his grammar of marking when an event took place.

Paul is 15 now. He has been in a special school and has been receiving special tutoring in language in the intervening years. We have just tested him again. We gave him 15 pairs of sentences which clearly referred to past time. In every pair one verb was marked with an 'ed' for past and one was not. We asked him to rank their naturalness on a scale of 1 to 7; 7 if the sentence seemed perfectly natural and 1 if it sounded totally unnatural:

Tracy usually walks to school every day.
1   She would have *walk* to school yesterday, but it was raining.
2   She would have *walked* to school yesterday, but it was raining.

Surely after all these years and all his training he would finally get it right. He did have a perfectly consistent response. He ranked all of the first sentences in these pairs 7 and ranked all of the second sentences 6, no matter whether the 'ed' occurred in the first or the second sentence. It is clear that he still does not have an internalized rule for marking past tense.

Was the problem just with number and tense? If so, it might be that he was somehow missing out on the little parts of a word like 's' and 'ed'. That would be puzzling because, as we showed above, it was clear that he could hear and produce both 's' and 'ed'. What we needed was an example of the same sort of grammatical rule which did not get marked in this way. Then we would be able to tell whether it was the form of the grammatical rule or the presence of the little addition to the word that was the problem. The perfect place to look for this distinction was in the aspect marking system of English. If you mark progressive aspect on the verb of a sentence then it means that the action is continuous, for example 'She jumped' versus 'She was jumping'. In English you have to put two different markers on the verb in order to indicate progressive aspect: a form of the verb 'to be' before the verb and an 'ing' after the verb. Based on the analysis of other languages like English, the theory of grammar shows that if you cannot construct the right grammatical rule for aspect then the effect would be different from the case of number or tense. The markers would not be absent. What should happen is that each of the two markers should be able to appear without the other. Therefore *progressive aspect* gave us just what we needed: a way of finding out whether the problem was with the underlying grammatical system or with the surface form of the word.

When we studied his spontaneous speech we found sentences like: 'This one is look.' 'The dragon drying hisself.' 'The witch is coming.' This seemed to indicate that it was the grammatical rule that was missing. To test *progressive aspect* we showed him little puppet skits which he had to describe. To our surprise and delight, he produced exactly what the theory of grammar predicts. Out of 19 items he used sentences with both 'be' and 'ing' seven times, e.g. 'The queen is sleeping.' He used sentences with just 'be' six times, e.g. 'The dragon is walk.' Sentences with just 'ing' appeared six times, e.g. 'The dragon jumping.' He seemed indeed to be randomly choosing between the two markers. So we asked him to make up sentences for these sorts of words. For the word 'starting' he said: 'I am start to clean up my room.' For 'ride' he said: 'I am riding a bicycle.'

He used the same alternate forms when he was asked to repeat sentences. 'They are dancing' was repeated as : 'They dancing.'

His use of progressive aspect was just what one would expect if he could not construct a correct underlying rule. Therefore, it seemed reasonable to suppose that he had the same problem in tense and number; he simply could not construct these kinds of grammatical rules. Were there any other clues that we could look for to decide the case? What we needed to find was some effect of not having tense besides just not putting on the 'ed' on the verb. We found one, and an improbable one at that. In lots of languages, but not in English, you can have a verb in a sentence which is not marked for tense. In these untensed sentences you can omit the subject pronoun if its referent is clear. In English you can never omit the subject of a sentence, because you always have to put a tense marker on the verb. Very young children seem to know this rule unconsciously. Before they learn how to mark tense on the verb they often leave off subject pronouns; as soon as they learn about tense and start marking it, they stop leaving off subject pronouns. If Paul really did not have a rule for representing tense then he should also sometimes omit pronouns when they were the subject of a sentence. And he did. He omitted them in spontaneous speech: 'Can watch them at the Forums.' And he repeated sentences like 'When they play, they get points' as 'When they play get points.'

All of this evidence pointed in the same direction: an inability to construct rules in the grammar which related the form of the word to particular meanings. Anyone who had trouble in constructing these special kinds of rules would make just the kinds of mistake which Paul made.

We could now be reasonably sure that he could not construct these kinds of rules. Now we had to find out what he could do. After all he was not mute. He spoke and wrote language well enough for people to understand him most of the time. What parts of language did he know that allowed him to make himself understood as well as he did? The fundamental thing which he had to comprehend if he wanted to be understood was how to construct a simple sentence. He had to know which words were nouns and which words were verbs and how to put them together. This is not as easy as it seems. Some verbs like sneeze are intransitive and do not take objects: you cannot say 'John sneezed the dog.' Other verbs like 'put' require two nouns after it; you cannot say 'John put'; John has to put something somewhere. In the test we gave Paul some of the verbs had too many objects, some had too few and others had just the appropriate number. He had to judge whether the sentence was correct, repeat it and then act it out. By making him act it out we could find out whether he really understood who was doing what to whom. He did the job almost perfectly. Not only could he recognize and correct the errors in the sentences, sometimes when the sentence had only one object, but could take two he corrected that too. When we gave him: 'The pretty girl brings the book' he said: 'I can make it better.' He repeated it and acted it out as: 'The pretty girl brings the book to the boy.'

Even in the tests which were not intended to test his knowledge of this part of grammar he made corrections of this sort. In one of the tests for aspect which we discussed above he showed at the same time that, although he did not know how to use aspect, he did know how to construct sentences. When we asked him to judge whether the sentence: 'I saying' was correct he responded: '"I saying." No good, you cannot say "I am saying." you have to say something.' When he repeated the sentence he added the 'am' which was necessary mark aspect, but he did not seem to recognize that the sentence was wrong without it. He was, however, very conscious that the full form of the sentence required something more.

His performance on this test told us several things about his language. It was clear that the kinds of rules which were needed to construct basic sentences were easy for him. Moreover, in this test he could understand instructions like 'Is this sentence a good sentence or does it sound funny to you?' So we could be reasonably sure that in the tests of the other kinds of rules he did not get things wrong because he did not understand how to take the test; he got things wrong because he did not understand those parts of language.

What we had shown was that there was a very particular part of grammar that Paul could not do. Paul made mistakes everywhere that these rules operated in English. And he made these mistakes in his spontaneous speech, in his writing, when we asked him to repeat sentences, when we asked him to judge whether sentences were grammatical and in all the other tests we could think of. It seemed clear that an important part of what was wrong with his language was that he could not build these rules.

The question we now had to ask was whether Paul was simply a special case or whether other children with a similar diagnosis had a similar problem. To answer this question we pored over the reports in the literature on these children. While these reports were not as detailed as one might like, they did show the same pattern of errors as we had discovered in Paul. Other children made precisely the same sorts of errors in number as he had. The reports in the literature tell us that these children say things like: 'three Christmas tree', 'two motor boat', 'a cups', just the sort of errors that we would predict. In discussing the language of these children, reports agree that they have problems marking plurals with 's' and they have problems marking past with 'ed'. When it comes to aspect the reports are quite different. Everyone seems to agree that these children do produce words with 'ing', but they report that they use it 'inconsistently', sometimes using it and sometimes not. They say the same thing about their use of 'be'. They cite examples just like the ones we saw in Paul's speech: 'Man is fall down', 'Man smiling', 'Dad taking camera'. And it is clear from reading quotations from their spontaneous speech that they too drop pronouns that are the subject of the sentence. It looks like Paul is not alone. Whatever is wrong with him is also wrong with some of the other children with this same diagnosis, probably not all of them, but at least some.

One other piece of the puzzle was to see if this was a special problem because of something about the structure of English or whether it could happen in other languages too. We did not have to wait long for an answer. At the same time that we were puzzling over Paul, a colleague, Harald Clahsen, was working on the same problem in Germany. He looked at several children in Germany with the same diagnosis and came to almost the identical conclusion. The problem that they had was not just putting the inflectional markers on the words, but with constructing rules in that part of the grammar that handled number, gender and tense. We now knew that the problem was not restricted to English. It was more general. Of course, because English and German are very closely related languages, we still need to find that children who speak very different kinds of unrelated languages have similar problems in order to be sure that it is the language facility in general that causes the problem and not just a peculiarity of the Germanic languages. At the moment we are looking at children who have similar problems learning Inuktitut, the language of the Inuit peoples of the far north. (The people whom we used to call Eskimos.) We know that there are Inuit children who have problems learning language. Now we want to see if they have the same problem. This will be especially interesting because Inuktitut is a very highly inflected language with very many rules of the kind that Paul and the other children have problems with.

Even if we understood exactly what was wrong with these children, and we don't (there are still problems with their language, especially pronunciation, that remain unexplained) and even if we could show that the problem affected all languages, a deeper mystery would remain. What causes these children to have problems with such a specific part of language? And why, after years of speech therapy, can they not learn the simple rules for indicating number and tense that every three-year-old with no special teaching knows?

Nobody really has the answer. There are some likely guesses. Perhaps they were deprived of oxygen at birth. Some of the children had eventful births, though there is no direct evidence to show that there was any shortage of oxygen, and anyway many of these children had perfectly routine births. And even if you assumed that there was a shortage of oxygen, why would it affect only language and only a subpart of language at that? Another guess is that perhaps the children have some very minor hearing loss. If they cannot hear perfectly well then they might not be able to hear little sounds like 's' and 'ed'. But this theory can not explain why they produce all three forms for aspect. They could perfectly well hear and pronounce 'be' and 'ing', but they still could not get it right. As is often the case, the answer came from several different places at once and was surprising to everyone.

The second part of the story: some British dysphasias

I will recount this part of the story the way that I found out about it, though for each of the participants involved in unravelling this story it unfolded differently. I was at Oxford and I was presenting a paper on the theory of dysphasia that I discussed above. One night a friend told me that there was going to be a programme on television that night about a gene for language. Now this appeared to me to be very silly. I had just spent the previous term teaching a graduate seminar about the evolution of language and no one had ever had the temerity to suggest that there was a gene for language. There were lots of people who thought that the ability to learn language must be innate because all children learned language in the same way and no other creatures ever did. Experiments that try to teach chimpanzees language have shown us that though they can learn many complex things, they cannot master language. The way that children acquire language is impressive. They learn language without being taught and without being routinely corrected when they make grammatical errors. In fact, studies have shown that they mostly ignore corrections of their grammatical errors. Telling them what the rule is does no good. They all discover the rules for themselves in about the same order. But even those people who think that there are good reasons to suppose that language is innate have not suggested that there is a gene for language. So it was with some scepticism that I went with my friend to find out about a gene for language.

To my surprise the evidence for this language gene was from a large family which had many members who had dysphasia. The programme showed the way the cases of dysphasia were distributed in three generations of the family, about half of the children in each family had dysphasia and half did not. The family tree looked just like the pictures of

Mendel's peas that I remembered from my genetics class. It surely seemed as if a single dominant gene was behind these cases of dysphasia. But all that was said about their language was that they had problems with grammar. No examples were given and all that the two dysphasics who were shown said was, 'My name is Timmy. I am 10 years old.'

I was more than curious to find out what these problems with grammar were. The next day I telephoned the speech therapist who had brought the family to everyone's attention. She invited me to come to the special school for language disordered children which she headed to talk about dysphasia. I gave a talk about the theory that some cases of dysphasia involved the inability to construct certain kinds of language rules and then I gave examples of the kinds of errors these dysphasics would make. Every time that I described one problem or another one of the teachers in the school would say 'That sounds just like this one,' or 'That child makes just that error.' I was intrigued that these dysphasics seemed to have the same sort of problems that we had already seen. But such anecdotal information could not be trusted to answer such an important question. I had to go back to Canada, but within two months I returned with a research assistant to test the family.

The family, especially the grandmother, could not have been more warm and welcoming. They wanted to find out what was wrong and they were happy and anxious to cooperate with all of the researchers who wanted to solve this mystery. We gave our tests not only to the dysphasics in the family, but also to several of the normal members of the family. If our theory of dysphasia was right then the dysphasics in the family should have no trouble with some of the tests, but they should be unable to do others. We could judge how impaired they were by measuring their performance against that of the normal members of the family who spoke the same dialect of English and had been raised in the same household. The results of the tests were unambiguous, almost too perfect to believe. On those tests which did not involve that part of grammar discussed above there was absolutely no difference between the scores of the normals and the dysphasics. In addition, some of the tests had been run on normal people outside the family and it was clear that the dysphasics were normal on these tests. But on the tests which involved such things as *number* or *tense* the dysphasics did no better than chance. There was one test which was designed to see whether they could see that the rules had been violated. It included 30 sentences of the form, 'The boy eats three cookie'. They were asked if it sounded like a good sentence to them and if they said that it was not good they were asked to correct it. On average, they got about 15 out of 30 right. They would have done just as well if they had flipped a coin. Even when they said the sentence was not good they were not very good at correcting it. One

17-year-old boy who had been in the special school for children with language problems since he was four, after much thinking said he thought it was not good. When he was asked to make it better he said, 'The boys eat *four* cookies.' The normals in the family were just like you and me. The error was completely obvious and did not need any thinking about. On average, the normals got 29 out of the 30 right and they quickly fixed exactly what was wrong.

This was the first time I had looked at adult dysphasics. The grandmother was in her seventies and her children were in their forties, and they did some very intriguing things. I was claiming that they did not have a rule for *number* and yet they could pass a test that required them to touch 'the book' one time and 'the books' another time. How could they do this if they did not know the rule for *number*? They were perfectly bright and it seemed possible, even likely, that they had simply learned that the word 'books' referred to more than one reading object in just the same way as everyone has to learn that 'children' refers to more than one child. But how could we test this? We could not simply test them on other words because they could have learned them in the same way. What we had to do was test them on words that they could not possibly know, words that we simply made up. So we quickly made up our version of an old test, showing them two pictures of imaginary creatures (figure 4.1) and, pointing to the single creature saying , 'This is a wug.' Then we pointed to the other picture with lots of the creatures and asked 'These are ____ ?' If they knew the rule for *number* this would be trivially easy. If they had not learned the rule, but had simply learned the meaning of each 's' marked plural word as a separate word then they would not be able to do this task. They could not do the task. Some of them managed to get a few right, but when they did it was clear that they were using a rule which someone had explicitly taught them. One woman puzzled over our question for several seconds, repeating it several times to herself. It was obviously very hard for her. Finally her face brightened and she whispered to herself, 'add an *s*, add an *s*.' She got the first few right using this rule, but when we got to the creature that was named 'a sas' her rule would not work. Instead of saying 'sasses', as all normal speakers of English would, she took her rule seriously and tried to add an 's' by simply prolonging the final 's' and producing something like 'sassss', a totally unallowable word in English.

The tests themselves told us a lot, but sometimes, as we have seen, the way in which they took the test told us even more. Three members of the family did something which surprised us all and revealed a great deal about how they were taking the test. Each member of the family was tested individually and alone. The very first test was designed to be the simplest. At the start of the test the experimenter took some objects out of a bag and put them on the table in front of the person taking the test. There were four balloons, four little books, four crayons and four coins. One balloon was put on the table. The same for all of the other objects. Each kind of object was presented as a single object and a pile of three objects. Once all eight piles had been arranged on the table the person taking the test was asked to 'Touch the book', then 'Touch the crayons' and so forth. It was clearly an easy task for everyone. We thought we knew what to expect. But three members of the family, when they were asked to 'Touch to books' touched not only the pile of three books but also the single book. Of course, they were right. They had indeed touched the books. In fact, in some sense, they were more accurate than the normals who all did just what we expected; they touched only the pile of three books. The same was true with the singular words. Sometimes when they were asked to 'Touch the coin' they carefully touched a single coin in the pile of three coins. Again, we could not say that they were wrong, though they did not do what we expected them to and what all of the other normals did. When we got back to Montreal we gave exactly the same test that we had given to the family to Paul and his mother and younger brother. We saw the same exact picture of which tests they were the same on and which they differed on. In fact Paul's scores were almost always the same as the average for the family. What was more surprising was that on the touching test he did precisely the same thing as the three dysphasics in Britain had done. What we dismissed at the beginning as just a fluke in the way they took the test now had to be thought of as behaviour that was somehow the result of their problem with language. Why should there be this difference between the way all of the normals took the test and the way some of the dysphasics did? In English we use one form of a word when there is a single object and another form when there is more than one object. The items were clearly arranged on the table to show this difference between singular and plural. All of the normals understood that the display on the table exemplified this contrast. Some of the dysphasics did not realize this. Their reaction was just what you would expect of someone who did not understand that there was a *systematic* contrast in English between singular and plural. They know that 'books' means more than one book and that 'coin' means only one coin and they showed that they knew what these words meant by touching all of the books in one case and only one coin in the other.

The tests also showed clearly that they could not change from one tense to another. In a test in which there were ten sentences of the form: 'Everyday he walks eight miles. Yesterday he _____ ?' they got on average three right out of ten, just as we predicted. They did not seem to have a rule for forming tenses. But when we looked at their spontaneous speech it was clear that the adults sometimes used regular past tense words with 'ed' when they wanted to refer to some action which took place in the past, though sometimes they did not: 'The mother bird was feeding her baby. They seem to be in danger because the dad climb up the tree.' Could we find evidence that they were learning past tense words with 'ed' one at a time just like they were learning 's' marked plurals? We were lucky to have a notebook from a ten-year-old in which he wrote a story every Monday about what he had done at the weekend. By using this notebook we could trace the development of his use of 'ed'. The pattern was very clear. Almost every time he used a regular past tense word he did not put on 'ed' the first time he used it. In the very first entry he got 'watch' wrong (figure 4.2). The teacher corrected it and he got it right the next time he used it (figure 4.3) but at the same time he got 'wash', 'dress' and 'eat' wrong. Again, when the teacher corrected the errors he got them right the next time. In the very last story of the year he still forgot to mark the past tense: 'On Saturday we went to the seaside and we stop in the car park.' He had no trouble learning individual words like 'watched' and 'dressed', but he never seemed to learn that

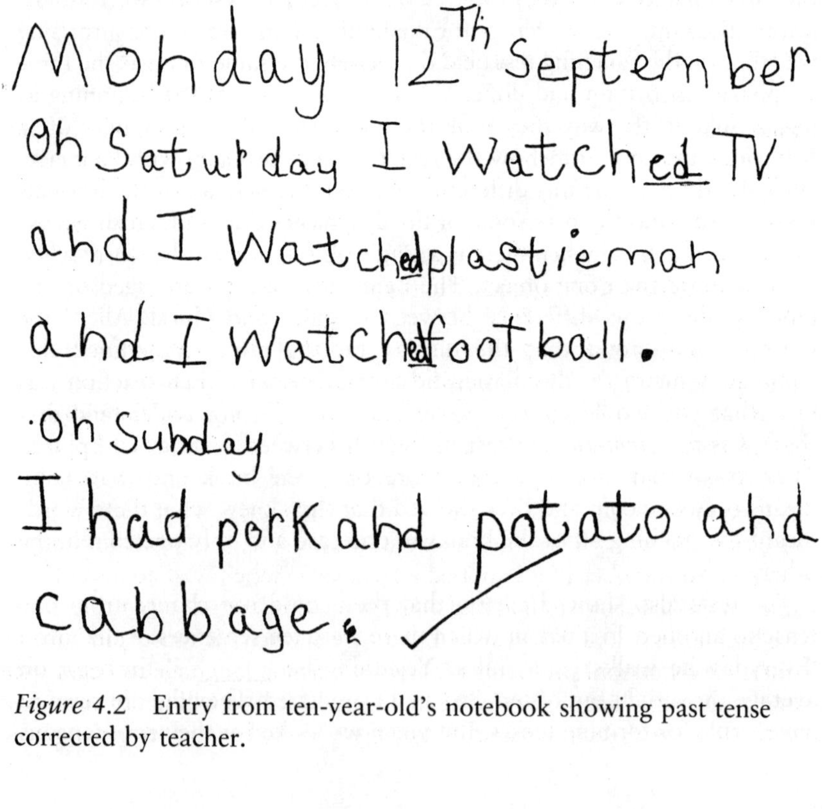

Figure 4.2 Entry from ten-year-old's notebook showing past tense corrected by teacher.

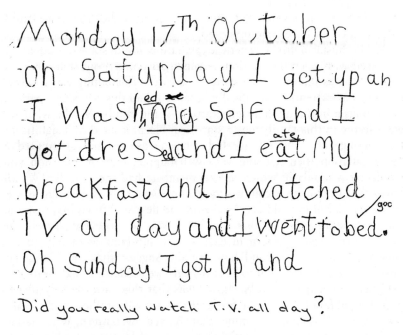

Figure 4.3 Later entry in notebook.

there was a general rule that related 'ed' with the meaning of past. But what about the four words that he did get right on the first try? When we studied these words more carefully we found out something surprising. Three out of the four words actually occurred much more frequently in normal speech in the past tense than they did in the present tense. He had learned the past tense because that was the word that he heard most of the time.

The British television programme had roused our curiosity. The speech therapists who had worked most closely with the family had said that the kinds of rules that we were talking about were just the kind that the members of the family had trouble with. And now the tests had clearly confirmed their observations. What we saw in this large family was precisely the same kinds of error that we had seen in Paul and the other children. Now another intriguing question arose. Could it be that the language difficulties that Paul had were also genetic? We had never heard that any of his relatives had had a problem with language, but then again we had never asked. So we asked and sure enough his father did have an uncle who had had problems both with learning language to begin with and with using language once he had learned it. We will never know if it was precisely the same sort of problem because this great-uncle is now dead. But still it meant that there was some indication that Paul's dysphasia could have been inherited.

Our enthusiasm for a genetic explanation for dysphasia had to be tempered with scientific caution. A geneticist pointed out that what we had so far was merely circumstantial evidence. This family was brought to everyone's attention specifically because it had this particular pattern of dysphasia in the different generations of the family. Maybe what we were seeing in this family was a statistical bleep, instead of a significant pattern of genetic inheritability. If dysphasia was randomly distributed in the population then it could very well happen that on occasion you would see a family in which several members had the disorder. We all know that if you flip a coin it should come up heads 50 per cent of the time overall, but it could very well come up heads 20 times in a row and still be random. The fact that this family was so large and showed the same distributional pattern in each of the sub-families of half of the children being affected and half not did suggest that their language disorder was inherited. But to be really sure we needed a broader range of evidence. What needed to be shown was that this pattern of dysphasia occurring in families was true for large numbers of families. And this did not mean just looking for families that showed this pattern. What had to be done was to select some children who had language problems and others that did not and then show that the families of the normal children were normal and the families of the language impaired children had other language impaired members. But even if it did show up clustered in families there might be some other explanation for this clustering. It might be the case that something strange was going on within the families that caused it. Perhaps these children were raised differently or there was some other factor in their environment which caused the language problem. If we really wanted a clinching argument that it was genetic it would have to be shown that people who shared exactly the same set of genes, identical twins, were much more likely both to have the problem than fraternal twins that did not share the same genes. All of these arguments are essentially statistical. If it turned out that every time you found a dysphasic child you also found another relative that had the same problem *and* if you could not find any other differences between the families which had dysphasia and those that did not *and* if identical twins were more alike in this respect than fraternal twins, then it would not be unreasonable to suppose that it was inherited, or at least that something or other that was inherited made children much more likely to have this disorder.

All of this statistical evidence would not really point to the gene itself. To do that you would have to look for a marker that would show up in a particular spot in the DNA of everyone who had the problem and not show up in the DNA of everyone who did not have the problem. There are ways to do this, but they are long and tedious and very chancy. I knew that there were geneticists working to find such a marker in this family. They had not found one yet but they were still looking. Even if they did find such a marker that distinguished the language impaired members of the family from the normal members it would still have to be shown that this marker told us something about the problem in general. It would have to be shown that at least some other people with language problems were distinguished with the same marker. And even if such a general marker were found it would not tell us what was wrong with their language. The detailed linguistic analysis would still have to be done.

A genetic basis for dysphasia? The latest news

I wrote a brief report about the family and what I knew about their problems. Even though the evidence was far from complete it was important to report that there was the possibility that there was a gene which affected part of language. If there were such a gene it would provide direct evidence that in some way the brain was constructed from the start to learn these rules of language and that brains which did not get constructed correctly could not learn them. If it were true it would be very important to know about; if it were not then others would have a chance to demonstrate how and why it was not. Only by making it explicit and putting it before the scientific community could other scientists have the chance of testing these ideas. This free exchange of information and ideas is the essence of science. Real science is about moving forward the frontiers of knowledge. It is less important to be right than to have your work lead to new insights. The article had precisely this effect. I heard from two colleagues who had both been working on the origins of dysphasia. Both of them independently had done precisely the kind of statistical study that my geneticist colleague had said was necessary. They both had compared the families of children with dysphasia to the families of children who were normal and they both came to the same conclusion: if a child has a serious problem with language then it is very likely that a parent or sibling will also have a language problem; if a child does not have a language problem then it is very unlikely that a close relative will have one. They were both cautious about interpreting their results: maybe it was genetic but perhaps it was environmental. It seems to me that you can put the environmental question the other way around. Perhaps you should ask how the normal children in these families escape from having language problems. In the large family that we studied there was a family of nine children. The mother and four of the children were dysphasic. Five of the children were normal. There seemed to be no sex bias, two girls and two boys had language problems and four boys and one girl did not. And they were distributed in age among the family. The first, the fifth, the seventh, and the ninth child had language problems. There was even a set of fraternal twins, one who had problems and one who did not. Our tests showed that the normal children were perfectly normal when we compared their results to those of other normal people outside of the family. The mother and the school reported that the normal children were always perfectly normal. They started to speak at about a year and a half and they had absolutely no problem with language. Now the question is how did they do it? While they were growing up they heard all kinds of errors from their mother and their sisters and brothers and cousins and uncles and aunts and grandmother. Yet somehow they knew that they should not pay attention to these errors, but instead they should construct rules like their friends and normal relatives. It would be hard to think of something in their environment that could account for this. Perhaps there is something, but no one has yet proposed it. The statistical results are complex, but they also do not seem to indicate that any simple environmental explanation could account for the way that the language problems are clustered in families.

Most exciting of all was finding out that one of these colleagues had actually performed a twin study. It was not yet published, but the results were clear; if a pair of male twins were judged to be identical then the probability that they both would be receiving language therapy was over 80 per cent, if they were judged to be non-identical then the probability fell to under 35 per cent. This was not surprising since it had been shown in the large statistical study that brothers had a 35 per cent probability of both having language problems. Now we had evidence of several different kinds about the pattern of distribution of language disorders; from a large family, from two statistical studies and from a twin study, that all pointed in the same direction: at least some component of language impairment in at least some patients is heritable.

That is where we are now. Each of the scientists involved in this quest is beginning to understand a piece of the puzzle. Evidence from lots of directions points to a genetic origin, but no one has yet located its site on the DNA. Nor do we yet know what this gene actually does to the developing brain that affects the way in which language is learned. Neurologists have done autopsies on the brains of some people who have had problems in learning to speak and to read and found that their brains are indeed constructed differently from normal brains but we do not yet know if these people had precisely the same sort of problem as that which we have been talking about here. We also do not have a good picture of the way that these people actually use their brains in processing language. We guess that they do it differently from normals and we are just beginning to develop tests to find out about how their brains actually process language. When it comes to the actual language which they do use we know a bit more. The evidence seems to be clear that all of the parts of language that are normally handled by certain kinds of rules are learned by these people as single items. This seems to show that some parts of language can be learned by using general intelligence rather than by an innate specific set of instructions for acquiring language. To do it this way you have to learn one word at a time. It takes a long time to do it this way, perhaps 40 years, and you never really get it right, but it can be done. What is perfectly clear, however, is that this is not at all the way normal children go about the job of acquiring language.

Though we now know somewhat more about the language of these people there is much more that we still do not know. We still do not understand what is wrong with their pronunciation or why they have this problem too. We have a hunch that they cannot construct general rules about the sound system of the language either, but we are just starting to understand this part of their problem. And we have only a very rough idea of what they cannot do in syntax. They do not make very many mistakes in syntax, but then again they do not try to construct very complex sentences. Could they have simply learned some very basic sentence forms and by sticking with these manage to communicate? From what we know about the syntactic complexity of the language that they do produce and the general complexity of the rules for syntax in general this seems unlikely, but the evidence is not yet in.

We have always known that some children, who are bright in every other way, do not learn language like other children. We do not yet know all the answers, but at least we have made real progress in finding out the right way to pose the questions.

Further Reading

This chapter was written to communicate something of the excitement of the discovery of similar language problems in different children; it would have slowed down the pace of the story to have given you dates and details in the text.

A more detailed, scientific description of the family with dysphasia is given in Gopnik (1991). Other studies on the genetics of language that suggest a genetic component (in some, but not all, cases) can be found in Tallal et al. (1989a, b) and in Tomblin (1989). The first genetic study of the British family with dysphasia is reported by Hurst et al. (1990).

My approach of trying to find a *motivated linguistic* account of the problem in dysphasia is shared with other investigators (Clahsen, 1990; Gopnik, 1990; Grodzinsky, 1990). In Gopnik (1991) there are fuller details, with linguists' labels, of the different tests of different parts of the 'grammar machine' for most of the British children.

References

Clahsen, H. (1990) *Child Language and Developmental Dysphasia.* Philadelphia, PA: John Benjamin.

Gopnik, M. (1990) Feature blind grammar and dysphasia. *Nature,* 344, 715.

Gopnik, M. (1990). Feature blindness: A case study. *Language Acquisition,* 1 (2), 136–64.

This is a more detailed account of the child described informally in this chapter. It provides data and analysis that suppport the argument that this child cannot construct general linguistic rules for grammatical features such as number, tense or aspect.

Gopnik, M. and Crago, Martha (1991) Familial aggregation of a developmental language disorder. *Cognition* 39, 1–50.

This paper investigates the etiology of developmental dysphasia and its linguistic properties. Data are presented that suggest that at least some cases of dysphasia are associated with an abnormality in a single dominant gene. The results of a series of tests on a large three-generation family, in which half of the members have dysphasia, are reported. These results show that abstract morphology is impaired in these subjects. It is argued further that the data are consistent with the hypothesis that the dysphasics learn the feature-marked lexical items of language as unanalysed lexical items. They do not have the underlying capacity to learn language by constructing paradigms.

Grodzinsky, Y. (1990) *Theoretical Perspectives on Language Deficits.* Cambridge, Mass.: MIT Press.

Hurst, J. A., Baraitser, M., Auger, E., Graham, F. and Norell, S. (1990) An extended family with a dominantly inherited speech disorder. *Developmental Medicine and Child Neurology,* 32, 347–55.

Leonard, Laurence B. (1989) Language learnability and specific language impairment in children. *Applied Psycholinguistics,* 10, 179–202.

Theories of language learnability have focused on 'normal' language development, but here is a group of children, termed 'specifically language-impaired' for whom these theories are also appropriate. These children present an interesting learnability problem because they develop language slowly, the intermediate points in their development differ in certain respects from the usual developmental stages, and they do not always achieve the adult level of language functioning. In this article, specifically language-impaired children are treated as normal learners dealing with an input that is distorted in principled ways. When the children are viewed from this perspective, Pinker's (1984) theory can account for many of the features of their language.

Pinker, S. and Bloom, P. (1990) Natural language and natural selection. *Behavioral and Brain Sciences*, 13, 707–84.

This paper addresses the question of whether language can be accounted for within a neo-Darwinian model. Evolutionary theory offers clear criteria for when a trait should be attributed to natural selection: complex design for some function and the absence of alternative processes capable of explaining such complexity. Human language meets these criteria. Grammar is a complex mechanism tailored to the transmission of propositional structures through a serial interface. Autonomous and arbitrary grammatical phenomena have been offered as counterexamples to the position that language is an adaptation, but this reasoning is unsound. Communication protocols depend on arbitrary conventions that are adaptive as long as they are shared. Consequently, language acquisition in a child should systematically differ from language evolution in the species, and attempts to analogize them are misleading. Reviewing other arguments and data, we conclude that there is every reason to believe that a specialization for grammar evolved by a conventional neo-Darwinian process.

Tallal, P., Ross, R. and Curtiss, S. (1989a) Familial aggregation in specific language impairment. *Journal of Speech and Hearing Disorders*, 54, 167–73.

Tallal, P., Ross, R. and Curtiss, S. (1989b) Unexpected sex-ratios in families of language/learning impaired children. *Neuropsychologia*, 27, 987–98.

Tomblin, J. B. (1989) Familial concentration of developmental language impairment. *Journal of Speech and Hearing Disorders*, 54, 287–95.

A questionnaire concerning the history of treatment of developmental language disorder was used to evaluate the prevalence of these problems within the immediate family members of second-grade children with and without language impairment. The data obtained from these families revealed strong evidence that such language problems are not randomly distributed across families but rather tend to concentrate within families. Although all family members of the language-impaired second graders demonstrated substantially increased odds for language impairment over those who came from families with normal second graders, a considerable range of increased odds for language impairment existed among the family members. These results are consistent with the hypothesis that the factors that contribute to developmental language disorders are at least in part genetic.

5

Developmental verbal dyspraxia: a longitudinal case study

Joy Stackhouse

'My mouth won't cooperate with my brain' was how Keith, aged 13 years, described his dyspraxic speech difficulties. This insight reveals that although he knew what he wanted to say, he could not programme, time and coordinate the articulatory movements required. These difficulties existed and persisted in the absence of any obvious cause such as muscular weakness or physical abnormality.

The term *dyspraxia* was originally used in the nineteenth century by Broca to describe the difficulties in programming speech that some adults experienced following a stroke (Edwards, 1984). These *acquired* speech difficulties were: observable groping for sounds in words (phonetic experimentation), breakdown in multisyllabic words, inconsistent and variable production of words and frustration that the words will not come out right. It was not until the 1960s that the term was applied to children with *developmental* speech difficulties. Morley (1967, p. 237) described a 'defect of articulation' where the muscles used for speech are: 'normal for involuntary and spontaneous movement . . . but are inadequate for the complex and rapid movements used for articulation and reproduction of sequences of sounds used in speech'.

One of the problems with these defining characteristics is that they are only clearly demonstrable in older children. For example, in the pre-school years the criteria mentioned above with reference to the adult stroke victim are inappropriate. It would be quite acceptable for a three-year-old to have trouble with multisyllabic words such as 'gorilla', 'photography' or 'preliminary'. It is characteristic of normal speech development to have some inconsistency and variability as the child experiments with new sounds and structures (Grunwell, 1987). This lack of a developmental perspective may account for why the term 'developmental verbal dyspraxia'[1] has proved controversial when applied to children. There have been conflicting findings as to what the key characteristics may be (Williams et al., 1981) and indeed whether dyspraxia exists at all as a clinical entity in children (Guyette and Diedrich, 1981).

A developmental speech disorder cannot be static as it occurs within a rapidly changing individual, so the search is on for the criteria that will identify the *young* child who will go on to develop the defining characteristics of the disorder. Keith quoted above is now 18. He clearly has dyspraxic speech difficulties according to the criteria laid down by clinicians working with adults. However, this has not always been the case. Furthermore, the serious speech difficulties that he has experienced have affected other areas of his development such as his literacy skills. By observing Keith's progress at four different points in his development: first preschool, and then at age eight, 14 and 17 years, the unfolding nature of the condition can be seen.

Keith: case history

Keith was the youngest of three children. His father was employed in a manual occupation and his mother stayed at home when her children were young. Keith was referred to speech therapy at the age of two years and six months as his mother and health visitor were worried that he was 'not talking'. His expressive vocabulary comprised a small number of single words: 'No, mummy, look' and he was not putting words together as expected. However, he played well and vocalized during play. His mother felt that he understood appropriately for his age and was non-verbally very communicative. She described him as a happy and affectionate child.

No hearing problems were evident on testing at eight months and on subsequent tests during the preschool years. Keith had passed all milestones apart from speech at the appropriate ages. Although there were no obvious neurological or physical problems, he was clumsy in his movements and had had difficulties feeding. Head circumference was two standard deviations above the norm and this was being monitored at the local clinic. Handedness was established late and Keith used both left and right hands during the preschool years. This was also true of other members of the family, some of whom were thought to have minor speech problems. 'Terrible spelling' was described as a family trait.

Preschool years

On the Reynell Developmental Language Scales (Reynell, 1969), administered when Keith was aged two years and eight months, he scored at the two years and three months level on verbal comprehension but only at the nine-month level on the expressive language section. The gap between his chronological age and verbal comprehension age closed during the preschool years and by the age of five years and five months, Keith's verbal comprehension was above age appropriate, being at the six-year level. However, the gap between his chronological age and expressive skills persisted: even when he started school at the age of four and a half, he had limited expressive language and very unintelligible speech.

Although there was no physical abnormality of the mouth, Keith found it difficult to copy oral movements and speech sounds. For example, at the age of three when asked to mimic sad or happy faces, there would be much grimacing before he could get the right expression. Sequencing sad and happy faces was impossible. On one occasion he was so frustrated by his attempts to make a whistling face in the mirror that he pushed his lips into the forward pouting posture by using his fingers. This illustrates a curious feature of dyspraxia. Keith was unable to adopt a whistle posture to command and yet could blow a kiss to his mother automatically. Similarly, he could easily lick ice-cream from a cone but he could not stick out his tongue when asked. As these are non-verbal activities, this phenomenon is known as *oral dyspraxia* as distinct from *verbal dyspraxia*.

By four years of age he talked a lot but was very difficult to understand because of his reduced sound system. This comprised mainly of 'b' and 'd' in the initial position of words. He could produce other sounds in isolation such as 'p' and 't' but did not use them in continuous speech. He did not use any fricative sounds (f, v, s, z, sh) or affricates (ch, j) but would blow through spread lips when trying to copy these. He found it impossible to produce 'k' and 'g'. Another feature of his speech at this age was the replacement of final consonants by a glottal stop – the sound commonly used instead of 't' in Cockney speech in words like 'bottle' and 'butter'. This gave the impression of a jerky or staccato flow of speech. Initially, his problems were not restricted to the consonant system: some vowels were also absent or mispronounced. However, the vowel system had developed appropriately by the end of the preschool years.

Keith's limited sound repertoire meant that many words were represented by the same form. For example, he would say 'dor' for *door*, *tore* and *core* or 'dee' for *D*, *tea* and *key*. He was therefore unable to use sounds to contrast meaning (phonological disability) because of his difficulties in producing sounds in sequences (articulatory disorder). At the age of four, Keith's production of the sentence 'I played football in the garden' sounded like 'I day du-or i e dar-en.' The 'little words' like *in* and *the* were not always clearly marked, and it was very difficult to tell at this stage to what extent there were syntactic difficulties. Certainly, morphological endings such as plurals, for example 'days', could not be marked. However, comprehension of grammatical structures and the mean length of utterance produced were age appropriate.

In spite of his severe articulatory difficulty, Keith made himself understood more often than you would expect. Context helped the listener and Keith would use gesture and exaggerated intonation to emphasize his points. He was also patient with the listener and did not mind repeating the information, although it often sounded different on repetition and not always nearer to the target.

He settled well in to the local nursery school. He made friends and was communicative with both teachers and peers. He enjoyed drawing and played well with formboards though clumsiness hampered his performance. This was particularly evident in activities such as bead threading and peg boards which he tended to avoid. Concepts were well developed and play was imaginative. However, he found it impossble to tune in to rhyming games and beating time with musical instruments was somewhat haphazard.

Keith aged eight years

On first meeting Keith at this age you would be struck by his outgoing and welcoming personality: a happy little boy keen on his pets and doing well in the Cubs. Although very chatty, he was still difficult to understand at times and the listener was reliant on contextual cues. In spite of a rather blank facial expression, he communicated well and occasionally used gesture to supplement his speech. Clumsiness was still evident. He was inclined to bump into things and had a dishevelled appearance. He was always one of the last to get dressed after swimming at school.

Keith was now able to produce all sounds to command but did not use the full repertoire in continuous speech. He used 'p, b, t, d, m, n, l, f, v and w' in simple words but 'k, g, th, s, z, sh, ch, j, r, y' did not appear very often. Non-English sounds also appeared as a result of distortions of the target sounds. For example, 'k' was particularly difficult for him even at this age. Sometimes, when aiming for 'k', his imprecise articulation would sound more like the sound at the end of *loch*. Similarly, some fricatives were realized as the Welsh 'll' as in *Llandudno*, particularly if there was an adjacent 'l' sound as in *slipper* or *falls*. Compared to the preschool years, there was an increased number of sounds at the beginning and ending of words which improved his intelligibility.

However, dyspraxia is not so much a problem with individual sounds as one of programming and coordinating sound sequences. Testing the prerequisite skills for this involves counting how many times the child can stick out his tongue or move it from side to side in five seconds. Norms exist for these diadochokinetic rates, but the relationship between these non-verbal measurements and sound articulations is debatable. Testing the child's ability to produce sound sequences involving articulatory place change may be nearer to real speech. For example, consider the articulatory movements required to produce the following sequence: 'p-t-k'. First, the 'p' sound is produced by the lips. Second, the tongue tip moves up to the alveolar ridge behind the teeth to produce 't'. Finally, for 'k', the back of the tongue lifts up to the soft palate at the back of the mouth. Although such measures are unreliable in the preschool years, by eight Keith clearly had reduced rates of oral movements and performed poorly on sound sequencing speech tests. For example, when asked to say 'p–t–k' quickly and three times he produced a different sequence each time as follows:

p–t–k (correct but very slowly and carefully produced)
p–k–t (the k was slightly distorted)
p–t–t (the sequence is now lost)

Needless to say, problems at this level do not bode well for performance in longer words which comprise rapid sound sequence changes. Consider the articulatory place changes required in the following words: *buttercup hippopotamus, pictorial*. As in the above sound sequence test, Keith would produce these words differently on separate occasions. It was not that he could not produce the sounds but rather that he could not programme and carry out the sequence within the word. For example, he produced *buttercup* in the following ways in a short space of time: 'buttertup, bukertup, butterpuk, bukerpup'.

At school, he was a popular boy with his classmates and he worked hard. Teachers, however, were exasperated by his untidy handwriting and disorganized presentation of work. He enjoyed looking at books and could recognize familiar words. Reading new material was difficult. He was unable to apply letter-sound rules and his reading was not developing as quickly as expected for his overall ability. Spelling was also difficult to decipher and appeared bizarre at times.

Keith aged 14 years

By the age of 14, Keith was quite intelligible in everyday conversation but would still trip up over longer words. The following speech errors illustrate typical dyspraxic difficulties:-

ambulance	→	ambe, a-be-lance, abulance
systematic	→	sinsemakit
classification	→	classikekation
bibliography	→	biglegrafefi

The first example shows how a word might be broken up into its syllables in order to plan the flow and how sounds may be omitted. The second example reveals the problem with clusters (a sequence of consonants without intervening vowels: sp, fl, tr, spr, skl). The 'st' has been replaced by an incoordinated 'ns' articulation. Note also the transposition of the sounds 't' and 'k' (metathesis) in the last syllable. The third and fourth examples show repetition of the same sound (perseveration) as a result of difficulties changing the position of the articulators rapidly. The flow of the word was particularly distorted in the last example.

These errors occurred even though Keith could articulate the sounds individually. The problem was therefore not one of sound production but of planning the flow of the whole word. In each case he could define the meaning of the words correctly but was beginning to avoid speaking such words in conversation even though they were within his vocabulary. If he could not think of a simpler word, he would circumlocute by describing what he meant.

Higher level syntax errors also occurred. At times Keith would sound non-fluent as a result of sentence planning difficulties. The following extract is taken from an interview where Keith reflected on his difficulties. Speech errors were few, but note the hesitations and syntax:

From er the age of two – from er eighteen months – I had er this problem called dyspraxia and since then I had a problem of speaking and pronouncing letters – and er se way of spelling which is dyslexia – and um from a age of two I did not speak for two years – til about four – and um had – I had problem with writing and understanding letters which from a speech therapist which I have managed to learn – and um from then I've managed to write and spell and I've been going to speech therapist for er ten years roughly and from then I've been – well – for them ten years I've been going roughly about once a week or sometimes for twice a week . . .

Intelligence tests administered confirmed that Keith was a boy of above-average intelligence and yet his reading and spelling skills were below age appropriate. Although he had progressed well with his reading and was now reading for pleasure at home, he was still underachieving given his overall IQ. What is more, his spelling was not just immature but showed signs of specific segmentation difficulties. Spelling errors were particularly evident in longer words that he had trouble pronouncing, for example:

mysterious	→	mistreriles
politician	→	polieytistioon
calculator	→	catltulater
machinery	→	michaengery

When asked how he tackled words that he could not spell, he replied: 'I listen for the sharpest notes and then think of words like them.' This would account for why in each case he has the correct number of syllables – the 'sharpest notes' of the word being the most salient beats. All of the above examples have four beats or syllables. He was also able to identify the beginning of each word. The problem arose identifying the sounds within the syllables, within the word, as a prerequisite to selecting the appropriate letters. Even non-speech-impaired adults will repeat an unfamiliar word in order to clarify its components prior to spelling it. This avenue was restricted for Keith since his articulation of multisyllabic words was imprecise and, more significantly, very variable. He was aware of this and stated that if 'I can't say it, I can't split it up.' It is difficult to work out the components of a word when their order changes on each repetition.

Keith aged 17 years

Keith was now a tall, well-proportioned, competent young man. Clumsiness was no longer apparent and he was enjoying his new hobby of sailing. Speech errors persisted but not enough to interfere with intelligibility. For example, he would separate clusters with a neutral vowel (intrusive schwa) as in *statistic* pronounced as 'setistic'. Other intrusive sounds occurred, for example *spaghetti* pronounced as 'spleghetti'; but in the main it was only multisyllabic words of four or more syllables that still showed speech programming problems, for example:

hippopatumus	→	hitopotanus
chrysanthemum	→	chrysanfefum
preliminary	→	plim, plewim, ple, pre, plelimewy

A Wechsler Adult Intelligence Scale was administered when Keith was 17 years and three months. He scored in the high average range even though there was a scatter of test scores. He had slow reaction times on auditory tasks but performed well on visual tasks. He still performed much better on reading comprehension tasks than those involving reading aloud, on which he had a reading age of 12 years and four months. He was inclined to confuse visually similar words. For example, he read *soloist* as 'socialist' and *pneumonia* as 'pandemonium'.

Keith had developed a good spelling vocabulary and could spell quite complicated words automatically for example: *especially, library, immediate*. On testing, he had a spelling age of 12 years and six months. Errors in spelling were now nearer the target. Compare his spellings of the following words with those produced at the age of 14 (see above):

mysterious	→	misterious
politician	→	politition
calculator	→	catulator
machinery	→	mechinary

However, some spelling errors indicated persisting speech and segmentation difficulties:

familiar	→	ferminiler
similar	→	simin, siminila, siminiler
slippery	→	slipperly
amateur	→	aminature

Keith could now perform well on segmentation tasks involving rhyme and identification of sounds at the beginnings and ends of words. However, more age-appropriate tasks revealed persisting high-level segmentation difficulties. One such task was a spoonerism test (Perin, 1983). Names of singers and pop groups are presented with the instruction to transpose the first sound of each word. For example, the spoonerism on *Chuck Berry* is 'Buck Cherry'. Keith found this difficult but persevered and scored 15/18 correct. Accuracy, however, was at the expense of speed: reaction time was slow and there was normally a long pause between the first and second name. He had particular difficulties with the following items:

Led Zeppelin → Zed Leppin
Johnnie Cash → Connie Jesh
Four Seasons → Sorf Feasons

When compared to his classmates, Keith also found that it took him much longer to produce a piece of written work. This proved to be a handicap in written examinations. Handwriting was now perfectly legible and his work appeared tidy. Help with organization of ideas and sentences was still needed but the content of his written work was imaginative and interesting. The following is an extract from an essay written in his last year of school (he confessed that this was not the first draft!):

Inmagine that you are in the fifth year of your secondary school, the end of the school year and prehaps school life is drawing near . . . So questions rush to your head while you speaking to your careers adviser . . . Perhaps one of the questions you might of asked in the careers room was 'What about if I want to do just practical you know no written work?' The careers lady would not worry you by sayying that all of the courses being offered to you for the next year in school are just examination courses. In fact there are many courses in the sixth form which last for six months and each pupil is given a certificate to prove that he/she has completed the course. To show any future employer . . . The 'earn as you learn' scheme which I have mentioned briefly before is an idea which may sound as a dream come true to those who otherwise may be unemployed. But a harsh note bits into the reality of the scheme and thats the amount of money which people are being paid also they are being paid such a low wage. That many employers will rather take on these Y.T.S. employees than pay other people a normal wage.

Discussion

Keith illustrates the wide-ranging problems experienced by children described as having developmental verbal dyspraxia. In addition to his speech problems, he also had language, learning and motor difficulties. Table 5.1 lists the characteristics of developmental verbal dyspraxia as cited in the literature (references for further reading are at the end of the chapter). The table is organized to show the different perspectives on this condition.

Table 5.1 Perspectives on developmental verbal dyspraxia

The speech perspective	*The clinical perspective*
General characteristics	**Genetic**
History of delayed speech development	Speech and/or learning problems often occur in other members of the family
Resistant to therapy	**Neurological**
Unintelligible	Soft signs, e.g. clumsiness
Articulation	Delayed lateralization of cerebral function
Inconsistent v. rigid pattern	Predominance in males
Phonetic experimentation	Feeding problems – chewing and sucking
Non-English articulation	Drooling
Errors increase as word length and complexity increase	**Oral examination**
Breakdown in continuous speech	Oral apraxia
Perseveration	Poor lip posture
Metathesis	Poor tongue tip control
Intrusive schwa	Slow or inability to perform diadochokinetic rates
Sound omissions, particularly in syllable final position	Problems with oral sensory-motor feedback
Voice, place and manner errors	
Vowel distortion	*The linguistic perspective*
May also show dysarthric features	History of delayed language development
Prosody	Verbal comprehension often significantly ahead of expressive language development
Inappropriate stress and intonation	Phonological disability
Variable speed – may have rushes of speech	Restricted use of syntax
Monotonous	Disordered verbal language development
Resonance	Non-verbal communication may be well developed and compensatory
Fluctuating nasality as a result of incoordination of the palatopharyngeal sphincter	
Incoordination of the vocal tract resulting in:	*The cognitive perspective*
dysphonia	Often a significant discrepancy between verbal and performance tasks
dysprosody	Problems with reading, spelling, writing and drawing
disorder of resonance	Poor auditory memory
inconsistent articulatory pattern	Sequencing difficulties
	Cross-modality difficulties
	Selective attention problems

Working through the list of characteristics, it is clear that Keith had most of them. Clinical observation revealed soft neurological signs. His vocal tract was incoordinated and his speech developed into a classic dyspraxic pattern. Language problems, particularly at the syntax level, were evident. Keith also experienced learning problems at school and had poor auditory memory and sequencing abilities. In contrast, visual tasks were not a problem for him.

Demonstration of so many dyspraxic features has only been possible by taking a longitudinal view of Keith's progress. The classic signs of verbal dyspraxia outlined in the introduction were not present in Keith's speech during the preschool years. He did not use multisyllabic words and would not grope for or experiment with sounds since he had so few in his output repertoire. However, there were indications that he would develop dyspraxic speech difficulties. The accompanying neurological signs of clumsiness and delayed lateralization may be the most significant factors here. Certainly, children can have equally severe articulatory difficulties in the absence of neurological signs and go on to achieve normal speech and language levels by the time they start school. Common causes of these difficulties may be chronic upper respiratory infections, fluctuating hearing loss and immature motor development (Stackhouse, 1984).

Children can be misdiagnosed as 'dyspraxic' on the basis of the severity of their unintelligibility. This measure in isolation is not very helpful since young children are often unintelligible because of the absence of sounds rather than because of the presence of oral incoordination and sound programming problems. Diagnosis on the basis of speech data alone can therefore be misleading. The total clinical picture and developmental pattern needs to be considered too.

Dyspraxic difficulties occur in varying degrees of severity within the same child as well as between different children given the same label. Keith had a very severe speech problem initially but now has mild speech difficulties and is perfectly intelligible. He is, however, still dyspraxic. It is the *persistence* of the difficulties rather than the *severity* that should alert us to the likelihood of associated language and learning problems.

The associated learning problems are usually most evident in the child's reading and spelling skills. However, it is not necessary to wait until a child fails at school before intervening. Warning signs in the preschool years may be present. Keith's general and oral motor incoordination and his poor performance on early sound-processing tasks, such as beating rhythms and rhyming games, suggested that he was at risk for later dyslexic difficulties (Bradley and Bryant, 1983). This concern indeed proved to be well founded.

As he had problems in developing alphabetic skills, Keith's reading progressed along mainly visual lines: he accommodated words into his visual memory through reading experience. Inevitably, his visual memory became overloaded which explains why visual errors were common. Reading new words was difficult because of the problems with letter-sound conversions, so he relied heavily on context for decoding unfamiliar material.

Spelling is even more reliant on sound-processing skills. Again, Keith has developed his spelling skills by learning whole words or chunks of words. Spelling novel material or multisyllabic words was difficult because of his inability to distinguish the components of syllables. This is particularly the case when the syllable contained sound clusters. Children with verbal dyspraxia have been found to have specific difficulties discriminating the order of sounds in clusters, particularly if the words are unfamiliar to them (Bridgeman and Snowling, 1988). For example, the difference between *lots* and *lost* requires precise identification of the order in which 't' and 's' occur. Arguably, this is because they are unable to use their articulation to hold on to the word while they perform various processing tasks. Keith was certainly aware that his repetition of words was variable and unhelpful. However, as his speech has improved, so has his spelling. Words are now decipherable even if not completely conventional.

It would be wrong, however, to assume that there is a one-to-one matching between the speech and spelling errors made by children with developmental verbal dyspraxia (Snowling and Stackhouse, 1983). Rather, the imprecise and variable speech production confuses the child so that the spelling outcome is unpredictable.

Identification and prognosis

Developmental verbal dyspraxia is much more than a speech problem. It is a medical condition where clinical features should be a central part of the diagnosis. It is a psycholinguistic disability within which problems may occur at the input and representational stages of information processing as well as at the more obvious speech output stage. It presents the child with educational problems, particularly where reading and writing are concerned.

The defining characteristics of the disorder will depend on the child's developmental level. The range of problems will unfold as the child progresses and more demands are placed upon him or her. Not all of the features listed in table 5.1 will be present all of the time. Some may not occur at all. However, for the label to be used with confidence, there should be evidence from each of the four perspectives during the child's development.

This may still seem an unsatisfactory identification procedure but it is preferable to the *diagnosis by exclusion* approach where the child is labelled dyspraxic because he has unintelligible speech and no other label fits. Some theoretical and philosophical problems are posed for the developmental specialist in the use of a label coined originally to describe acquired speech difficulties in adults. However, the label does serve to focus attention on a group of children who because of the pervasiveness of their verbal difficulties require specialist teaching and speech therapy. That said, it may be better to forget the label when planning remediation and therapy activities! Even if the criteria listed in table 5.1 are applied, a group of children labelled as dyspraxic will still be very heterogeneous. As they progress, they will develop compensatory strategies dependent on their cognitive, linguistic, motor and social strengths. Remediation and therapy activities need to link up with these compensatory strategies and be planned within a psycholinguistic and educational framework.

Prognosis for children with developmental verbal dyspraxia will depend on the interplay of their strengths and weaknesses and what opportunities are available to them. However, if diagnosis has been accurate, then dyspraxic difficulties will remain throughout their adult lives. These may or may not be apparent. Keith still avoids multisyllabic words and transposes sounds particularly when tired, for example 'par cark' for *car park*. He is now in full-time employment and attends college on a day-release basis. Reading is not a problem for him but he worries about his spelling. Even though he no longer needs regular speech therapy, he recently requested help with preparation for his sailing exams. This hobby has now taken a serious turn and he hopes to qualify as an instructor. This will involve him in the speaking and spelling of a whole new set of articulatorily complex vocabulary and illustrates the long-term needs of such 'children'.

It is impossible to make predictions about an individual's progress from the initial presentation of the condition. It would seem that the more pervasive and persisting the speech and associated problems, then the more limiting might be employment prospects. Some children will require further regular speech therapy after leaving school. Others like Keith require a lifeline: the knowledge that they can obtain help when confronted by new obstacles that adult life may bring. Still others will disappear all together but may turn up later at speech therapy or adult literacy classes.

When he was 14, Keith offered the following advice to others with speech difficulties: 'If you have any problems to see a therapist, to always try and write letters. Enjoy it. Do not take it as thing you never get out of it cause if you try you will.' This illustrates one of the most important prognostic factors – a positive attitude! It has certainly paid off in Keith's case.

Acknowledgements

The author would like to thank Keith for his participation in this study and Bill Wells for his helpful comments on this chapter.

Note

1 The term developmental *verbal* dyspraxia rather than the more commonly used developmental *articulatory* dyspraxia has been adopted deliberately to emphasize that children with the type of speech difficulties described will have extensive speech and language problems and not just an articulatory difficulty. However, you will find that these terms, along with apraxia and dyspraxia of speech, are used interchangeably in the literature.

Further Reading

Crary, M. A. (1984) A neurolinguistic perspective on developmental verbal dyspraxia. *Communicative Disorders*, 9, 33–49.

Ekelman, B. L. and Aram, D. M. (1983) Syntactic findings in developmental verbal apraxia. *Journal of Communication Disorders*, 16, 237–50.

Gordon, N. and McKinlay, I. (1980) *Helping Clumsy Children*. Edinburgh: Churchill Livingstone.

Grunwell, P. (Ed) (1990) *Developmental Speech Disorders*, Churchill Livingstone.

Stackhouse, J. (1989) Relationship between spoken and written language disorders. In Mogford, K. and Sadler, J. (eds) *Child Language Disability* Multilingual Matters, Clevedon.

Stackhouse, J. and Wells, B. (1991) Dyslexia: The obvious and hidden speech and language disorder. In Snowling, M. and Thomson, M. (eds) *Dyslexia: Integrating Theory and Practice*. Whurr Publishers Ltd.

Stackhouse, J. (in press) Developmental Verbal Dyspraxia I: A Review and Critique. *British Journal of Disorders of Communication*, March, 1992.

References

Bradley, L. and Bryant, P. (1983) Categorising sounds and learning to read: a causal connection. *Nature*, 301, 419.

Bridgeman, E. and Snowling, M. (1988) The perception of phoneme sequence: a comparison of dyspraxic and normal children. *British Journal of Disorders of Communication*, 23, 3.

Edwards, M. (1984) *Disorders of Articulation*. New York: Springer Verlag.

Grunwell, P. (1987) *Clinical Phonology*, 2nd edn. London: Croom Helm.

Guyette, T. W. and Diedrich, W. M. (1981) A critical review of apraxia of speech. In Lass, N. J. (ed.) *Speech and Language Advances in Basic Research and Practice*, vol. 6. New York: Academic Press.

Morley, M. (1967) *The Development and Disorders of Speech in Childhood*, 2nd edn. London: Churchill Livingstone.

Perin, D. (1983) Phonemic segmentation and spelling. *British Journal of Psychology*, 74, 129–44.

Reynell, J. (1969) *Reynell Developmental Language Scales*. Windsor: NFER-Nelson.

Snowling, M. and Stackhouse, J. (1983) Spelling performance of children with developmental verbal dyspraxia. *Developmental Medicine and Child Neurology*, 25, 430–37.

Stackhouse, J. (1984) Phonological therapy: a case and some thoughts. *Bulletin of the College of Speech Therapists*, 381, 10–11.

Williams, R., Ingham, R. J. and Rosenthal, J. (1981) A further analysis for developmental apraxia of speech in children with defective articulation. *Journal of Speech and Hearing Research*, 24, 496–505.

6

Developmental Reading and Writing Impairment

Maggie Snowling and Nata Goulandris

David

In 1896, a general practitioner, Dr Pringle-Morgan, writing in the *British Medical Journal*, reported the case of a 14-year-old boy who, despite obvious intelligence, had failed to learn to read. Fortunately, few children these days have to wait until they are teenagers before a reading impairment is diagnosed. However, there are still regrettably many forms of developmental dyslexia which may go unnoticed or not understood. David's specific learning difficulties were of this type.

David was known to us for some time before his difficulties were identified. A colleague had been keeping a 'neighbourly' eye on his progress because this had been causing some concern at home. David is the eldest son of professional parents. The majority of family members have been university educated, gaining good degrees, with the exception of an uncle and a cousin who were dyslexic and had struggled through school. There was nothing exceptional about David's early development; he reached his developmental milestones at the usual time and from an early stage was a bright, inquisitive little boy with a good spoken vocabulary. He was and is, however, physically rather clumsy.

From a baby, David had been interested in books but had rejected any attempts by his parents to teach him to read. When he went to nursery school he settled well, proceeding to Infant Class when he was rising five. At this stage, formal reading tuition began but progress was slow. In his second year of school, he hated reading and became extremely upset if even the slightest thing went wrong. There was an increasing divergence between the kind of books that he liked read to him and the books in his reading scheme. The school did not feel that David had a problem but, none the less, his headteacher agreed to give him some additional help herself. This resulted in a noticeable increase in his technical reading ability but he still did not bridge the gap between himself and his peers, whom he increasingly began to avoid. When listening to his reading, David's parents noticed that he had no idea of how to read a word which he did not know: what he read would usually make sense but he did not use initial sounds or any other conventional clue. For instance, he once read 'roof' as 'floor' and then decided it must be 'ceiling'.

During his third year at school, David's parents arranged for him to have some special lessons at a private teaching centre. He made very obvious progress and after three months, his reading had really taken off. But spelling and writing then emerged as considerable problems. David's parents were perplexed: 'Maybe his school was right when they suggested that all we had to do was wait and David would develop reading and writing skills. Alternatively, maybe he wouldn't have made these leaps forward without the additional help that he has had outside of school'. It was at this point that we first saw David. He was almost eight years old.

David presented as a confident and outgoing boy who was mature for his age. He used words well in conversation and was able to discuss a wide range of topics, often showing more sophisticated knowledge than we had ourselves! We began by giving him a test of general intelligence. On this test he gained an impressive score within the very superior range; his language skills were particularly good and he gained the highest score possible on a test of verbal reasoning. He also did extremely well on a test of mental arithmetic and has continued to prove to be an able mathematician. So, there was no doubting that David was a highly intelligent boy: his reading and writing development was clearly out of step with other aspects of his intellectual development.

The only clue at this stage to a possible 'cause' of David's problems with literacy was that he had some specific perceptual problems. In marked contrast to his excellent performance on many sub-tests of the IQ battery, he had specific difficulties with a test requiring the assembly of objects from their parts (a test reminiscent of jigsaw puzzles), and a copying test requiring rapid eye–hand coordination. These difficulties were consistent with reports of David being clumsy but 'went against the grain' as far as we were concerned. Current theories of dyslexia tended to reject visual problems as a cause, and point instead to verbal deficits. Could it be that although David's language skills were good, he had subtle verbal memory problems which were preventing him from learning the relationships between printed and spoken words and his 'visual problems' were not closely related to his reading and writing difficulties?

Many dyslexic children have verbal short-term memory problems. The capacity they have for holding speech-based information in mind is limited and this places a constraint on their ability to retain spoken words while dividing them into individual speech segments (phonemes). This step is thought to be crucial for mastering the alphabetic principle of how speech sounds map onto letters. It also can limit their ability to blend sounds together to make words, a step crucial for reading phonically.

To explore David's verbal memory we asked him to listen to sequences of numbers presented at the rate of one word per second, and then to repeat them back in the same order. David surprised us; he could repeat eight digits forwards without error – adult performance at only seven years and nine months! This could not be the source of his problem. What about long-term verbal memory? Perhaps David would have difficulty retaining newly presented verbal information over longer periods of time. To test this, we asked him to study 20 pictures of common objects for two minutes, after which we asked him to tell us what he had seen. Again his performance was good; he recalled twelve of the items, as many as a typical 11½-year-old.

So, David did not perform like a 'typical' developmental dyslexic on these verbal memory tests. Rather, it turned out that his problems were indeed in the visual sphere. We asked him to study a set of abstract visual figures, presented one at a time, for five seconds each. Immediately after this, he drew the figures one by one. In contrast to his performance on the verbal memory tasks, David's performance was poor. He had difficulty reproducing the details of the designs and frequently misrepresented their order. Thus, in addition to the perceptual problems noted during David's attempts at performance tasks on the IQ scale, he had visual memory difficulties. Hence, we were forced to hypothesize that David's slow start with reading and spelling skills might be associated with his visual processing weaknesses. Reading and writing are visible language skills; although David's spoken language was excellent, he found it difficult to cope with the visual demands which literacy skills posed.

If our hunch was correct, then we predicted that David would have a particular sort of reading difficulty. When children learn to read, it is thought that they begin by remembering words wholistically and only later begin to be able to sound them out phonically (e.g. c-a-t = 'cat'). At a later stage, children's reading becomes more flexible; they continue to be able to decode by sound, but also they can recognize familiar sequences in words, such as complex spelling patterns and morphemes, and can read new words by analogy with previously learned ones. Acquisition of this last stage depends upon being able to analyse words into visual units and to match these to stored sound and meaning components. Given that David had difficulty with tasks requiring visual perceptual skills, we anticipated that he might have a poor sight vocabulary (his development in the first stage of literacy would be limited), he would be able to read words phonically by sound but he would have more difficulty with complex spelling patterns. This was exactly what we observed. When shown words in isolation, David often sounded them out, taking some time to do so. Errors such as reading *shepherd* as 'sheepherd', *ceiling* as 'selling' reflected his reliance on phonics. As anticipated, his phonological reading strategies were intact: he made only two minor errors when asked to read aloud a set of 12 non-words like 'zuk' and 'skag', a perfectly adequate performance for his age.

Fortunately, as well as his proficient phonological strategies, David had other skills at his disposal, namely his general language abilities. He was able to use these to good effect when presented with prose. He used context to help him to predict words (e.g. to predict that 'ball' was a better completion for the sentence 'he played with a bat and ____ ' than 'bell'), and he was well able to monitor the meaning of what he was reading. In fact, at seven years nine months, David's accuracy when reading connected text measured at the nine year three month level, with comprehension even further in advance at almost an 11-year level. It is relevant, if a little surprising, that in developmental dyslexia it is usually the case that reading comprehension is in advance of decoding skill. It is amazing that even when a dyslexic is heard to stumble through a demanding text, his or her understanding of it may be excellent; David's understanding of what he read enabled him to decode words which he would have been unable to decipher if presented in isolation.

Thus, David seemed to manage to compensate for his visual weakness in learning to read. However, the strategies he had adopted were not conducive to learning to spell. Relying upon context directs attention away from the letter-by-letter structure of words and, in an irregular spelling system such as English, this provides crucial information for spelling. Without such knowledge, the reader is forced to spell words the way in which they sound, violating spelling conventions. This is just what David did. Whilst his reading comprehension measured at the 11-year level, his spelling was only just age appropriate. He wrote slowly and effortfully, writing hay as 'hae', boat as 'bowt', dream as 'drem', sight as 'sit' and large as 'lrgu'. He also made letter reversal errors, writing good as 'goob' and bed as 'ded'. Indeed, five minutes of David's written work (figure 6.1) was well below the level expected given his excellent verbal skills.

On the basis of this assessment, we recommended that David should receive specialized teaching using multisensory methods. It was important to introduce him systematically to the spelling patterns and rules of English – the conventions which he would not abstract for himself because of the reading style he had adopted. He also needed structured assistance with hand-writing skills to improve pencil control and increase writing fluency. But, perhaps what David had needed more was sympathetic understanding. Despite our attempts to help and his parents' efforts to support David, his school did not really recognize the problem. David's written work was undoubtedly poor. He became increasingly frustrated because of the inordinate amount of time it took him to produce even a poor piece of written work. This all went unnoticed and his teachers were critical of the 'presentation' of his work. David's morale dropped, his behaviour deteriorated and he became frankly depressed. While David made an average rate of progress with reading and spelling as a result of the help he was receiving, there were increasing worries about his self-concept. This extremely articulate, talented child, a wizard with computers, had become the class clown; he was opting out. He was constantly reprimanded by his headteacher. The School Psycho-

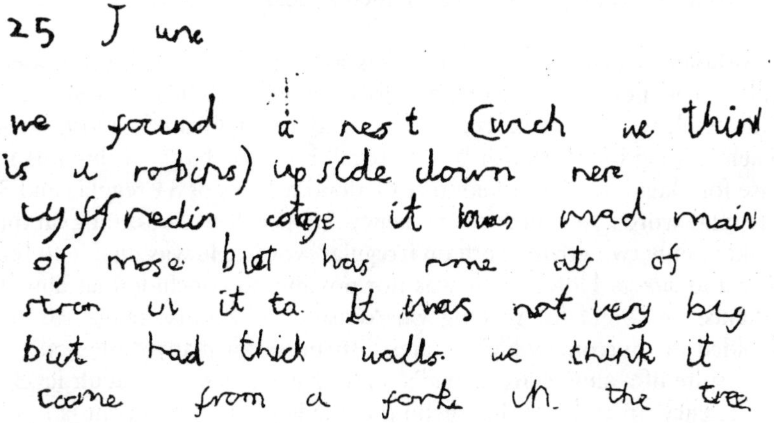
25 June

we found a nest (wich we think
is u robins) up sCde down nere
uffredin cotge it was mad main
of mose but has rome at of
stron ui it ta. It was not very big
but had thick walls. we think it
came from a fork in the tree

Figure 6.1 David's free writing at 7 years, 9 months: 'We found a nest (which we think is a robin's) upside down near Uffredin cottage. It was made mainly of moss but has room out of straw in it too. It was not very big but had thick walls. We think it came from a fork in the tree.'

logical Service had definite views: 'It would seem that David's reading weaknesses had some structural base but he has developed an attitude to reading and being helped which probably lies in his relationships at home.' Family therapy was recommended. But we could not really agree that this was the appropriate way to proceed. Instead, we closely monitored David's work at school and in remedial lessons, and we informally counselled his parents at regular intervals.

We last saw David when he was 10 years 9 months. His reading had forged ahead and, on a standardized test of single-word reading, he gained a Reading Age of 14 years, entirely to be expected given his age and intelligence. Thankfully, David could read for academic purposes. We anticipated that a possible problem was that he might be over-relying upon a phonic approach. If that were ttue, then we would expect him to have difficulty in distinguishing the meanings of pairs of words which sound the same but are spelled differently; homophones such as pear–pair. To test this, we asked him to read and then to define 40 homophonous words (e.g. bury, root, rain). He did exceptionally well making only seven errors; he could not read *pique*, *magnate* or *weighed* and he misread *plumb* as 'plump'. Interstingly, the other errors consisted of a mispronunciation followed by a correct definition:

suite → 'suit'   →   part of a hotel
corps→ 'corpse'   →   part of army
route → 'roater'   →   way someone goes

Although David's performance was average for his age, there was a minor tendency for him to read words the way in which they sounded. This tendency to 'regularize' words leads to significantly more errors when reading irregular words than regular words. To see if this was the case for David, he was asked to read aloud a series of 31 regular and 31 irregular words, matched for frequency. He performed at ceiling on this, making only two errors, both on irregular words. He was unable to read *litre* and *suede*. However, it was not possible to conclude that David's reliance on sound for reading was outside the normal range. He had avoided the outcome which creates difficulties for many dyslexics.

In spite of a slow start, David's reading has reached an adult level of proficiency. In contrast, his spelling remains poor. Attainment is in line with chronological age but well below expectation given age and IQ. When devoting full attention to seplling as, for example, when formally tested, David tries hard and successfully applies the spelling rules he has been taught. This is, however, a slow laborious process. When his aim is to commit ideas to paper, as in the preparation of an essay, his spelling performance deteriorates and there are many errors. When asked to write for ten minutes about a roller-coaster he had designed and built, together with another boy for his science project, he produced the sample shown in figure 6.2. The construction of the roller-coaster is described with careful attention to detail, and we are told that the boys are using the computer to make an animation of it. We are then told how the model works. A considerable amount of technical skill has been used to bring this model to fruition, but David's attempt to describe it is much less good than expected of a highly intelligent boy.

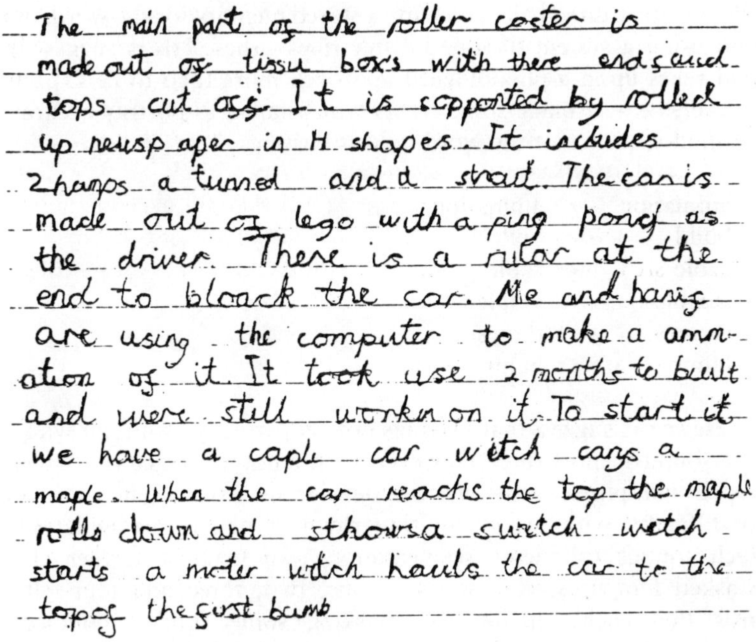

The main part of the roller coster is made out of tissu box's with there ends and tops cut off. It is sopported by rolled up newspaper in H shapes. It inclides 2 ramps a tunnel and a srait. The car is made out of lego with a ping pong as the driver. There is a rular at the end to block the car. Me and hanif are using the computer to make a ammation of it It took use 2 months to built and were still workin on it. To start it we have a caple car wich carys a maple. When the car reachs the top the maple rolls down and sthows a switch wich starts a motor wich hauls the car to the top of the fust bump

Figure 6.2   David's free writing at 10 years, 9 months: 'The main part of the roller coaster is made out of tissue boxes with their ends and tops cut off. It is supported by rolled up newspaper in H shapes. It includes two ramps, a tunnel and a straight. The car is made out of lego with a ping pong as the driver. There is a ruler at the end to block the car. Me and Hanif are using the computer to make an animation of it. It took us two months to build and we're still working on it. To start it we have a cable car which carries a marble. When the car reaches the top the marble rolls down and throws a switch which starts a motor which hauls the car to the top of the first bump.'

David's spelling errors are primarily phonetic. In the piece described above, he wrote:

coaster	→	coster
tissue	→	tissu
straight	→	strait
block	→	bloack
which	→	witch

If it is accepted that there are at least two ways in which a word can be spelled – either directly by accessing a stored memory for the word, or by sound using a system of sound–letter rules – these errors suggest that David relies upon a phonological approach more than to be expected. However, he also made some errors which failed to portray accurately the sound sequence of the word he was writing:

animation	→	ammation
build	→	biult
cable	→	caple
marble	→	maple
throws	→	thows
bump	→	bumb

These errors suggest that David is not yet perfectly proficient with the use of sound-spelling rules. However, we did not think that the tendency to spell non-phonetically was serious in his case, as he had never had difficulty with tasks requiring rhyming or the manipulation of speech sounds (phoneme segmentation). To make a further check, we asked him to spell a series of one, two, three and four-syllable words (ten each). If he was masking some subtle phonological difficulty, then we expected an increasing tendency to make non-phonetic errors with an increase in syllable length. David spelled only 3 three-syllable and 1 four-syllable word correctly. Quantitatively, his performance was significantly poorer than that of other ten-year-old children (whose reading was actually worse than his). However, qualitatively, he made a similar proportion of phonetic errors as them – he could use sound–letter spelling strategies just as well. Give his pattern of strengths and weaknesses, we would anticipate that he should be able to spell regular words as accurately as other people, but will have more difficulty with less consistent or exceptional spellings.

Stephen

The tendency for specific reading difficulties to run in families has been recognized for most of this century, and in recent years there has been a gradual accumulation of evidence that dyslexia may have a genetic basis. David's brother Stephen, some two years younger, is also dyslexic. From the outset the two boys had seemed different in terms of personality and temperament; Stephen was much more easy going. There were also developmental differences: unlike David, Stephen had been slow to reach his language milestones. First words did not appear until well after he was two years old. When he began to speak, he was difficult to understand. His hearing was tested and found to be normal and language comprehension was good. Speech therapy was started to improve intelligibility and this continued until Stephen went to school; he remains under review and has short periods of therapy from time to time. His parents commented that his speech was full of 'how d'you say?' and 'what d'you call it?'

Despite his speech problems, Stephen settled well at school, although reading proved to be difficult. Because the family were alerted to the possibility of dyslexia through David, Stephen was assessed early and we first saw him when he was seven years two months old. We found Stephen to be a sociable little boy. He was a good communicator who used a wide range of spoken vocabulary. However, his speech was quite difficult to follow: there were immaturities of both phonology (the way in which we use sounds) and syntax.

Like his brother, Stephen proved to be a bright boy. He gained a superior IQ score and did particularly well on tests of verbal reasoning and vocabulary, usually held to be the best predictors of educational potential. He also was good at maths. In spite of his speech problems, he gained an above-average score for a test of verbal short-term memory, suggesting that he had the normal capacity for learning auditorily presented material. He did marginally less well on performance tests tapping perceptual processes but the discrepancy was not as large as it had been in David's case.

To explore Stephen's memory skills further, he was given the tests requiring the memorization of pictures and the reproduction of abstract designs which were described earlier. His performance was strikingly similar to that of his brother: he scored at the 11½-year level on the picture-recall test but did less well on the visual memory test where his performance was just age appropriate. So, in many respects, the two boys were alike in terms of their strengths and weaknesses. But Stephen had additional difficulties; we suspected that he might have difficulty on tests requiring awareness of the properties of spoken words, especially if he were asked to manipulate components of spoken words. Neither of these tasks should be easy for a child with marked speech problems.

Our first attempt to explore phonological awareness was by means of a test of rhyming skill. Stephen was presented with a picture of an object which he had to match to one of two alternatives. One of these depicted an object which rhymed with the target, the other was a distractor which was either semantically similar or started with the same sound. For instance, 'spoon' had to be matched either to 'moon' or to 'knife'; 'coat' had to be matched to 'boat' or 'cup'. Stephen could always reject the semantically related distractors but he was confused when the distractor started with the same first sound as the target. On a second test, he had to listen to a series of four words, three of which rhymed and one of which did not, for example, bun, *rub*, fun, gun. Stephen found this task very hard indeed. Generally, he was performing at between the five- and six-year level on these tests of sound awareness. These tests are held to be good predictors of reading and spelling achievement. While David had had no difficulty with them, Stephen had. If he were already 'at risk' of reading failure because he presented a similar profile of skill as his brother, then his difficulties with sound processing would surely exacerbate his difficulties.

At this stage in his development, Stephen's reading and spelling skills were very much at the beginner level. Thus, it was difficult to make a formal assessment of them. We recommended that Stephen receive remedial assistance with reading in conjunction with speech therapy to promote sound awareness, as we felt that this would be important to ensure satisfactory progress with literacy skills. We reviewed his case a year later. In the intervening period his remedial therapist had worked hard to help him build his auditory skills (segmentation, blending), to promote decoding skills for reading (he was already good at using context imaginatively) and had begun to teach simple spelling–sound correspondences for spelling. She had noted definite progress, Stephen having worked extremely hard.

Indeed, Stephen had made good progress but attainment was still significantly below expected levels. To complicate matters further, a mild bilateral sensorineural hearing loss had been discovered. At eight years four months, Stephen's Reading Age was just six years eleven months on a test of single word reading and his spelling measured at the six year ten month level. His writing was really quite difficult to decipher (figure 6.3). He was now really beginning to lag behind his peers, and most certainly behind his intellectual equals. But his placid temperament was keeping him buoyant.

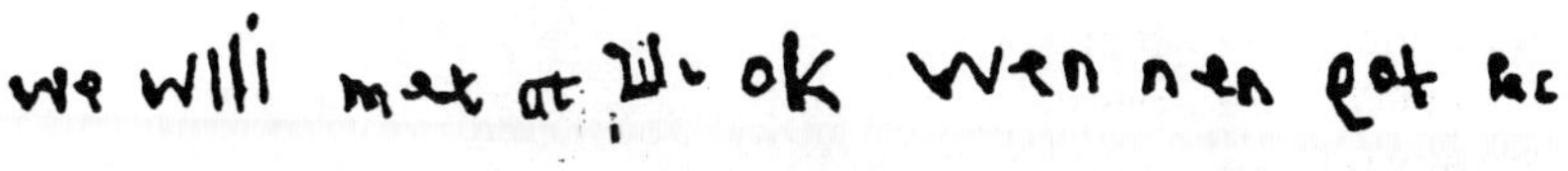

we will meet at 12 ok when nen get ke

Figure 6.3 Stephen's free writing at 8 years, 4 months: 'We will meet at 12 o'clock when they get back.'

To explore the strategies which Stephen was using in his reading, he was asked to read aloud 31 regular words which could be sounded out and 31 irregular words which we assume have to be read visually. He read 19 regular words correctly and four irregular words. This surprised us as it suggested he was relying upon a phonic approach even though he had the kind of speech problems which one would normally expect to create difficulties for this process which requires the blending of sound segments. Confirmation of his reliance on phonological strategies would come from a high proportion of regularization errors on irregular words. Stephen read *choir* as 'choyer', *wolf* as 'wollf', *sword* as 'swored' and *vase* as 'vaise', but generally he did not do this excessively for his age. Frequently his errors reflected a phonic analysis followed by a guess at a real word sounding similar to his decoding attempt; thus, he read *flood* as 'flude . . flowed . . flute!', *sign* as 'sigunt . . segun . . second!' Stephen was obviously bringing his general language resources to bear to support his decoding skill. This was confirmed by his better performance on a test of prose reading where accuracy and comprehension were rated at age-appropriate levels. When contextual cues were completely removed and vocabulary knowledge could not be used, reading was much less good. So, Stephen failed to score on a test of non-word reading, pronouncing *pedbim* as 'plebe' and *romsig* as 'rosing'.

It appeared then that Stephen was learning to read using phonological skills but, in isolation, these were inadequate tools, possibly because of his speech difficulties. To facilitate his reading, Stephen was also making use of general language resources: vocabulary knowledge and knowledge of the world, a testament to his intelligence and also to the good teaching he had received. Interestingly, his performance on sound-awareness tests had also improved and he now scored at around the seven-year level on these tests. His articulation was still faulty and his verbal repetition well below age-appropriate levels.

If Stephen was making use of a phonological approach to reading, would he also be in spelling, or would his problem with sound segmentation and speech preclude this? On a standardized spelling test he made a mixture of phonetic errors and semiphonetic spelling errors of the type frequently made by young children, such as reducing consonant clusters and misrepresenting vowels. Phonetic errors included:

honey   →   huny
pencil   →   pensall
always   →   allwase

Semiphonetic errors included:

thumb   →   fum
earth   →   irf
cold   →   cod
young   →   yug

To see how well Stephen would cope when spelling words containing more than one syllable, he was given the same spelling test as his brother containing one, two, three and four-syllable words. He spelled all of the one-syllable words correctly and, although only one of the two-syllable versions was correct, the remainder were phonetically accurate. This is entirely as expected if Stephen's reading ability is taken into account. It seemed to be his reading and not his speech which was placing a constraint upon progress. Stephen's spellings of three-syllable words were acceptable versions for an eight-year-old boy and included:

membership   →   mempship
cigarette   →   sigerret
refreshment   →   refrshmot

Only four-syllable words created any significant difficulty:

congratulate   →   congochlat
geography   →   geogcfy
calculator   →   cakderlater.

Thus, it seems to be the case the Stephen can use phonological spelling strategies. Given his weakness in visual memory, might his spelling of irregular words which are exceptions to spelling rules be lagging behind his spelling of regular words? To explore this, we asked Stephen to spell 12 regular and 12 irregular words all of which were familiar to young children. He showed a striking regularity effect, spelling nine regular but only three irregular words correctly. Spelling errors on irregular words included 'rsc' for ask, 'dus' for does, 'rite' for write and 'rser' for answer. Stephen does seem to have more difficulty in memorizing the letter-by-letter sequences of words than his level of intelligence and reading skill predicts. In this respect he is very like his brother. Clearly, he requires continuing remediation of his reading and spelling to bring them up to

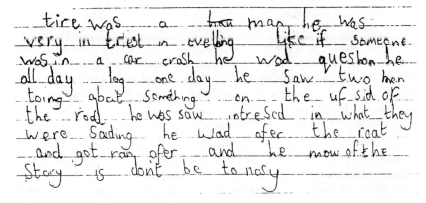

Figure 6.4 Stephen's free writing at 10 years: 'Tyre was a man. He was very interested in everything like if someone was in a car crash he would question all day long. One day he saw two men talking about something on the other side of the road. He was interested in what they were saying. He went over the road and got run over and the moral of the story is don't be too nosy.'

levels appropriate for his educational needs (figure 6.4). This help needs to be focused for the time being on the development of a sight vocabulary for reading and on knowledge of English spelling conventions as well as exceptions to these rules.

Perhaps unsurprisingly, Stephen's parents have reacted with a more relaxed attitude to his difficulties than to those of David. Moreover, Stephen is milder mannered than his older brother, he has been less frustrated by his problems and, to date, has not lashed out at the world regarding them. Stephen is a year behind where his brother was in reading and spelling at the same age, but perhaps he has had less reason for frustration: his perceptual problems are proportionately less serious than his brother and his position in the family may possibly cushion him from particular implicit expectations.

Theories of dyslexia

Cognitive theories of dyslexia stress the role of specific language factors in the determination of reading problems. While IQ is undoubtedly the most important predictor of reading skill, phonological awareness is also important. This means that one can reasonably expect a child who has reading difficulties to have problems with phonological awareness. In the case of the two boys described here, only Stephen showed this pattern. In other respects too he showed characteristic 'dyslexic' symptoms: he had problems with non-word reading, he had word-finding difficulties and his verbal repetition was poor. However, neither he nor David had verbal short-term memory problems. What does this tell us about our theories of dyslexia, and what can we learn about reading and spelling development from this evidence?

First, these data show up the inadequacy of explanations of reading failure which are based on the results of correlational studies or on group studies comparing dyslexic children with normal readers. Such studies make generalizations which do not necessarily apply at the level of individuals. Secondly, by looking at how David and Stephen's development proceeded, we form a very different picture from that portrayed by one-off snapshot studies of dyslexia.

A number of general statements can be made about the status of reading and spelling from the examination of these dyslexic children. First, although reading is a language skill, it is clearly dissociable from other language skills; recall that both boys had an excellent spoken vocabulary and their verbal reasoning was good. They were also good at mathematics and, like many dyslexics, did not have difficulties with digit symbols. Instances of children who read well but who have poor verbal and intellectual abilities have been described and they provide an important point of contrast. These cases indicate that reading can develop (or fail to develop) in isolation from other skills. Yet strangely, in the case of developmental dyslexia, it seems to be the availability of other language skills which fuels the development of reading. Both David and Stephen appeared to be relying heavily upon their general language resources to compensate in the early stages for their weak decoding abilities. In development then, although the reading system seems encapsulated, its interaction with other cognitive systems provides an important compensatory resource.

Arguably, David and Stephen were forced to learn to read in an atypical fashion because of their weak visual perceptual and visual memory skills. Yet, in David's case at least, the eventual outcome for his reading development was entirely normal. He did, however, continue to experience spelling difficulties; this underlines the fact that spelling is not just the converse of reading. While it cannot be denied that aspects of spelling knowledge are learned through reading experience, David's case suggests that the stored knowledge which is used for reading need not be accessible for spelling. David was forced to rely almost exclusively on a phonological approach to spelling, although he made use of other knowledge in reading, as shown by his ability to distinguish between homophones which would otherwise be confused.

In what ways do David and Stephen seem different from other children who are learning to read and write? To consider this question, it is necessary to have a framework based on the normal development of literacy skills. Developmental theorists generally hold that in the first stages of literacy development, reading is visual in nature and makes use of the same memory strategies as children use to memorize other aspects of their visual environment. Reading is based on partial cues, for instance one or two of the letters in the words or perhaps their whole shape. At this stage, referred to as the *logographic*, spelling is rudimentary and may consist of a few rote spellings. Gradually the child attempts to write down words in the way in which they sound. Their attempts are partial as the ability to segment phonologically is not yet proficient. Hence, children might write 'chan' for train or 'sore'for story. Their attempts are gradually perfected until phonetic spelling is possible and, at this stage, they start to use letter-sound rules for reading words. This transforms their reading as they are now able to tackle unfamiliar words using a 'phonic' approach. This phase of development is known as the *alphabetic*; reading and spelling are based on sound. There is a final stage of development when reading first, followed by spelling, becomes automatic and free of sound. This phase, the *orthographic*, is the stage of adult literacy when reference can be made to a stored body of knowledge about the orthographic characteristics of words, for reading and for spelling.

The details of these models of reading and spelling have not been fully worked out. However, a good deal is known about the end-point from experimental studies of proficient reading and spelling. It is reasonable to expect that children may reach the end-point in different ways, that progress towards them might be hindered in a variety of ways in cases of developmental disorder and that in some cases, adult proficiency may not be attained.

Both David and Stephen were bright boys who, in the normal course of events, should have learned to read quickly, as indeed they had learned to do maths. However, they both had perceptual weaknesses and their visual memory was poor. They both had a slow start, being unable to retain the visual features of words which are necessary in the early logographic stages to begin to build a sight vocabulary. In both cases, they were assisted by a remedial approach which emphasized the alphabetic links between letters and sounds. In David's case, transition to the alphabetic phase brought with it a 'taking off' of his reading, fuelled by general language skills. There did not seem to be such an easy ride for Stephen. This was most likely because, in addition to his visual problems, he had problems with phonological skills. Although he mastered simple letter-sound correspondence rules, he found it difficult to use these out of context; his non-word reading was less good than expected. Perhaps even more than David, Stephen was forced to rely on contextual cues. Perforce this meant that he looked at words superficially and he did not abstract knowledge of the exceptions in the English spelling system. It follows that his ability to spell irregular words was exceptionally weak, although he managed remarkably well in spelling regular words which followed spelling rules. The last time we saw Stephen, this was the status of his dyslexic difficulties. In David's case, reading development had proceeded further to enter the orthographic phase. It was impossible to show any abnormality in his single word reading. But his spelling was impaired and here, he remained with the alphabetic phase.

In cases of acquired dyslexia, selective impairment of either the visual or the phonological reading system is possible. It is much less common for such pure disorders to be identified in developmental dyslexia. This is at least in part because of the dynamic nature of children's reading: in short, it changes with time. In childhood, the reading system is evolving and its development can become impaired at different stages depending upon the extent to which underlying, prerequisite skills are intact. Many dyslexic children, for example, have phonological difficulties which hinder their transition into the alphabetic phase of development. This was not true of David and Stephen whose visual memory deficits had hampered their development at the earlier, logographic stage. In development, it is also the case that reading and spelling are to an extent interdependent. Much spelling knowledge is derived from reading. Hence it is usually the case that reading is in advance of spelling skill and children do not have reading problems without spelling difficulties. If we did not know of David's earlier problems, we might be tempted to say that he experienced spelling problems in the absence of reading difficulty. These data must make us cautious about theorizing about the nature and cause of developmental difficulties in the absence of longitudinal evidence.

Other major factors which must be taken into account when trying to understand the cognitive manifestations of a developmental reading or writing impairment are the ways the problem might change in relation to maturation and intervention and how it may be modified in interaction with other skills. It could conceivably be argued that David had learned to read simply because, as time had passed, he had slowly learned more and more words by sight, pushing him into the second phase of development. In effect, his development was slow but along normal lines, a maturational problem. However, it is almost certainly the case that David's general language skills had helped him on. The printed words children encounter are almost always embedded in context. Therefore, it is possible to use language skills to help read words which otherwise can not be deciphered. Stephen did this to a very great extent. In addition, a major factor in his development was the availability of teaching to promote the phonological skills so vital to transition to the alphabetic phase.

It will be interesting to see the eventual outcome for both David and Stephen, and indeed for their younger brother who is yet to embark on the road to literacy! So far, notwithstanding the support which Stephen is having, their development is remarkably similar. We have speculated that their difficulties stem from an inherited disposition, but it is indubitable that their progress has been, and will be, determined by the complex interaction of their cognitive strengths and weaknesses with the demands of learning to read and the teaching to which they are exposed. Personality and temperamental factors will in addition be important in sustaining their motivation and will to succeed.

Acknowledgement

This work was supported by a grant from the Medical Research Council of Great Britain.

Further Reading

This chapter presents a cognitive view of dyslexia. Developmental dyslexia is, however, a subject which has attracted multidisciplinary interest, as exemplified by the reviews suggested below. Discussion of its genetic basis can be found in Pennington (1990) which summarizes recent research on the heritability of dyslexia. Its biological bases do not, however, influence educational practice and Yule and Rutter (1985) view dyslexia from the viewpoint of educational and clinical psychology. An alternative, educational perspective is provided by Aaron (1989). Understanding the nature and development of dyslexic children depends upon a theory of the normal acquisition of literacy. For discussion of some theories, see Oakhill and Garnham (1988), Goswani and Bryant (1990), and Ehri (1991). The predominant view of dyslexia is that it is a verbal deficit, specifically affecting phonological skills. Evidence is reviewed by Bryant and Bradley (1985) and Hulme and Snowling (1991). For a detailed information-processing account, see Seymour (1986) and, for a broader overview, see Snowling (1987).

References

Aaron, P. G. (1989) *Dyslexia and Hyperlexia: Diagnosis and Management of Developmental Reading Disabilities*. Boston, Mass.: Kluwer.

Bryant, P. E. and Bradley, L. (1985) *Children's Reading Problems*. Oxford: Blackwell.

Campbell, R. (1987) One or two lexicons for reading and writing words: can misspellings shed any light? *Cognitive Neuropsychology*, 4, 487–99.

Campbell, R. and Butterworth, B. (1985) Phonological dyslexia and dysgraphia in a highly literate subject; a developmental case with associated deficits of phonemic awareness and processing. *Quarterly Journal of Experimental Psychology*, 37A, 435–75.

Coltheart, M., Masterson, J., Byng, S., Prior, M. and Riddoch, J. (1983) Surface dyslexia. *Quarterly Journal of Experimental Psychology*, 35A, 469–96.

Ehri, L. (1991) Reconceptualising the development of sight-word reading and its relationship to decoding. In P. Gough, Ehri, L. and Treiman, R (eds.) *Reading Acquisition*. New York: Lawrence Erlbaum.

Frith, U. (1980) Unexpected spelling problems. In U. Frith (ed.) *Cognitive Processes in Spelling*. London: Academic Press.

Frith, U. (1985) Beneath the surface of developmental dyslexia. In K. E. Patterson, J. C. Marshall and M. Coltheart (eds) *Surface Dyslexia*. London: Routledge and Kegan Paul.

Frith, U. and Frith, C. D. (1980) Relationships between reading and spelling. In J. F. Kavanagh and R. L. Venezky (eds) *Orthography, Reading and Dyslexia*. Baltimore: University Park Press.

Goswami, U. and Bryant, P. (1990) *Phonological Skills and Learning to Read*. London: Lawrence Erlbaum.

Goulandris, N. and Snowling, M. (1991) Visual memory deficits: a possible cause of developmental dyslexia? *Cognitive Neuropsychology* 8, 127–154.

Hulme, C. and Snowling, M. (1991) Phonological deficits in dyslexia: a 'sound' reappraisal of the verbal deficit hypothesis. In N. Singh and I. Beale (eds) *Current Perspectives in Learning Disabilities*. New York: Springer-Verlag.

Lovegrove, W., Martin, F. and Slaghuis, W. (1986) A theoretical and experimental case for a visual deficit in specific reading disability. *Cognitive Neuropsychology*, 3, 255–67.

Marsh, G., Friedman, M., Welch, V. and Desberg, P. (1981) A cognitive–developmental theory of reading acquisition. *Reading Research: Advances in Theory and Practice 3*. New York: Academic Press.

Oakhill, J. and Garnham, A. (1988) *Becoming a Skill Reader*. Oxford: Blackwell.

Olson, R., Wise, B., Conners, F., Rack, J. and Fulker, D. (1989) Specific deficits in component reading and language skills: genetic and environmental influences. *Journal of Learning Disabilities*, 22, 339–49.

Pennington, B. F. (1990) The genetics of dyslexia. *Journal of Child Psychology and Psychiatry*, 31, 193–202.

Pring, L. and Snowling, M. (1986) Developmental changes in word recognition: an information processing account. *Quarterly Journal of Experimental Psychology*, 38A, 395–418.

Seymour, P. H. K. 91986) *Cognitive Analysis of Dyslexia*. London: Routledge and Kegan Paul.

Snowling, M. (1981) Phonemic deficits in developmental dyslexia. *Psychological Research*, 43, 219–34.

Snowling, M. (1987) *Dyslexia: a Cognitive Developmental Perspective*. Oxford: Basil Blackwell.

Snowling, M. and Frith, U. (1986) Comprehension in 'hyperlexic' readers. *Journal of Experimental Child Psychology*, 42, 392–415.

Snowling, M., Goulandris, N., Bowlby, M. and Howell, P. (1986) Segmentation and speech perception in relation to reading skill. *Journal of Experimental Child Psychology*, 41, 489–507.

Snowling, M. and Hulme, C. (1989) A longitudinal case study of developmental phonological dyslexia. *Cognitive Neuropsychology*, 6, 379–401.

Stevenson, J., Fredman, G., McLoughlin, V. and Graham, A. (1987) A twin study of genetic influences on reading and spelling ability and disability. *Journal of Child Psychology and Psychiatry*, 28, 229–47.

Torgesen, J. and Wagenar, R. (1988) Blending and segmentation processes in beginning readers. *Journal of Experimental Child Psychology*, 49, 364–76.

Yule, W. and Rutter, M. (1985) Reading and other learning difficulties. In M. Rutter and L. Hersov (eds) *Child and Adolescent Psychiatry: Modern Approaches*. Oxford: Blackwell Scientific.

7

Deaf to the meaning of words

Sue Franklin and David Howard

Theoretical papers on the types of auditory comprehension disorder found in stroke patients have existed for nearly a hundred years (Ziehl, 1896). Traditionally, two types of comprehension deficit, or 'word deafness', have been proposed. One is an inability to analyse the sounds of speech (word-sound deafness), the other an inability to reach the meaning (word-meaning deafness). Subsequently, an impairment at an intervening level, an inability to distinguish the word forms from the word sounds has been suggested (word-form deafness). While cases of word-sound deafness have been well described (Goldstein, 1974), and at least one detailed case of a patient with word-form deafness exists (Howard and Franklin, 1989), cases of word-meaning deafness have been described rarely and at an anecdotal level (Bramwell, 1897; Kohn and Friedman, 1986). The characteristics of word-meaning deafness comprise an inability to hear the meanings of words despite being unimpaired at understanding written word meanings.

This chapter describes Derek B who, since his stroke, finds it difficult to understand what people say to him. His is a very specific problem. While he can hear words, he is unable to understand their meanings. This chapter will seek to give an idea of what this must be like for Derek, and how we have been able to characterize his problem in spoken word comprehension. We will begin with a brief description of Derek's life before his stroke and an account of what happened when he had the stroke, before describing the speech and language assessments we carried out.

Biographical details

Derek left school at 15 and went on to do a great variety of jobs. These included being a joiner, a draughtsman, an electronics inspector, a publican, a newsagent and a chauffeur. At the time of his stroke, when he was 54, he was working for a travel agency, managing a motorcycle dispatch rider service. He is married with four (grown-up) stepchildren and lives in North London. He is an amusing and naturally gregarious person, with a lively interest in politics; before his stroke, he was a successful amateur photographer.

At the age of 37, Derek had two coronary heart attacks, and has continued to suffer from angina and high blood pressure. When he was 45 he was diagnosed as being diabetic, for which he continues to receive treatment. He was 54 (in 1984) when he had the stroke which affected his speech. A CT scan carried out several years later showed evidence of a left middle cerebral infarct.

The first thing Derek can remember after his stroke is being in the hospital on the second day. He heard one of the doctors standing at the bottom of his bed say 'B____ can go home.' That was good enough for him and he promptly got out of bed and started walking down the ward. When they tried to stop him he became very agitated, so they let him go.

As soon as Derek arrived home, he went to the bathroom to shave. He picked up the can of shaving foam and began scraping it along his chin, as though it were a razor. He then sprayed foam all over the bathroom. At this point, his wife understandably felt very worried about how she was going to manage to look after him. In desperation, she went to the library and took out all the books she could find on what she learned was called 'dysphasia', the language impairment which often followed a stroke. She worked with Derek every day, beginning with the alphabet. At first he was completely unable to speak, but by the end of a month he was speaking in whole sentences again.

However, it soon became clear to Derek that his biggest problem was not speaking, but *understanding* speech. 'I thought I was deaf, couldn't hear it.' If there were a number of people talking it would just sound like a 'mumble' to him, with just the odd word clearly audible. In a one-to-one situation, with no background noise, he was usually able to pick out key words in what the other person was saying. (Figure 7.1 shows Derek's cartoon version of what having a stroke is like.)

Figure 7.1   Derek's drawing of how it feels to have a stroke.

Following recovery

We first saw Derek 18 months after his stroke. He had been fortunate in getting a place at the City Dysphasic Group, a speech therapy group funded by charity, where he was able to receive three full days of treatment per week. He had made a good general recovery and had no remaining problems from his stroke except for his dysphasia. He continued to drive a car and, although he was now unable to work or afford to continue his hobby of photography, he had taken up an entirely new hobby. This was marquetry, at which he quickly became highly proficient and received many commissions to carry out. The first Christmas following his stroke, he made a card to send to the staff at the Dysphasic Group (figure 7.2).

Figure 7.2 Derek's Christmas card.

Derek's *speech* was fluent and it was easy to understand what he was trying to get across, although he would often hesitate when unable to find the correct word. This is an example of a conversation with him:

Therapist: What do you think about religion? what about the Church of England, say?

Derek: I had too much as a child. As soon as I was school I said 'no more' because I had to go three times every Sunday, morning lunch and afternoon and evening. And I'd so much of it, I I don't want to do it anymore. So I'm just not bothered any more; I'm not interested.

Therapist: Was it a Catholic church?

Derek: No no.

Therapist: Church of England?

Derek: I was in the – it was during the war. And my uncle is in a farm, a little village, as I, I was a – an S, E–S–C– I don't know. During the war, when I used to go from London – out–

Therapist: You mean an evacuee.

Derek: That's right. Yeah. And from 9 until 14 I was living there. And everybody in the village had to go by church. And when at the – I – at the end of the war I said 'that's it I'm not going to the church any more' and I haven't.

Much of the time, Derek would *understand* what was said to him, but he was obviously concentrating very hard both on listening and on watching the speaker's face. He was obviously relying very heavily on the context to work out what he was hearing, so an abrupt change of subject would leave him floundering. Sometimes he would look puzzled and ask the speaker to repeat what he or she had just said, often several times. Occasionally, even this strategy would not work and he would just give up trying to understand. Rarely, he would reply completely inappropriately, indicating that he had misunderstood, but it was more usual for him either to comprehend or simply not get it all. He still found that his comprehension was worse when he was among a group of people talking.

A model of auditory comprehension

We decided to investigate Derek's auditory comprehension impairment in a more systematic way than had previously been done. For the sake of simplicity, we will only describe experiments looking at his understanding of single words, although we will later discuss the way in which his single-word comprehension deficit may affect his understanding of connected speech. In order to understand what is going wrong with Derek's comprehension of speech it is necessary to consider what stages we go through in understanding a word; that is, we need to consider a model of auditory word comprehension.

Such a model can be seen in figure 7.3, taken from Franklin (1989). Comprehension requires at least three levels of processing. The acoustic information going into the ear is analysed by the brain. This analysis is then used to 'look up' the particular word in a lexicon of word forms. Once an entry in the lexicon has been reached, this can be used to look up its meaning. This model is derived from experiments with non-brain damaged individuals, but predicts that it should be possible, following brain damage, to have an impairment at any of the three levels: auditory analysis of the spoken input; the auditory lexicon; or, the process of access to central representations of word meaning.

These three levels correspond to the three types of word deafness which were described in the introduction: the first is a problem in hearing the sounds of speech, the second an inability to gain access to a word form, the third to derive the heard word's meaning. In all three cases,

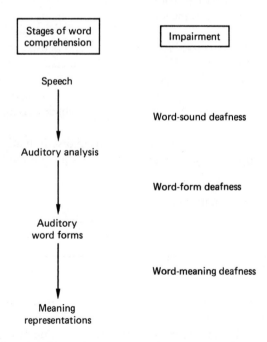

Figure 7.3   Levels of impairment in auditory comprehension.

hearing itself is normal, but in the first case patients are unable to repeat the words they hear as well as being unable to understand them. In the case of the problem in getting to the word or the word's meaning, repetition may be intact because the words can be repeated as if they were a meaningless string of sounds.

Is Derek 'word deaf'?

Our first hypothesis was that Derek's problem was an inability to recognize speech sounds. This was also suggested by the fact that he kept telling us 'I can't *hear* the words', despite the fact that his hearing, tested by standard pure tone audiometry, was found to be completely normal. A problem at this level could mean that when he hears word like 'pack', he may not be sure whether the sound at the beginning is a 'p' or a 't' or an 's', or he may have a similar problem with either the 'a' or the 'k' sound, or he may not 'hear' all of the sounds. To test this hypothesis, we gave him a number of tests, in which he was required to demonstrate exact recognition of the sounds he heard in words.

The tests consisted of hearing two syllables or words, and deciding whether they were the same or not. Half of the time they were (e.g. 'pack'/'pack'); and half the time they differed very slightly (e.g. 'pack'/ 'pad'). Some of the tests used real words, but others used non-words (e.g. 'mip'/'mip' or 'mip'/'mig'). The results of these tests are shown in table 7.1. It can be seen that Derek is well able to decide whether these strings sound the same or not, irrespective of whether they are made up of words or non-words, and even when he is not sure which part of the word is going to vary.

So Derek does not have obvious problems in discriminating the sounds he hears. However, he may be doing these tests just on the basis of them

Table 7.1   Minimal pair tests

Phoneme discrimination	Score	Example
Consonant Vowel (CV) syllables	0.95	ba/ba, ba/ma, ba/sa
Consonant Vowel Consonant (CVC) non-words	0.89	fes/fes, mip/mig
Consonant Vowel Consonant (CVC) words	0.94	face/face, roam/road

being meaningless sounds where he is detecting minimal changes; he does not actually have to know the identity of the speech sound he hears. He was therefore given another series of tests where he heard a string of sounds and had to decide whether they corresponded to a real word or not (lexical decision test). The strings either made up real words ('yes' condition) or non-words which differed from real words by only one sound ('no' condition). So for example for 'book' Derek would have to decide 'yes, that's a word', but for 'boak' he should decide 'no, that's not a word.' In order to do this type of test correctly, it is necessary not only to recognize which speech sounds are being heard, but also to look up in an auditory input lexicon whether those sounds correspond to a known word.

The lexical decision tests given to Derek are shown in table 7.2. As can be seen from the results, irrespective of how difficult this task was made in terms of which words were used, Derek had no difficulty in responding correctly. So not only is he able to recognize the speech sound he is hearing, he is also able to utilize those sounds to 'look up' words in his mental lexicon for heard words. Thus our original hypothesis, that he was 'word-sound deaf', was not supported. Intriguingly, however, there were many occasions when he heard a word, said correctly 'yes, it's a word' yet added 'but I can't hear it'!

Table 7.2 Lexical decision tests

	Auditory	*Visual*
Easy lexical decision ($n = 50$)	0.98	0.98
320 item test	0.96	0.98
Syllable length		
1	0.98	
2	0.93	
3	0.93	

Is Derek 'word-meaning deaf'?

With the previous tests, we demonstrated that Derek was not word deaf in the sense that he can discriminate between different sounds and even 'look up' words he hears in his mental 'lexicon'. So he must, by default, be impaired in actually reaching the word meanings. The next series of tests we did, therefore, were tests where Derek had to understand the meaning of a word in order to respond correctly. The most usual way to test for understanding the meaning of a word is a picture selection test, where one of the pictures corresponds to the word the subject hears.

If Derek is having a problem understanding the meanings of words, then he should have a particular problem in distinguishing between things with very similar meanings, for example choosing between a picture of a tiger and a picture of a lion when hearing the word 'tiger'. In order to test this he was given the word-to-picture matching test from the PALPA (Kay et al., 1990). In this test the subject has to choose between pictures of the correct word (e.g. 'axe'), a word closely related in meaning (e.g. 'hammer'), a word more distantly related in meaning (e.g. 'scissors') and two other words. In fact, Derek had little problem in selecting the correct picture: out of 40 items he made just one error (he pointed to the vest when asked to point to the 'underpants'). Although Derek seems to have failures of understanding in conversation, he has no real difficulty in understanding single spoken words where they have meanings that can be pictured.

Is Derek 'deaf' for abstract words?

From studies of patients with reading impairments following stroke it has become clear that many have a particular problem with words which are abstract, and therefore difficult to picture (e.g. 'series') as opposed to those which are concrete or easy to picture (e.g. 'clay'). Our next hypothesis was therefore that Derek's comprehension problem was limited to abstract words. This would explain his good performance on the picture-word matching test, since words that can be pictured are by definition concrete. In order to establish whether Derek was able to comprehend abstract words he was given the synonym judgements test (Coltheart, 1980). In this test Derek heard two words and had to decide whether they had similar meanings or not. So, for example, he would respond 'yes' if he heard 'flower/blossom' but 'no' if he heard 'flower/boat'. The important aspect of this test is that half of the word pairs are made up of concrete words, like the examples given above, but the other half are pairs of abstract words, for example 'irony/sarcasm' or 'irony/kingdom'.

The results of this test were quite dramatic. Derek correctly judged 34/38 concrete words, but only 23/38 abstract words. Not only was he significantly worse on the abstract words, but his performance on the abstract words was not significantly better than you would predict from someone just guessing (a chance score in this test is 19/38). Since he was relatively good at the concrete word items, it could not be the case that he was unable to understand the task. This suggested, therefore, that he was having a particular problem in understanding abstract words. To verify this we gave him another test which compared his ability to comprehend abstract words and concrete words. He was given matched lists of concrete and abstract words and asked to give single-word definitions for the words he heard. Examples of his definitions are given in table 7.3. He was able to give appropriate definitions to 38/40 concrete words (e.g. 'radio' → 'TV', 'clay' → 'wax'), but only 18/40 abstract words were appropriately defined (e.g. 'cult' → 'ghost', 'theory' → 'idea'). Derek produced few actual errors; either he produced an appropriate definition or he simply said he had no idea what the word was.

Derek's performance on this test is as predicted; he again demonstrates an inability to get to the meanings of abstract words. It is important to note that the 'lexical decision tests' described in an earlier section included abstract words, so that even though Derek insists that he has no idea what word he has heard, he can still judge that it was a real word.

Table 7.3   Examples of definitions for heard and read words

	Heard	*Read*
Concrete	river → lake mouse → elephant rabbit → rat	River → stream mouse → elephant rabbit → rat
Abstract	meek → no idea → no sullen → dull	meek → bold idea → theory sullen → smile

Is Derek's comprehension problem specific to words he hears?

If Derek has a problem understanding abstract words, this may be accounted for in one of two ways. First, it might be because of an impairment to the representation of the meanings of abstract words. If this were so then the problem would be apparent irrespective of whether Derek is trying to comprehend words he hears or words he reads. That is, his written comprehension of abstract words will be as impaired as his understanding of these words in spoken form. The second account is that he is unable to get to the word meanings from the auditory lexicon. According to this account there would be no impairment to the meanings themselves, and therefore there would be no corresponding difficulty in written words.

To test these possibilities, Derek was given the synonym judgements test and the word definition tests in written form; he was unimpaired at these tasks, even with the abstract words (a summary of results for both the auditory and written versions of the tests are given in table 7.4). This demonstrates that Derek has a 'deafness' in the sense that it is an impairment of auditory processing alone, although of course it is a deafness for word meanings. The impairment can therefore be located precisely at the level of getting to the meaning of the word from the auditory lexical form.

Table 7.4   Tests of spoken and written comprehension

Test	Spoken stimuli		Written stimuli	
	High imagery	Low imagery	High imagery	Low imagery
Synonym judgements ($n = 38$)	0.95	0.61	1.00	0.95
Word definitions ($n = 40$)	0.93	0.43	1.00	0.90
PALPA word-to-picture matching test ($n = 40$)	0.98			

Repeating abstract words

Derek has a second impairment in addition to his word-meaning deafness. When he hears strings of sounds he is unable to repeat them unless he can understand them. In order to make sense of this it is necessary to consider the model of speech comprehension once more. Clearly, one way of repeating words is to understand the word heard (e.g. 'cat'), think of the meaning of the word (e.g. furry animal that miaows) and then produce its name ('cat'). However, there must be another way to repeat, since it is possible to repeat words which have never been heard before (as long as they are made up of English sounds). So, for example, it is perfectly possible for any English speaker to hear 'floip' and repeat it correctly, even though this is a novel combination of sounds. In order to do this, it must be possible to translate heard sounds directly into speech.

Now if Derek was able to use this way of repeating, he should be able to repeat words even when he cannot understand them; he would just be repeating them as if they were strings of speech sounds he had never heard in that particular combination before. If, however, he were unable to repeat in this way he would be forced to repeat words by comprehending their meanings; his difficulty in understanding abstract words should therefore be reflected in a difficulty in repeating them.

To see whether Derek could repeat words without using meaning we simply asked him to repeat 'made-up' words, such as 'flon', 'clup', etc. The following list shows his responses in this task:

clup	→	no response
chet	→	like chess
thack	→	fact
snit	→	/smes/
flad	→	thread
lon	→	long
prug	→	/fud/
teep	→	teak
weg	→	not watch
droom	→	show
glun	→	thump
hom	→	up
juss	→	no response
chark	→	jake
lut	→	wake
mive	→	no response
skilt	→	skill
hesh	→	race
vike	→	phrase
trob	→	no response

It can be seen that he cannot repeat a single made-up word correctly. Therefore, we would predict that his repetition will show the same difficulties as his comprehension, since he cannot repeat words sound by sound, but must look up their meaning.

We therefore gave him the abstract and concrete word list to repeat, that we had previously given him for definition. Table 7.5 shows the

Table 7.5   Repetition of abstract and concrete words: example responses

Abstract (20% correct)	Concrete (80% correct)
answer → correct	river → water
type → DK	radio → correct
fear → /f/ – no	window → correct
theory → fairy	army → correct
modern → DK	heart → correct
idea → DK	plant → plants
late → liver	summer → today, no
easy → answer	clay → DK
unit → DK	square → DK
chance → DK	ball → correct
issue → DK	road → correct
deal → DK	book → correct
rest → correct	doctor → correct
moral → DK	wall → correct
fine → DK	blood → correct
care → DK	market → correct
piece → correct	hair → correct
trade → business	pool → correct

DK = 'don't know'.

results. As predicted, he found it difficult to repeat words, and he had a particular difficulty with the abstract words. Further confirmation that he was repeating via meaning came from the fact that he made a number of errors which were related in meaning to the word he was trying to repeat.

Does Derek 'hear' any of the meaning of the words he is trying to repeat?

We pointed out earlier that most of Derek's errors in the word repetition and definition tasks were 'don't know' errors, and that he often insisted that he had no idea what the words were that he was hearing. We thought it would be interesting to test whether he had any (even unconscious) information about these words. We therefore asked him to repeat some words, and when he said he did not know what the word was, we showed him two written words. One of these words was related in meaning to the word he had just heard. So, for example, he was asked to repeat 'crisis', and when he was unable to do so he was shown two words, 'evidence' and 'emergency' (and would, we hoped, select 'emergency' as being related in meaning). Could he reliably point to the target word rather than the one unrelated in meaning, even though he had 'no idea' what the heard word was? Using a list of 100 concrete and 100 abstract words, he was able to select 131/136 synonyms for the words he was unable to repeat. The fact that he could reliably point to the synonym of the word he heard means that he must have possessed at least some information about the meaning of the word, even though he was not aware of this.

How does his impairment for abstract words affect Derek's communicative ability?

Obviously, if Derek can only comprehend concrete words, he can only talk about concrete subjects. Apart from practical conversations (e.g. about shopping), people tend to use a large number of abstract nouns. This is particularly debilitating for Derek in that there is no other way apart from language that abstract concepts can be communicated; they are language-specific. Consider for example the concrete word 'apple'. If you were trying to get across to someone that it was an apple that you were talking about, but they could not understand the word, how would you do it? Well, you might be able to point to an apple and communicate the meaning that way; or you might be able to draw it; or you could gesture picking it off the tree and eating it. Or you could even give a verbal definition, hoping that you would give enough extra information to enable the person to understand. So you could say 'it's a fruit which grows on a tree, is red or green and you make cider from it'. Consider, however, an abstract word like 'debut'. You cannot point to it, or draw it; you cannot gesture a 'debut', and although you can give a verbal definition, it will be very difficult to give one that defines that word and that word alone.

There is another sense in which incomprehension of abstract words is a problem. We have only described Derek's comprehension of single words, but consider the comprehension of sentences. Take, for example, two sentences:

1 Priscilla walks puppies.
2 Priscilla will be taking some of the puppies for a walk.

The first sentence comprises three fairly concrete words, and would be easy for Derek to understand. It is, however, not a particularly informative or common type of sentence. The second sentence is of a much more usual form, in that it contains several words which relate directly to the grammatical form of the sentence. These are the words 'will', 'be', 'of', 'the', 'for' and 'a'. All these words are abstract in that they do not refer to anything that can be pictured. Since Derek will be unable to understand these words (because they are abstract) he will have considerable problems understanding the fine detail of the sentence. For example, in the case of sentence 2 he might know that the speaker is talking about Priscilla, and something about the dogs and something about walking, but he will not know whether a past, future or possible event is being described.

Intriguingly, this problem also affects how Derek 'hears' his own speech. Although he speaks in complete sentences he believes that he speaks 'telegrammatically'. So he says that where his wife would say 'I'm going shopping' he thinks he is saying 'I go shop'. So this is what he hears himself saying even though he is actually saying 'I'm going shopping' too.

What does Derek's impairment suggest about normal language?

It can be seen that even such a specific impairment as abstract word-meaning deafness is devastating for Derek's ability to communicate with others. But what does the existence of such a deficit tell us about language itself?

The fact that Derek can have a problem at the level of getting to meaning demonstrates very clearly the separability of written and spoken comprehension processes. Of course, written and spoken comprehension must be separable at early processing stages in that one deals with auditory stimuli and one with visual. However, one might expect that both types of information would reach a single word-form system. However, experiments with normal subjects in cognitive psychology have suggested that there are separate word-form systems for spoken and written words, as demonstrated in Morton's 'logogen' model (1980). The fact that Derek can get to semantics from visual word forms but not from auditory word forms strongly supports a model which has separate routines for access to meanings from heard and written words.

Morton's model also proposes that the word-form systems constitute a separate level of processing from a meaning or 'semantic' system. Again, the fact that Derek is able to reach word forms, but is then unable to get to the meaning, is further support for such a model. What Morton's model (and its descendants) does not predict is that there can be an inability to reach meaning which is specific to abstract words. Whether this is simply because abstract words are in some sense more 'difficult' or whether it represents some kind of category-specific deficit, similar to the anomia for proper names described by Semenza and Zettin (1988), is as yet unclear.

References

Bramwell, B. (1897) Illustrative cases of aphasia. *Lancet*, 1, 1256–9. (Reprinted in 1984 as 'A case of word meaning deafness', *Cognitive Neuropsychology*, 1, 249–58.)

Coltheart, M. (1980) Analysing acquired disorders of reading. Unpublished manuscript, Birkbeck College, London.

Franklin, S. (1989) Dissociations in auditory word comprehension: evidence from nine fluent aphasics. *Aphasiology*, 3, 189–207.

Goldstein, M. (1974) Auditory agnosia for speech ('pure word-deafness'): a historical review with current implications. *Brain and Language*, 1, 195–204.

Howard, D. and Franklin, S. (1989) *Missing the Meaning?* Cambridge, Mass.: MIT Press.

Kay, J., Lesser, R. and Coltheart, M. (1991) *Psycholinguistic Assessments of Language Processing in Aphasia (PALPA)*. Hove: Lawrence Erlbaum.

Kohn, S. and Friedman, R. (1986) Word-meaning deafness: a phonological-semantic dissociation. *Cognitive Neuropsychology*, 3, 291–308.

Morton, J. (1980) The logogen model and orthographic structure. In U. Frith (ed.) *Cognitive Processes in Spelling*. London: Academic Press.

Semenza, C. and Zettin, M. (1988) Generating proper names: a case of selective inability. *Cognitive Neuropsychology*, 5, 711–21.

Ziehl, F. (1896) Ueber einen Fall von Worttaubheit und das Lichtheim'sche Krankheitsbild der subcorticalen sensorischen Aphasie. *Deutsche Zeitschrift fur Nervenheilkunde*, 8, 259–307.

8

The write stuff: a case of acquired spelling disorder

Janice Kay

By any standards, EST is a brave man. He was still in his early forties when he was diagnosed as suffering from a brain tumour considered at that time to be inoperable. He continued working as an engineer for the next ten years, helping his wife to bring up their young family, while the neurological episodes associated with the tumour – dull painful head-aches, loss of sensation in his right arm and hand – grew alarmingly more frequent. At the same time, he noticed that during these episodes, he would have difficulty with his speech, principally with finding appropriate words that remained stubbornly on the tip of his tongue. As it turned out, the tumour was benign and slow-growing but, even so, his physical symptoms eventually began to prove life-threatening and surg-ery could no longer be delayed. A CT scan taken just before the operation in 1977 showed the tumour to be as big as an orange, filling much of the area where his temporal lobe should have been. A second scan, taken a few years ago, showed the area where the tumour was to have been replaced by lines of scar tissue which looked a little as if a running stitch had been tacked round a hole in a swatch of material and pulled tight.

It must have taken all of what the neurosurgeon called 'his robust Lancastrian personality' for EST to cope with coming round from the operation to find that he was unable to speak. A week later, he woke in the middle of the night to find that he could say 'lunk' or 'gunk' or something like that. And that is what he remembers shouting, at the top of his voice, waking the whole ward. He says he was relieved that he was able to say something, even a meaningless word, because it was a promise of a return to being able to communicate again.

Over the following months, with speech therapy help, he did indeed regain a certain fluency in his speech, though not to the extent that he had before the operation. His difficulty in word-finding is considerably greater than before, and it frequently disrupts the tempo of his conversation. Often this difficulty pitches him in unanticipated directions, because in trying to find a replacement for the intended word, he finds himself unable to generate the alternative and he is forced to search for a third word that may do instead. Perhaps the most frustrating aspect of this is that he generally has a perfectly clear idea of what he wants to say: the difficulty is finding the appropriate word to express it. A common enough phenomenon, particularly for anyone who is elderly, pregnant or under stress, but imagine experiencing this problem to a pathological degree, so that even trying to produce relatively common words like 'envelope' or 'ashtray' is a considerable struggle. His difficulty is in finding words, not in articulating them: he is well able to repeat words that he cannot produce spontaneously.

Stuff and nonsense

A difficulty in finding words, referred to clinically as *anomia*, is arguably the most common accompaniment of acquired language disorders. A syndrome in which anomia itself is the principal and pervasive sign is much more unusual. *Anomic aphasia* (alternative terms are *amnesic aphasia* and *nominal aphasia*) is characterized by problems in word-finding which occur however a response is elicited. The person with anomia will have difficulty in finding the name of an object whether the object is presented visually, tactually, as a picture or as a corresponding spoken description, even though he or she may fully understand what the object is. Thus, Alfred E, the subject of an early study by Potts (1901), was unable 'to name paper, a penholder, an ink-well and a watch, but he could tell at once what they were used for, and whether or not they were named correctly by another . . . [he] was equally unable to name the objects when felt or heard, as in the case of the watch; or objects smelled or tasted' (Potts, 1901, p. 1239).

Anomic speech is as fluent as the word-finding difficulty permits, grammatically correct and well articulated, though the problem in finding vocabulary words generally results in conversation which is relatively 'empty' of content and littered with non-specific words like 'stuff' and 'thing' as the following excerpt from patient AL in Allport (1983) demonstrates. Patient AL had been asked to describe a picture of a disastrous scene in a kitchen:

> You never do *that* with a place there, you push it and do that [gestures to cooker controls]. That is the same thing underneath there's one to do that as well. *That* you don't have to do either . . . I don't know what's happened to that, but it's taken that out. That is mm there without doing it, the things that are being done – you know the thing I mean? . . . That's the same thing too; that's all wrong. What else is there? . . . Oh yes, she's doing some stuff here and it's really rather bad to do things there. You don't do *that*; you take it and do it, slow . . .

It has been known for some time that the more common the word, the more likely it is to be retrieved (Howes, 1964; Rochford and Williams, 1965). An ability to repeat words is generally preserved (though not in the case of Alfred E).

It can be demonstrated experimentally that EST's ability to find words is strongly determined by how often they occur in the language by showing him pictures of words with names that are either common or more unusual, such as 'telephone' and 'butterfly'. It is good practice to match the words for other variables like syllable length which may affect word retrieval. In EST's case, however, whether a word has one syllable, like 'gun', or many syllables, like 'hospital', does not affect his ability to produce it, as long as it is high in frequency.

In a paper published a few years ago (Kay and Ellis, 1987), we tried to assess how much EST understands of the word he is attempting to find, since it is clearly unsatisfactory simply to rely on a person's own report. Even an apparently accurate gesture is not a reliable guide to the degree of comprehension a patient has (Riddoch et al., 1988). One finding that convinces us that he actually does have detailed knowledge of the thing he is trying to name is that he can easily choose between two uncommon, closely related pictures (such as 'artichoke' and 'asparagus') when he is given the spoken name of one of them, even though he is unable to produce that name spontaneously. On being shown a picture of an 'artichoke' and asked to name it, his response was typical: 'Dear, we'll be here till Christmas – not this year, next year. [JK: It's an artichoke.] I'm just up to lettuce and then cabbage, not got to blooming artichoke . . . I'm very, very pleased I've got round to cabbage!'

Another factor that suggests he can have a precise target in mind is that his naming attempts are often similar in sound to the target. What is more, they sometimes have the same number of syllables and begin with the same sound (a 'strawberry' was called a 'sumberry', for example).

Sometimes he estimates the number of letters in the word and tries to spell it. To a picture of a 'crocodile', for example, he said, 'seizing . . . bite you . . . begins with 'c' . . . 11 letters in it, no 7 or 8 . . . 'h' . . . ch . . . 'c' . . . 8 (letters) in it . . . 'r', 'cr', crow, cray . . . '. Shown a picture of a 'stool', he said, 'stop, step . . . seat, small seat, round seat, sit on the . . . sit on the stuh, steep, stone . . . it's stole, stay, steet'.

If EST's difficulties lie not in understanding word meanings but in finding their spoken form, where is the actual problem? We have charcterized it in the following way. Assume that there is a store or 'mental lexicon' of all spoken words that we know. Psychologists refer to the store as a *speech output lexicon* because it contains information about the sounds of words that are prepared for speaking (output) rather than listening (input).

Detailed knowledge about the meaning of a particular word is usually sufficient to pinpoint its corresponding entry in the speech output lexicon. The process of going from the meaning of the word to its word form is not infallible, however, and depends on the 'strength' of the connection between the two types of information. More common words (words that are spoken more often in the general run of conversation) will have stronger links than less common ones and, it is assumed, will be less vulnerable to damage. Our interpretation of EST's word-finding disorder was that the activation between word meanings and their corresponding sound forms is reduced, with the result that names for less common things are more difficult to retrieve. We also suggested that, for some less common items, some sounds in the word can be retrieved, so that EST is often able to make a stab at the target that sounds something like it, as in 'stop' or 'steet' for 'stool'. These responses consist of real words and word-like sounds in approximately equal number. In some cases he is unable to say anything about the sound form of the target (even though he knows what it is) and these examples turn out to have the lowest frequency names of our sample.

Our view was that the word forms themselves were largely unimpaired and this hypothesis was based on two circumstantial pieces of evidence. First, EST was sometimes able to find the name for a picture that he had been unable to retrieve on a previous occasion, suggesting that the word is available in the lexicon even though it cannot always be accessed. Put another way, it is difficult to predict on any occasion whether EST will be able to retrieve a particular word, other than by whether it is high or low in frequency: he is likely to be able to find it if it is a common word, but not if it is more unusual. One would expect a different outcome if there was permanent damage to a selection of the words in the lexicon: there would be a subset of names that he would be consistently be unable to retrieve correctly and a further subset that he would be consistently be able to produce. (Of course, one could argue that such damage might be *transitory*, so that a name can be retrieved with ease on one occasion but not on another.)

Our second piece of evidence appeared more convincing. EST's ability to repeat picture names is considerably better than his ability to produce them spontaneously and is not affected by how often they occur in speech. He was able, for example, to repeat perfectly a set of uncommon words like 'artichoke', even though he had earlier been unable to generate them in response to pictures and had no idea about their sounds. At the same time, his ability to repeat nonsense items like 'archilope', derived from the words, was very poor. Although it may seem a strange thing to do, most of us can do a task like this; we are perfectly able to repeat a novel utterance like 'archilope'. But we cannot do it by consulting our mental lexicon for how it is pronounced, because we will not have an entry for it. It is likely that we do it by using a procedure which allows us to 'echo' novel combinations of sounds. Given that EST was good at repeating real words, but poor at repeating made-up words, we believed it was doubtful that he was repeating by echoing. Rather, it seemed more likely that he *was* using his speech output lexicon when we asked him to repeat words, although he was unable to use it successfully if he only had the meaning of the word to guide him – that is, when he was required to name a picture or to find a word in spontaneous speech.

Recently, Zingeser and Berndt (1988) and Miceli et al. (1991) have reported the language behaviour of patients who, like EST, show a strong frequency effect in picture naming, but who make *few* sound-based errors, illustrating that the two symptoms do not always co-occur. Ellis et al. (1991) suggest that effects of word frequency reflect damage to the connections between word meaning and word sounds, while phonological errors (in the absence of symptoms such as syllable-length effects) indicate damage to the storage of sound forms themselves (or to even later stages prior to speaking). In EST's case, then, this means that his word-retrieval difficulties stem from *two* levels of damage: first to connections between the meaning and the lexicon and second to the lexicon itself. Now, if EST has damage to the speech output lexicon, how are we to explain his good word repetition abilities? One reason could be that when he repeats words, unlike when he tries to name a picture, he has the option of using two procedures, even though both are impaired. He can try to echo what he hears and he can try to match what he hears with the corresponding word in the speech output lexicon. By combining information from these separate sources, his word repetition appears, to all intents and purposes, near-perfect.

The write stuff

As well as profound difficulties in naming, EST also has problems in reading and spelling. An avid student of the stocks and shares pages of *The Times*, it is a great trial to him that he is unable to read through the other pages as he used to. Instead, he is forced to decipher one word at a time, often pronouncing unusual words like 'colonel' and 'coup' as they look (as koll-un-el and k-uw-p), even though he knows their meaning and would once have been able to produce them correctly. The reason why he is unable to read aloud words fluently may be because the lexicon that he needs to consult to say them is the same one that he has difficulty in using in spontaneous speech and in picture-naming, namely the speech output lexicon. The reason why he produced literal soundings of the written words will become clearer as we examine how EST *spells* words following his operation.

A fascinating aspect of EST's case is that the problems he experiences in reading are mirrored in spelling. Once again the disability seems to relate to his word-retrieval difficulties in speech and it is the *interaction* between speaking words and spelling them that is the focus of this paper. Researchers interested in acquired speech and language disability try to understand precisely what goes wrong with a particular skill, such as written spelling, by investigating the impaired mechanism in great detail and by trying to relate it to how the skill operates in the absence of brain damage. To understand fully EST's case, it is therefore necessary to go into a little more detail about how word retrieval in speech, reading and writing is normally achieved. But first, we need to see how EST actually spells. Figure 8.1 illustrates a small sample of his spontaneous writing.

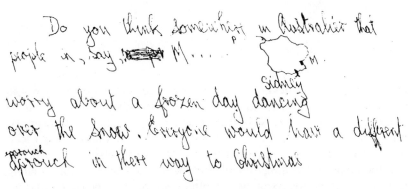

Figure 8.1   A sample of EST's spontaneous writing.

There are a number of things to notice about the piece. First, although it has a grammatical structure, the word-retrieval difficulties that he has when he tries to describe people, places and things out loud are also manifest when he writes (thus, he is unable to retrieve Melbourne and Perth, but indicates their first letters and locates them on his map). Secondly, it is clear that some of the words he uses are mis-spelled ('Australier', 'Sidney', 'aprouch' for approach and 'there' for their). Not only does he sound out certain words when he reads them aloud, but he also often spells words as they are sounded. 'Approach' for example, is spelled as 'aprouch', whereas prior to his operation, he considered himself to be a good speller and would not have made such an error.

Written English is made up of many words which are not spelled the way they sound. 'Colonel' is an example; others are 'yacht', 'meringue', 'scissors' and 'answer'. Some of them, like 'many', 'one' and 'two', are very common. This state of affairs has come about because of a variety of interesting historical reasons. One is the influx of spellings borrowed from invaders (such as 'people' and 'piece' from the Normans), or from trading partners ('school' and 'yacht' from the Dutch). Another is the over-zealous tinkering with the etymologies of words that was prevalent during the great revival of learning that swept through Europe at the end of the fifteenth century ('scissors' for example, was given the letter 'c' on the assumption that its root was the Latin *scindere*, to cut; in fact, it derives ultimately from the late Latin *cisorium*, cutting instrument). Good descriptions of the evolution of written English can be found in Strang (1970) and Scraggs (1974). Many other languages, Italian and Spanish are examples, are considerably more regular in their sound-spelling correspondence, so that once you learn the rules, you can take a good crack at spelling or pronouncing a new word.

Spelling procedures: routes to successful spelling

In order to spell a large number of English words successfully, one has to know precisely their written forms because following rules for sound-spelling correspondence will produce a wrong, if plausible, answer. To turn this into psychologist's terminology, we can say that in these cases, the appropriate lexical entry in a *spelling lexicon* must be addressed. We can look up the spellings of all the words we know in this spelling lexicon. On the other hand, we are often required to spell things that we have not come across before, say when writing down a new address (Phollet Road or Shapter Street). In this case, we use our knowledge about sound-spelling correspondences to construct a spelling, because the new word form will not be stored in our lexicons. We can only guess, though; the correct spellings may be Follett and Schaptor.

There are therefore two logically possible ways to spell an item: first, by using a procedure which specifies whole-word spellings and which must be used to spell unpredictable or exceptional words correctly; and, secondly, by using a procedure which encapsulates what we know about the ways sounds can be spelled and which enables us to spell 'by rule'. Using this procedure we can spell novel items (let us call them non-words), and it also provides us with an alternative way of spelling rule-governed, regular, words (words such as 'bus' which are made up of sounds that have perfectly predictable spellings). Damage to each of these procedures has readily specifiable consequences. If the spelling lexicon (or access to it) is impaired, there will naturally be a difficulty in spelling words, but this difficulty will only really be noticeable when trying to spell exceptional words like 'colonel', because there is another way of spelling regular words. Regular words and non-words will be spelled correctly using the sound-spelling procedure, providing this routine remains intact. Reliance on sound-spelling rules means that exceptional words will be spelt literally according to how they sound (like 'kurnal' for 'colonel').

What happens if the pattern of damage is reversed, so that sound-spelling procedures are impaired while the use of the spelling lexicon is intact? In this case, familiar words (whether exceptions or regular) will be spelled correctly; it will be exceedingly difficult to construct spellings for non-words, however, although, for obvious reasons, this is not a problem that is immediately apparent!

Beauvois and Derousné (1981) produced the first detailed case study of a patient who appeared to be unable to spell using the lexicon, a disorder which they termed *lexical agraphia* (agraphia is the technical term for writing disorders). True to what we have just said, their French-speaking patient was perfectly able to spell even long and complex non-words, while word spelling was governed strictly by the number of sounds in a word that had an ambiguous or exceptional correspondence. Thus, completely regular words in French such as *madame* were generally spelled correctly. But if they were slightly ambiguous (e.g. *en* in *mental*), the patient showed some difficulty and when they were very ambiguous (e.g. *an* and *s* in *anchois*), he was very poor indeed. English-speaking patients with similar patterns of performance have since been described (Hatfield and Patterson, 1983; Roeltgen and Heilman, 1984; Goodman and Caramazza, 1986; Baxter and Warrington, 1987), though most showed impairments that were less severe or less pure than the original case (Shallice, 1988, table 6.1, p. 133).

There have also been examples of patients who are impaired in using sound-spelling rules. The observation that such cases exist allows one to say that there is a *double dissociation* between word-specific disorders and disorders of sound-spelling knowledge in spelling. In *phonological agraphia*, the patient cannot spell novel combinations of sounds that he hears (like 'dasp' and 'biffle'), but still has relatively normal word spelling, with no superiority of regular over exceptional words (Shallice, 1981; Bub and Kertesz, 1982).

How does EST spell words?

A glance at EST's written spelling shows that he often spells words as they sound and that he is particularly affected when they have exceptional spellings. Although clinical evidence suggested that EST's spelling may conform to the pattern of lexical agraphia, we tested for this disorder in a more controlled way. He was asked to spell to dictation a list of 40 words with regular sound-spelling correspondences and 40 words with exceptional correspondences. The words, taken from the PALPA battery (Kay et al., 1992), are matched so that they do not differ on other variables such as word length that are known to affect spelling ability. He was able to spell 38 of the 40 regular words correctly, but only 20 exceptional words, a statistically significant difference. His spelling errors were principally errors which sounded like the targets (giraffe → giraphe, guard → garde). Spelling aloud was affected in the same way as written spelling. He spelt aloud 37 of the 40 regular words correctly, but only 18 exceptional words (again this difference is statistically significant). 'Giraffe' was again spelled as 'giraphe' and 'guard' was spelled as 'gard'. These findings show that EST's spelling disorder is not a straightforward motor difficulty in writing and must reflect damage to more central *cognitive* processes that are common to both written and oral spelling. EST's difficulty in spelling exceptional words indicates that, for some reason, he is often unable to retrieve appropriate *word* spellings. The interesting question is why not.

Spelling picture names

Recall that EST's ability to name pictures is strongly influenced by the frequency of its name (how often it occurs in conversation or in written language). We attributed this finding to a difficulty in successfully activating speech forms of words. Now spelling a word (spontaneously or to dictation) may also involve this procedure: perhaps we look up the correct sound form of a word in the speech output lexicon and use this information to get hold of the correct spelling in the spelling lexicon (many of us are familiar with the experience of hearing an 'inner voice' saying the word before we spell it). This may not be the only way to spell a word. Another may simply be to use the *meaning* of the word directly to look up the correct entry in the spelling lexicon, and this avoids any need to first 'name' the word covertly. Now, the interesting question is what happens when EST is shown a picture and asked to write down its name? We know what happens when he is asked to say aloud what it is. If EST has to retrieve the spoken name before he can *spell* it, then he will experience the same type of difficulty in writing down a picture name. On the other hand, if he simply uses his knowledge of what the picture represents to retrieve the correct spelling, then he should be able to write down the names of pictures without difficulty. To find out what he does, we showed him 20 pictures and simply asked him to write their names. Half of the names were high in frequency (e.g. 'heart') and half were low in frequency (e.g. 'comb'). It turns out that he was not very good at spelling the picture names; he only managed to write down ten of them. However, in written naming, as in saying the picture names, he was far better at spelling pictures with common names (he successfully wrote eight of the high-frequency names, but only two of the low-frequency ones).

In a second task, we showed EST a set of 42 pictures, 14 each of one-, two- and three-syllables, taken from the Cambridge 300 picture set (Howard, personal communication). In one session he was asked to write down the names of the pictures and it was stressed that he should not try to vocalize the name, either overtly or covertly. In a second session, one day later, he was asked to *say* the names of the pictures. You can see what he said and what he wrote in table 8.1. It is clear that success in naming the pictures aloud is not affected by syllable length (a finding that replicates what we had observed in our original investigations) and neither is spelling picture names. It is also clear that his ability to spell is strongly related to his ability to say the name aloud: if he can name a picture, he can usually spell it (though he sometimes produces literal spellings such as 'televishon' instead of 'television'). If he is unable to name it and can only provide a verbal description, then he tends to produce a similar 'anomic' written description.

There is, then, a strong contingency between spoken and written naming. Spelling picture names appears to be based on prior retrieval of word phonology and both are strongly affected by word frequency. A careful look at his spellings also suggests that spelling individual words may be driven by sound-spelling correspondences rather than by actual *word* knowledge, because words with ambiguous spellings were often

Table 8.1 A comparison of written and oral naming

Picture	Spoken naming response	Written naming response
cup	+	+
blouse	clothes	clothes
tray	have a meal	–
worm	snail near enough	floor crawling
mug	cup, no	cup
cheese	+	+
logs	tree, cut lengths of the tree	wood for burning
spade	handle, I know that's not right	handle
arch	church	door for church
noose	tie for your . . .	to kill a man years ago
frog	4 letters	F---
bat	flies away in middle of the night	bird, night time
hook	no	anker
nose	+	+
razor	shave	shaver
bonnet	woman's hat	girl's hat
cowboy	horse with man from Yankee-land	horse with a man
rocket	+	+
mermaid	sea-girl	sea-girl
knitting	stitching	kniting

ladder	no	–
tractor	car . . . travelling about on grass	van
necklace	girl's . . .	lady's hair, ring
butter	+	+
zebra	horse in Africa	horse in Africa
marrow	to eat	to eat
hammer	+	+
baby	kid	child – one year
telescope	+	You can see a distance with
cigarette	+	Fag alight
sausages	+	+
caravan	+	+
telephone	+	+
banana	B, eat it	+
spaghetti	Italy, to eat	Italy for eating
pyramid	in the Arabs, many years ago	Arabs built hear, 1000s of years ago
television	+	+ (television)
stethoscope	doctor's . . .	Doctors for child seeing health
envelope	letter, but . . .	letter
skeleton	200 years ago, dead old bugger	Old Dead Man Years ago
celery	eat that stuff	To eat
battery	+	+
Total correct	13	13

spelled as they sound ('anchor', for example, was spelled as 'anker', 'chair' was written as 'chare', 'scissors' as 'sissors').

Spelling to dictation

When EST is asked to write down the name of a picture, it appears that he first needs to *name* it. Because spoken naming is impaired, so is written naming. One of the findings that brought us to this conclusion was that both tasks are affected by word frequency in the language. We were interested to see whether EST's ability to spell words to dictation would also be affected by word frequency. If did not logically follow that it would. Think about what one has to do in each of these tasks. In naming a picture we *have* to retrieve the correct sound form of the target. In spelling to dictation, the correct sound form is *specified* as we hear it (though we may have to transform it into a speech code and maintain it for long enough to consult our spelling lexicon). In this respect, we can think of spelling a word to dictation as being similar to repeating a word: the procedures that we use in identifying what we hear and locating its speech form may be the same in both cases. We know that EST is good at word repetition and that the frequency of a word plays no part in his success. Word frequency may likewise have little effect when he spells to dictation, unlike when he looks at a picture and has to write down its name. To see whether this was true, we gave him 40 high-frequency and 40 low-frequency words from the PALPA battery (Kay et al., 1992) to write to dictation. The words were matched for imageability, regularity, syllable and letter length. He spelt 23 high-frequency words correctly and 19 low-frequency words, a slight difference which does not approach statistical significance and may well have happened by chance (further-more, we have looked for an effect of frequency using several different sets of words, but always with the same result). Spelling to dictation was none the less poor: just over half the words were spelled correctly. This is again because many of the words (high and low frequency alike) were spelled as they sound: 'character' was written as 'carricter', for example, 'system' as 'sistem' and 'idea' as 'iddear'). For EST, then, the sound of a word may be easier to evoke in spelling to dictation than in written naming: spelling to dictation can take advantage of the two procedures available in spoken word repetition. However, the fact that he still makes phonic errors implies that this advantage does not fully carry over into spelling to dictation: it is still regulated by sound-spelling procedures rather than by the speech output lexicon, presumably because the lexicon itself is impaired.

The integrity of the sound-spelling procedure: a caveat

From all that we have said about lexical agraphia and the way EST spells, he should be able to write non-words successfully to dictation. So we asked him to spell 24 non-words from the PALPA battery. In fact, he found it very difficult to do: he managed to produce acceptable spellings for only 13 (note that we accept any possible spelling of the sound as correct, so that 'gloap', 'glope' and even 'glowp' are all permissible renderings of 'gloap'). How does this fit in with our overall account of his difficulties? It occurred to us that this problem might have little to do with EST's spelling capabilities and rather more to do with his difficulty in *repeating non-words* that we mentioned earlier. And this is what seems to be the case. We asked EST to repeat 30 non-words: ten were mono-syllabic, like 'cleast', ten had two syllables, like 'drattle' and ten had three syllables, like 'ipical'. He only managed to repeat 16 successfully, producing errors that were similar in sound, but not quite right (thus, 'cleast' came out as 'cleace', 'ipical' as 'ickickle'). He found it particularly difficult to repeat polysyllabic non-words and only produced three correctly. However, we also observed that when he could repeat the non-word correctly, he could also spell it: his ability to use sound-spelling procedures seems to be perfectly adequate as long as he has the right input. There is a general lesson to be learnt here: in examining in detail any type of acquired language disorder, it is worth keeping in mind that the patterns of performance that one expects to find (given a working hypothesis about the nature of the particular disorder) are to some extent tempered by their interaction with other components of the language system.

Conclusion

Let us summarize how EST appears to spell. He used to be a good speller. To be a good speller you need to know how particular words are spelled; we have formalized this as being able to have access to a *spelling lexicon*. EST must be able to do this sometimes because he can spell some highly irregular words (such as 'yacht', 'answer' and 'routine'). But otherwise he has to rely on knowledge about how sounds, rather than words, are spelled. We know that this is what he does, firstly, because he is better at spelling regular than irregular words and, secondly, because if a word has an unusual or ambiguous spelling he tends to get it wrong in a characteristic way: words are spelled phonetically, so that 'sword', for example, is spelled as 'sord' and 'mortgage' as 'morgidge'. We have tried to find why EST has such difficulty in spelling words. Part of the reason seems to be because of the profound problems that he has in finding their speech forms, whether in general conversation or in specific tasks like picture naming. For EST, spelling is often contingent on first naming the word. We know, however, that spelling does not have to be based on a sound code. Brain damage, for example, can severely disrupt speech forms of words, but leave writing relatively well preserved (Ellis et al., 1983; Patterson and Shewell, 1987). This implies that information about word meaning can be used *directly* to retrieve correct spellings, although this does not seem to be an option that is readily open to EST.

The effects of brain disease on EST's ability to communicate are far-ranging. This chapter attempts to give a flavour of what these difficulties might be and how they might be explained within a simple model of language structure. In everyday life, EST meets these problems with a tenacity that sometimes belies their severity. Tom Wolfe wrote *The Right Stuff* about the courage of fliers to push their planes to the limits of the sound barrier and beyond; he might equally have written it about people such as EST.

Acknowledgements

I would like to thank Andrew Ellis for commenting on an earlier version of this paper. I would also like to thank the Wellcome Trust for their financial support as part of their University Award scheme. Most of all, I would like to acknowledge EST's patience and persistence over many years, and to thank him for his help in preparing this chapter.

References

Allport, D. A. (1983) Language and cognition. In R. Harris (ed.) *Approaches to Language*. Oxford: Pergamon.

Baxter, D. M. and Warrington, E. K. (1987) Transcoding sound to spelling: single or multiple unit correspondences. *Cortex*, 23, 11–28.

Beauvois, M-F. and Derousné, J. (1981) Lexical or orthographic agraphia. *Brain*, 104, 21–49.

Bub, D. and Kertesz, A. (1982) Evidence for lexicographic processing in a patient with preserved written over oral naming. *Brain*, 105, 697–717.

Ellis, A. W., Kay, J. and Franklin, S. (1992) Anomia: differentiating between semantic and phonological deficits. In D. I. Margolin (ed.) *Cognitive Neuropsychology in Clinical Practice*. New York: Oxford University Press.

Ellis, A. W., Miller, D. and Sin, G. (1983) Wernicke's aphasia and normal language processing: a case study in cognitive neuropsychology. *Cognition*, 15, 111–44.

Goodman, R. A. and Caramazza, A. (1986) Aspects of the spelling process: evidence from a case of acquired dysgraphia. *Language and Cognitive Processes*, 1, 263–96.

Hatfield, F. M. and Patterson, K. E. (1983) Phonological spelling. *Quarterly Journal of Experimental Psychology*, 35A, 451–68.

Howes, D. (1964) Application of the word frequency concept to aphasia. In A. V. S. De Reuck and M. O'Connor (eds) *Disorders of Language*. (CIBA Foundation Symposium.) London: Churchill.

Kay, J. and Ellis, A. W. (1987) A cognitive neuropsychological case study of anomia: implications for psychological models of word retrieval. *Brain*, 110, 613–29.

Kay, J., Lesser, R. and Coltheart, M. (1992) *Psycholinguistic Assessments of Language Processing in Aphasia (PALPA)*. Hove: Lawrence Erlbaum.

Miceli, G, Giustolisi, L. and Caramazza, A. (1991) The interaction of lexical and non-lexical processing mechanisms. *Cortex*, 27, 57–80.

Patterson, K. E. and Shewell, C. (1987) Speak and spell: dissociations and word-class effects. In Coltheart, M., Sartori, G. and Job, R. (eds) *The Cognitive Neuropsychology of Language*. London: Lawrence Erlbaum.

Potts, C. S. (1901) A case of transient motor aphasia, complete anomia, nearly complete agraphia and word blindness occurring in a left-handed man; with special reference to the existence of a naming center. *Journal of the American Medical Association*, 36, 1239–41.

Riddoch, M. J., Humphreys, G., Coltheart, M. and Funnell, E. (1988) Semantic system or systems? Neuropsychological evidence re-examined. *Cognitive Neuropsychology*, 5, 3–26.

Rochford, G. and Williams, M. (1965) Studies in the development and breakdown of the use of names. Part IV: The effects of word frequency. *Journal of Neurology, Neurosurgery and Psychiatry*, 28, 407–13.

Roeltgen, D. P. and Heilman, K. M. (1984) Lexical agraphia, further support for the two-strategy hypothesis of linguistic agraphia. *Brain*, 107, 811–27.

Scraggs, D. G. (1974) *A History of English Spelling*. Manchester: Manchester University Press.

Shallice, T. (1981) Phonological agraphia and the lexical route in writing. *Brain*, 104, 413–29.

Shallice, T. (1988) *From Neuropsychology to Mental Structure* (esp. chapter 6). Cambridge: Cambridge University Press.

Strang, B. M. H. (1970) *A History of English*. London: Methuen.

Zingeser, L. B. and Berndt, R. (1988) Grammatical class and context effects in a case of pure anomia: implications for models of language production. *Cognitive Neuropsychology*, 5, 473–516.

9

The two-legged apple

Jennie Powell and Jules Davidoff

When we first met NB in March 1989 she was 27 years of age and had been almost completely paralysed in all four limbs since the age of 20. The paralysis resulted from brain damage following a road traffic accident while on holiday in France. Cerebral CT scans in 1987 showed gross atrophic changes, with the occipital poles of both hemispheres particularly affected. She has virtually no residual vision except for a rough appreciation of luminance level.

NB is cared for in the family home, on a 24-hour basis, by care attendants appointed and supervised by her elderly parents. Despite her severe handicap, NB has remained amazingly cheerful, seemingly surrounded by a certain radiance of personality which is infectious. The family report that they do not see her as a different person since the accident and that her essential character has not been changed. NB's parents, however, describe her language as 'flowery', stating that it was not like this before the accident when she 'used more normal words'. The household welcome company of all kinds and visitors drop in, more to be inspired by NB than vice versa. Before the accident, NB had wanted to train as a chiropodist. She had obtained six 'O' levels, but had failed at 'A' level. Her interest in biology, however, was still evident.

Spoken language abilities were good with no evidence of any specific word-finding difficulty. There was some residual dysarthria which at times necessitated the listener requesting NB to repeat herself. Despite good spoken language skills, conversation was hampered by a memory loss for recent events. She would forget, for example, what she last ate or events of the previous day. Nevertheless, NB is able to assimilate some new information. For example, she is able to learn the names of therapists and helpers which she rapidly distinguishes by the sound of their voice.

NB could not consistently give the correct day, month, year, approximate time, her age or year of birth. She was, however, 100 per cent accurate in giving her name, date and month of birth, address, names of family, and whom she lived with. NB could also consistently supply the name of the current Prime Minister, the Prime Minister's political party and the name of the opposition leader.

Earlier psychological assessment indicated that remote memory was also partially damaged. For example, NB has no recollection of gaining the Duke of Edinburgh Award and it took some prompting before she remembered that she had been abroad several times. There was, however, recall of certain events in her life such as the names of schools attended, names of close friends and summer vacation jobs.

Assessment 1

We were asked to see NB following reports that she seemed to have difficulty in retrieving the appearance of objects. As a preliminary assessment (Assessment 1), NB was presented with the names of 130 items and, for each, was asked whether it had legs. If the response was 'yes', she was then asked if the given item had two, four, six, eight or more legs. NB was only correct on approximately two-thirds of these questions. The errors were remarkable. For example, two legs were assigned to an apple, a cat and a shirt; four legs to a cockerel, a watermelon and a chisel; six legs to a peacock, a camel and a tiger; eight legs to a fox, a worm and a snake, while an owl was said to have no legs and a zebra 'eight or more'.

NB does not appear to have much idea of what objects look like. So, we felt it important to obtain NB's introspective comments on her ability to visualize objects. Extracts of a conversation with one of us (JP) are recorded below.

JP: Can you see pictures in your mind?
NB: Yes.
JP: Are they clear?
NB: No.

JP: Are they sort of fuzzy?

NB: Yes.

JP: Are some things clearer than others?

NB: Yes, like if for example you ask me was a pig fat I would say yes. Or did a cow have a rather obnoxious smell then I would also say yes.

JP: Can you see a pig?

NB: I can just about see it.

JP: If I said to you 'What shape is an orange?' what would you say?

NB: Round.

JP: How do you know?

NB: Because I felt.

JP: Can you see an orange in your mind?

NB: No not really.

JP: What does a television look like?

NB: A television is usually attached to the wall and it has channels . . . Part of it where the sound comes out.

JP: Can you see a TV in your mind?

NB: I think so yes.

JP: Can you see it clearly?

NB: No, not very clearly at all.

JP: Do you see part or does it look as if it's in a haze?

NB: The latter. It all looks roughly the same.

JP: What do you mean?

NB: I can not see the corners of it.

JP: What can you see?

NB: I can see the microphone, the place where the sound comes out.

JP: Is that all you can see?

NB: Yes, but I know that it must have a button or somewhere to switch it on and off and change the channels.

JP: Can you see that button?

NB: No.

JP: Can you still see the microphone?

NB: Yes.

NB: I imagine that you are quite tall and brunette. Are you?

JP: Did you see me in your mind?

NB: Yes.

JP: Can you see a car in your mind's eye?

NB: No.

JP: Can you see any part of it?

NB: Yes, the windows.

JP: Just the windows?

NB: Yes and the door.

JP: Are you saying that because you see it or because you know it must have one?

NB: I think I am saying it because I know that it must have windows. But the door I think I saw.

JP: Imagine a banana. What do you see?
NB: A juicy fruit.
JP: Can you see the shape and the colour?
NB: Yes, it is fat and juicy.
JP: Can you see all of it?
NB: No, I can not see the root of it.
JP: Imagine an apple. What colour is it?
NB: Yellow.
JP: What shape is it?
NB: It is like a little stick.

Theory

For some as yet unknown reason, selective impairments of knowledge are more likely to occur from diffuse than from focal brain damage. NB has diffuse damage and, therefore, may help us understand how object knowledge is organized. There have been several proposals for the organization of knowledge in normal people (Collins and Loftus, 1975; Rosch, 1975; Warrington, 1975). Brain damage has given us two principle insights into that organization. The first concerns the possibility that the knowledge store may be organized hierarchically with specific knowledge being held under category headings; the second refers to the possibility that the store may be divided into a number of differing types.

Hierarchical models of stored knowledge have been found useful in understanding impairments from neurological damage (Warrington, 1975; Diesfeldt, 1985). For example, patients with diffuse brain damage may show preserved knowledge of a more general (superordinate) kind but lose more detailed information. Thus, they may know that an object is an animal but be unable to retrieve its country of origin and appearance. A goose, for example, is described as 'an animal but I've forgotten precisely'. There is a 'blunting of their knowledge of words and of the significance of objects' (Shallice, 1988). The loss of knowledge is manifest without the loss of intelligence as measured by abstract problem-solving abilities (Warrington, 1975).

Another way of looking at superordinate knowledge is to regard it as different from, rather than encompassing, other knowledge. We might then regard superordinate knowledge as referring to the function of an object. Such models of stored knowledge (Warrington and McCarthy, 1983; Davidoff, 1991) contrast functional and sensory attributes of objects. Fabrics, for example, are distinguished by their sensory properties; conversely, body parts are primarily distinguished by their function. Warrington and McCarthy (1983) propose the following explanation of their patient, VER: 'Consider differentiating between two types of item:

a wallet and a purse compared with a cabbage and a cauliflower. In the first case, sensory attributes are relatively unimportant (wallets can be of very different shapes, colours and sizes) whereas in the second it is these very sensory attributes which are crucial.'

The second important aspect of stored knowledge is to consider the number of distinct areas into which it may be divided. These divisions have been inferred from the loss or preservation of certain aspects of knowledge following brain damage. Many specific deficits as well as preserved islands of knowledge have now been reported. They include disorders for inanimate objects (Nielsen, 1946), animate objects (Warrington and Shallice, 1984), indoor objects (Yamadori and Albert, 1973) and body parts (Goodglass et al., 1966). One conclusion from these observations could be that each category of object is stored separately. Alternatively, Allport (1985) argues for an organization of object knowledge based on independent 'modules' concerned with sensory properties. An object may be represented across a number of these modules (tactile, visual, auditory, etc.). Depending upon the category of object, different sensory modalities are important to distinguish between category members; colour may be more important for fruit than for flowers, and smell more important for flowers than fruit.

NB's comments suggest that the loss of visual knowledge is much greater than the loss of knowledge which can be stored non-visually; this has important implications. It suggests that, for her, separate stores of object knowledge have been differentially impaired. Her comments also imply that there could be some duplication of knowledge across different types of stores. Thus, she may be able to answer questions which appear to be purely visual without actually accessing stored visual knowledge. When asked the shape of an orange, NB responded correctly with 'round' despite claiming that she could not see it in her mind. She stated that she knew it was round because she felt it. This could suggest that knowledge about an orange's shape may also be stored factually or in a tactile store remote from stored visual knowledge.

A further possibility is that when NB attempts to imagine objects she may be visualizing 'parts' of an object and not the whole. This partial visualization appears to be supplemented by factual, non-visual knowledge. Note, for example, her comments regarding *seeing* 'the place where the sound comes out' on a television but not being able to *see* a button to switch it on and off despite knowing that it must have one. Another interpretation derived from her introspection is that her visual imagery is based on stores of knowledge that have been distorted. Thus, the shape of an apple is reported as: 'like a little stick'. These alternatives may be difficult to decide between. She may be imaging only part of objects and, for example, have imaged the stalk of an apple and treated it as the whole object.

To further our understanding of NB, we constructed tests which concerned these different proposals for the organization of knowledge. We contrasted the knowledge concerning living versus non-living objects (Warrington, 1975) with the knowledge concerning visual versus non-visual attributes of objects. Two detailed assessments were constructed. The same 130 items constituting the 'legs test' described above were used in both assessments. These 130 items can be divided into two broad categories: animate and inanimate. Each of these broad categories was comprised of items from six specific object categories. These were: animate – body parts, vegetables, fruits, insects, animals and birds; inanimate – furniture, kitchen utensils, vehicles/transport, clothes, tools and musical instruments.

Assessment 2: yes/no format

Four questions were devised for each item, two regarding visual attributes of the item and two regarding non-visual attributes that we call general/factual knowledge. For one of the two visual and one of the two general questions the correct response was 'yes', while for the remaining two questions the correct response was 'no'. All the positive questions were used as negative questions for an alternative item from the same specific category. The total number of questions was 520. Examples are recorded below:

Questions for 'gorilla'

Visual 'yes':   Is a gorilla black in colour?
Visual 'no':   Are a gorilla's legs quite thin?
General 'yes':   Is a gorilla thought to be a quite intelligent animal?
General 'no':   Is a gorilla sometimes used to carry people's belongings long distances?

The assessment was devised to identify a selective impairment of knowledge. It was important to ensure that questions were of matched difficulty level with regards to accuracy for all four sections. We confirmed the difficulty level by administering the test to 20 undergraduates. In particular we wanted to make sure that the visual questions were, if anything, easier than the non-visual questions. The results are shown in table 9.1.

Table 9.1   Normal student performance on Assessment 2 (yes/no format) (% correct)

	Animate		Inanimate	
Visual		General	Visual	General
92.7		88.3	90.3	89.1

Assessment 2 was administered to NB twice over eight sessions in four days in September 1989. Each question was presented auditorily, with NB allowed repeats of any question. Great care was taken to ensure that she did not tire. The results of both presentations are recorded in table 9.2.

The questions were answered well, but not perfectly, by undergraduates. However, it is obvious that NB performed very much worse than these undergraduates. In particular, visual questions were answered very poorly; indeed, NB was at chance level. The general questions were answered a little better. The preservation of some general knowledge is confirmed by the consistency of these responses.

The results showed no difference in the retention of knowledge for animate and inanimate objects. However, we felt uneasy that this represented the true state of affairs. While Assessment 2 ensured that groups of questions were matched by difficulty level using the criterion of accuracy, there was the possibility of ceiling effects hiding differences between conditions. The result of brain damage could be to emphasize small differences in difficulty. So, we made a more determined effort to equate the difficulty of our questions.

Table 9.2   NB's performance on both presentations of Assessment 2 (yes/no format) (% correct) in September 1989

	Animate		Inanimate	
	Visual	General	Visual	General
1st presentation	54	65	51	64
2nd presentation	54	64	53	59
1st + 2nd combined	54	64	52	62
Items consistently correct over 1st and 2nd presentations	41	59	44	57

Assessment 3: forced choice format

Assessment 3 was constructed using a forced choice format. The respondent is faced with a choice between two answers to a question. The correct answer is known as the target and the incorrect answer as the distractor. For Assessment 3, each item was used once as a target for a visual question and once as a target for a general/factual question. Each item was also used once as a distractor for a visual question and once as a distractor for a general/factual question. Distractor and target items were always taken from the same specific object category. The total number of questions was 260. Two administrations of the assessment were prepared, allowing the position (left *v.* right) of target and distractor to be reversed for the different administrations. Examples are recorded below:

Questions for 'drum'

Visual: Which, if you look down on it, has a top that is shaped like a circle – a drum or a violin?

General: Which do soliders sometimes use when they're on parade – a guitar or a drum?

Assessment 3 was administered to 20 undergraduates and postgraduates. Latencies and accuracy for each question were obtained and are recorded in table 9.3. It should be noted that the accuracy levels are artificially low for this assessment as they were obtained under time pressure. Considering accuracy data alone, the groups of questions would appear to be well matched for difficulty. But the latency data show that the general questions are in fact markedly easier than the visual questions. Furthermore, visual questions about inanimate objects are particularly difficult. These data highlight the difficulty in making comparisons between fields of knowledge and stress the wisdom of using several procedures when attempting to identify selective neuropsychological impairments.

Table 9.3   Normal student performance on Assessment 3 (forced choice format)

	Animate		Inanimate	
	Visual	General	Visual	General
Accuracy (% correct)	91.9	94.8	92.3	91.8
Mean latency (s)	1.37	1.11	1.47	1.17

In order to ensure that a true comparison of visual versus general knowledge could be made for NB, it was necessary to extract a sub-set of questions from Assessment 3 that were matched for both accuracy and latency. To produce this sub-set, all questions were first 'banded' by latency. For each band, mean reaction times, percentage correct and number of questions falling within the given band were recorded. Combining the questions within the latency bands 1.0–1.3 seconds and 1.3–1.6 seconds created a sub-set of questions well matched for both latency and accuracy (see table 9.4).

Assessment 3 was administered twice over four sessions in two days in November 1989. Each question was presented auditorily with NB allowed repeats of any question. Great care was taken to ensure that she did not tire. NB's performance on the sub-set of questions from Assessment 3 which was matched for both latency and accuracy is recorded in table 9.5. Apart from general questions concerning inanimate objects, NB performed better than chance ($P < 0.05$) on the other sections of the test. However, it is also clear that she does not answer

Table 9.4 Sub-sets of questions in Assessment 3 (forced choice format) matched by mean latency and accuracy

	Animate				Inanimate		
Visual		General		Visual		General	
Lat. (s)	Acc. (%)	Lat. (s)	Acc. (%)	Lat. (s)	Acc. (%)	Lat. (s)	Acc. (%)
1.25	94.5	1.25	94.4	1.28	96.4	1.26	95.4
$n = 52$		$n = 36$		$n = 37$		$n = 23$	

Table 9.5 NB's performance on matched accuracy and latency sub-set of questions from Assessment 3 in November 1989

	Animate		Inanimate	
	Visual	General	Visual	General
No. correct	34/52	30/36	28/37	13/23
	33/52	32/36	23/37	15/23
% correct	64	86	69	61

these sections equally well. NB obtained 86 per cent for general questions concerning animals as opposed to only 64 per cent for visual questions which is a reliable difference ($P < 0.05$).

Discussion

We are now in a position to come to some conclusions concerning NB's store of object knowledge. She retains a small amount of information concerning the visual properties of knowledge. The actual amount of retained information, however, is not large and could be an overestimate. It could reflect the extent to which visual knowledge may be doubly represented. Even blind people have, for example, a limited verbal knowledge of the colours of objects (Wyke and Holgate, 1973). To explain NB's results we must presume that there is an impairment to those structures concerned with visual knowledge. These structures may be closely linked to perceptual mechanisms (Farah, 1985) but the cause of her lost imagery cannot be put down to her loss of vision. Even though those who go blind report a loss of visual imagery, NB's impairment is almost total. Furthermore, NB shows other (non-visual) loss.

The retention of greater general knowledge is more differentiated. At first (Assessment 2), it appeared to be better retained than visual knowledge for both animate and inanimate categories but this was due to the inanimate questions being rather easy. When the questions were equated for difficulty, it was found that the retention of general knowledge was far superior for the animate category. The retention of general knowledge for the inanimate category was, in fact, no better than the retention of visual knowledge. Thus, the results of our testing show that NB has an island of preserved knowledge. It concerns not all general knowledge but only that concerned with animate objects.

NB has confirmed the usefulness of both divisions of knowledge considered in the 'Theory' section above. Our conclusions are based on the assumption that her pre-morbid knowledge reflected the population averages. Others might not agree with that assumption. It could be that NB, like many teenage girls, was not interested in the functions of tools and other inanimate objects. If this were the case then we might be underestimating her preserved general knowledge for inanimate objects. However, we prefer to believe that NB reflects our normal sample and shows us how mental representations of knowledge are divided. They divide between visual and non-visual representations of objects and also according to whether they are animate or inanimate objects.

Further Reading

McCarthy, R. A. and Warrington, E. K. (1990) *Cognitive Neuropsychology*. London: Academic Press.

References

Allport, D. A. (1985) Distributed memory, modular systems and dysphasia. In: S. K. Newman and R. Epstein (eds) *Current Perspectives in Dysphasia*. Edinburgh: Churchill Livingstone.

Collins, A. M. and Loftus, E. F. (1975) A spreading-activation theory of semantic processing. *Psychological Review*, 82, 407–28.

Davidoff, J. B. (1991) *Cognition through Colour*. Cambridge, Mass: MIT Press.

Diesfeldt, H. F. A. (1985) Verbal fluency in senile dementia: an analysis of search and knowledge. *Archives of Gerontology and Geriatrics*, 4, 231–9.

Farah, M. J. (1985) Psychophysical evidence for a shared representational medium for visual images and percepts. *Journal of Experimental Psychology: General*, 114, 93–105.

Goodglass, H., Klein, B., Carey, P. and James, K. J. (1966) Specific semantic word categories in aphasia. *Cortex*, 2, 74–89.

Nielson, J. M. (1946) *Agnosia, Apraxia, Aphasia: their Value in Cerebral Localisation*. New York: Hoeber.

Rosch, E. (1975) Cognitive representations of semantic categories. *Journal of Experimental Psychology: General*, 104, 192–233.

Shallice, T. (1988) *From Neuropsychology to Mental Structure*. Cambridge: Cambridge University Press.

Warrington, E. K. (1975) The selective impairment of semantic memory. *Quarterly Journal of Experimental Psychology*, 27, 635–57.

Warrington, E. K. and McCarthy, R. (1983) Category specific access dysphasia. *Brain*, 106, 859–78.

Warrington, E. K. and Shallice, T. (1984) Category specific semantic impairments. *Brain*, 107, 829–53.

Wyke, M. and Holgate, D. (1973) Color-naming defects in dysphasic patients. A qualitative analysis. *Neuropsychologia*, 11, 451–61.

Yamadori, A. and Albert, M. L. (1983) Word category aphasia. *Cortex*, 9, 112–25.

10

The smiling giraffe: an illustration of a visual memory disorder

M. Jane Riddoch and Glyn W. Humphreys

On our first meeting, Dennis was making his way uncertainly down a dark corridor in a rehabilitation hospital. Through windows, a small quadrangle was apparent with a number of empty benches, and a black cat was attempting to lift her offspring onto a concrete ramp. It was a rather dismal autumn day. Dennis, however, appeared uninterested in the outside world. As he walked he had his eyes firmly fixed on a yellow line running the length of the passageway and through a set of double doors marked with green plastic strips, where we stood. He stopped as we greeted him, but seemed unable immediately to establish our position. His therapist had explained to us that his vision was very restricted and that he was only able to see small parts of his environment at a time. He was not blind, however, and the therapists had been perplexed at his inability to find his way from his ward to the room for occupational therapy. It was for this reason that his route had been carefully marked with bright coloured strips in order to help him to find his way.

Dennis was 47 years old and was undergoing rehabilitation for a head injury he had sustained two years before. He was a trained electronic engineer and, at that time, was employed as an electronic tester. Since the age of 20, Dennis had suffered from epilepsy. Although on regular medication, he was still prone to occasional fits. He was at work and just climbing a ladder when one such fit occurred. He lost consciousness momentarily and fell backwards from the second step of the ladder hitting his head. Although the distance was small, the results of the fall were severe and were to have devastating consequences. He fractured the back of his skull and the blow also caused internal damage both to the front and back of his brain (specifically, to the right frontal and to both occipital lobes).[1] As a result of the damage, bleeding caused further pressure inwards onto the soft brain tissue. Two days after admission to hospital, Dennis became drowsy and then completely unconscious. An emergency operation was performed to relieve the pressure within the brain and it was considered necessary to remove Dennis's right frontal lobe.

Dennis recovered well from the surgery in that he had none of the physical effects that are common following brain injury, such as hemiparesis. However, his initial ability to see was very impaired, and he was reported as being 'cortically blind', that is, blindness due to damage to the parts of the brain which receive and interpret visual signals rather than damage to the eyes. He was eventually discharged from hospital to a rehabilitation unit where the main objective of therapy was to facilitate independence in everyday life. Over a two-year period, Dennis's sight gradually improved. Tests showed that while he had no vision in the left half of each eye (clinically, this is termed a left hemianopia), vision in the right half of each eye was present and sufficient for him to watch the television and (for instance) to be able to read the number plates of cars. Despite this, Dennis was very impaired at recognizing the people he saw on television, or even his close family that he saw in real life. His problems in visual recognition were indeed quite profound and extended beyond faces to many common objects: he was unable to identify fruits and vegetables, animals and many household objects. Further, the problem was one of *recognition* rather than naming. He was typically unable to tell us other kinds of information about the objects or faces he failed to name, and on many occasions he would misidentify an object as something that looked similar (such as naming a paintbrush as a knife). Such visual errors should not occur if he knew what the object was but was unable to recall its name. In general, he complained that many objects, and all faces, no longer seemed familiar when he looked at them.

What could account for the kind of recognition loss experienced by Dennis? The first point to note here is that the recognition loss is not general. Dennis was able to recognize people from their voices; when we played him a tape of animal noises he correctly named each animal; he was able to name objects placed on his hands, even when prevented from looking at them. The problem is one of visual recognition.

Seeing but not recognizing

Could the visual recognition loss be related to his hemianopia, which prevents him from experiencing half the visual world? Loss of vision for a part of the visual field can occur as a result of interruption in the pathways of the nerves travelling from the retina of the eyes to the occipital lobes, the primary recipients of visual signals in the brain. In Dennis's case, the likely cause of the field loss is a lesion of his right occipital lobe. However, as we shall show, it is improbable that any simple loss of visual field could produce problems of the sort experienced by Dennis.

A standard way of testing whether a patient can see objects that they may fail to recognize is to ask them to copy what they see in front of them. When asked to do this, Dennis produced quite passable copies, even when he could not identify the object concerned. For instance, figure 10.1 shows an example of Dennis's copy of a picture of a giraffe; however, when shown the original picture he was only able to identify the giraffe as being 'some kind of animal', and he had no idea which particular animal it was. In some instances, Dennis was unable to identify even the general category that an object belonged to. For instance, although Dennis was able to copy a picture of a penguin (also shown in figure 10.1) without error, he said that the object was an animal, noting that it was standing upright, had long hair and a small tail. Apparently, Dennis was able to see the animals, but he was unable to recognize them.

However, it can be argued (and with some justification) that copying is not a good test of vision. It may be possible for patients to copy even if they do not see an object normally. For instance, a reasonable copy may be produced if a patient sees only part of an object at a time, providing they are able to scan around the object appropriately. In contrast, patients may try to identify the object from just the parts they see within a glance, so producing visual misrecognitions. Indeed, it may be difficult for patients to ignore their 'first guess' even when they scan the complete object when copying. Thus, once Dennis misidentified the penguin as an animal from its body and tail, he may have 'fit' the rest of the object into that description as he scanned around it. Certainly he did not suddenly realize the object was a penguin once he had copied it.

In fact, we do not think this kind of 'first guess' explanation is correct for Dennis, but we point it out to show something of the complexities of visual recognition problems, and to indicate why further tests are really required to assess the nature of the impairment in a given patient. To understand the kinds of test that are needed, we must consider the

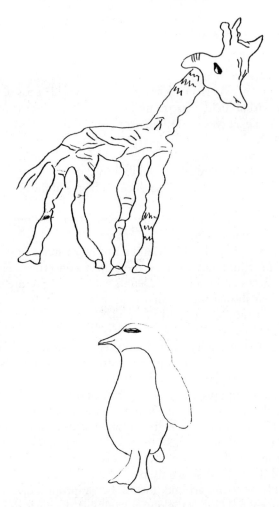

Figure 10.1   Dennis's copies of a giraffe and a penguin.

processes likely to underlie our astonishing ability to recognize many thousands of objects from vision. It is to such considerations that we now turn.

The complexity of visual recognition

Visual recognition seems easy. Within a tenth of a second we can recognize all manner of objects, even when they are shown quite out of context. We can recognize objects seen from very many different viewing positions, and when the objects impinge on different parts of our retinas. However, imagine trying to build a machine that is able to do this: that is able to transform light as it falls on a two-dimensional surface (such as our retinas) into coherent descriptions of three-dimensional, moving objects, that can be uniquely matched with memories of all objects that the machine knows about. This is not so easy. Indeed, despite the sophisticated nature of current digital computing systems, and despite their superhuman abilities in some spheres,[2] computer vision systems have not yet approached the visual expertise of an 18-month-old child. Visual recognition is in fact highly complex; it is the astonishing efficiency of visual recognition in most humans that hides the complexity of the processes involved.

Although computer vision systems have still to prove successful, it is nevertheless the case that attempts to develop artificial systems have furthered our knowledge of how visual recognition proceeds. In particular, it has been useful to consider some basic design points and basic processes that need to be incorporated into any visual system, artificial or natural, in order for it to recognize objects as efficiently as humans. We will briefly outline three proposals, one concerning a design point and two concerning specific processes that characterize visual recognition.

Modularity

One of the pioneers in the field of computer vision, David Marr (1982), pointed out that, in designing any complex system, it is useful to put together a number of small components, each of which can be removed or altered without drastically affecting the rest of the system. This is the design principle of modularity. Consider applying this principle to vision. The visual world is composed of objects varying along many dimensions in terms of their shape, colour, size, depth, movement etc. Not all of these dimensions vary with one another. When an object moves its colour does not change. Its shape may change (e.g. consider a person walking, where the relative positions of the limbs change over time), but only in certain proportions which are determined by the nature of the object. Its depth and size, however, will change according to the direction of movement. It follows that it would be sensible to design a visual system in which depth, movement and size were anlysed together, so that correlations between the three kinds of information can be derived. However, colour and shape should be analysed separately, so that variations in movement are not mixed up with constant shape or colour information.

Interestingly, it turns out that there is neurophysiological evidence that, in the brain, the processing of movement and depth is separated from that of shape and colour (see Livingstone, 1988). It is for this reason that, after brain damage, people can have selective problems with colour but not movement perception, or with movement but not shape perception etc. It is because of the modularity of vision that we can witness selective disturbances in visual recognition in patients such as Dennis.

The existence of different visual descriptions

Visual recognition involves going from the nerve impulses created when light falls on our eyes to our memories of objects. In attempting to design computer vision systems, it becomes obvious that such nerve impulses should not be matched directly with object memories. The nerve impulses change according to many incidental attributes in the image: for instance, according to the light reflected onto an object. It would be impossible to recognize the object using a description of such impulses since the description would be constantly changing, even though the object stays the same. Visual recognition must be based on descriptions that are somewhat abstracted from the image itself. There is not space here to go through the various candidate descriptions that might be constructed *en route* to visual recognition, our point is only to note that different visual descriptions are probably created, and that recognition problems might result if patients have difficulty constructing certain descriptions. One description that seems important is that which allows us to recognize that an object remains the same when seen from different views; if patients are impaired at constructing such a description, they will fail to see that stimuli in different views are equivalent.

The need for different memory representations

A final point here concerns the kind of memories that allow us to recognize objects. We have many kinds of stored knowledge about objects. Take a bee. We might know that it has two wings, a sting in its tail, that it lives in a highly organized community with other bees, that there are many workers but only one queen, that they have yellow and black stripes etc. However, only some kinds of knowledge can be matched with information that can be derived from an image, and so only some kinds of information may be used directly in visual recognition. For instance, colour and shape may be important, but knowledge about the social organization of bee hives is likely not to play a direct role in recognizing a single bee seen in isolation. Given the principle of modularity, it is even possible that these different types of knowledge, lets call them visual and functional knowledge, are represented in different 'modules'. This would allow certain efficiencies. For example, one kind of knowledge can be updated without necessarily leading to amendments to the other.[3] Using Dennis as an example, we will indeed argue that, in the brain, visual and functional knowledge are represented independently of one another.

Dennis's vision revisited

Let us return now to consider Dennis's vision. We argued above that different visual descriptions may be constructed *en route* to visual recognition, and that one kind of description allows us to judge that objects remain the same when seen from different viewpoints. Tests of vision that are more analytic than simple copying can assess whether patients are able to construct particular visual descriptions. For instance, if it can be shown that a patient can judge whether objects are the same across different viewpoints, it may be assumed that relatively 'high level' visual descriptions of objects can be derived, and that the patient's recognition impairment is not due simply to poor vision.

Dennis performed extremely well on tests requiring him to match photographs of objects taken from different views. He could judge that the objects shown in figure 10.2 were the same, even though their images are very different. Thus he seemed able to derive relatively abstract visual descriptions. However, he remained unable to recognize the objects involved. Dennis also performed well on other tests of vision. For instance, he could pick out pictures of different objects when they were overlayed, a task which is difficult if patients cannot separate 'figure' from 'ground'. These findings suggested that poor vision was not the reason for Dennis's recognition problem.

Memory for objects

Whilst Dennis has a constricted visual field, it seems he does not have a problem seeing objects within his unimpaired visual field, and he can perform many difficult visual discrimination tasks. Such good performance would be unlikely were his vision so restricted that he could only

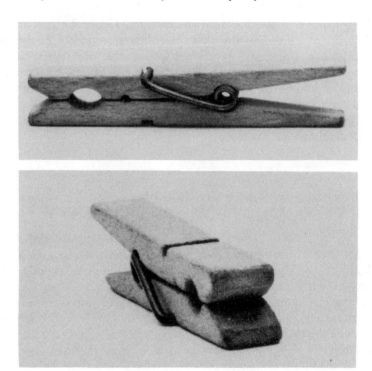

Figure 10.2   Examples of photographs used in the unusual views test. The patient has to decide whether the two photographs could be of the same object.

scan parts of objects at a time, guessing what the objects were from seeing a few of their parts. Why then is his visual recognition so poor?

Visual recognition involves more than seeing objects; there are many objects that we have never encountered and which we would not recognize, but nevertheless we may see them perfectly well. Visual recognition involves matching incoming visual signals with stored knowledge about objects. When a match occurs, the object is recognized.[4] Might Dennis be so poor at visual recognition because his memory for objects is in some way impaired?

Memory for objects can be tested in a variety of ways. Perhaps the simplest is to ask people to draw objects from memory. Whilst drawing from memory can be difficult for many people, they will still include the correct features of objects: they give elephants tusks and a trunk, even if the precise shape is not correct. However, Dennis was unable to do this. Figure 10.3 shows his attempt to draw a giraffe from memory. Compare it with figure 10.1 (his copy of a line drawing). The two bear no

Figure 10.3 Dennis's drawings of a giraffe and an owl from memory.

relationship to each other. Note though that it was not the case that Dennis had forgotten what he was supposed to be doing when drawing the giraffe from memory. As he was drawing, Dennis remarked that 'giraffes have long legs' and that the 'giraffe was kneeling at a waterhole for a drink'.

Most of Dennis's drawings from memory were not so bizzare as the giraffe, but nevertheless, he quite commonly placed the wrong attributes on objects. Figure 10.3 also shows his drawing from memory of an owl, where he has given the owl teeth and shoes. Interestingly, Dennis's difficulties in drawing from memory appeared to be confined to certain categories of object: he had especial difficulties with many living objects such as fruits, vegetables and animals. With other categories no real impairment was apparent. For instance, compare Dennis's drawing of a bed and a screw in figure 10.4 with that of the giraffe and the owl in figure 10.3.

Is this problem in drawing certain objects due simply to the use of a difficult task, namely drawing? Though this seems unlikely, we further assessed Dennis's knowledge of objects by simply asking him to tell us about them. Here again Dennis had difficulty with particular classes of object. For example, when asked to define a giraffe, Dennis's reply was: 'A giraffe spends most of its time jumping, It has strong back legs and small front legs. It chews the cud. It's of medium size but I can't think what it looks like. It's light brown in colour.' When asked about a carrot he said: 'I don't know if it's a fruit or a vegetable. It's curved, red in

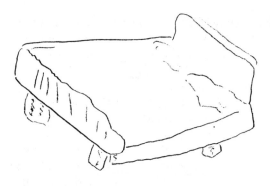

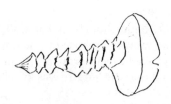

Figure 10.4   Dennis's drawings of a bed and a screw from memory.

colour and quite sweet. I would say that it is more ball shaped than cylinder shaped.'

Clearly, Dennis's problems arise in a variety of tasks. Moreover, the items that he was poor at drawing from memory tended to be the same ones that he had difficulty in defining, and they also tended to be the same items that he failed to recognize. That is, Dennis was consistently able to recognize certain items, and he consistently failed with others. This consistency suggests that Dennis's knowledge about some items was impaired, and that this was the reason behind his poor drawings, his poor definitions and his poor visual recognition. Due to his impaired knowledge, Dennis was never able to recognize certain items, nor to define them or to draw them for memory.

On the difference between visual and functional memory

But what kinds of knowledge might be impaired? Above, we pointed out that we have different kinds of knowledge about objects. It turned out that, in Dennis's case, only some kinds of knowledge were impaired. Instead of asking Dennis to provide us with definitions of objects, we gave him some, but we constrained the definitions so that they contained only certain kinds of information. In one set they stressed the visual appearance of objects. For example, the 'visual definition' of a bee was: 'a small black and yellow striped flying insect'. A second set of definitions stressed functional knowledge about the objects. The 'functional definition' of a bee was: 'an insect that lives in hives and makes honey'. Dennis did poorly on the 'visual definitions', failing to produce the correct name on over half the trials; in contrast, he named nearly all the objects from 'functional definitions'. We again noted that, when visual definitions were generated for different classes of object, Dennis tended to find those for living things hardest. Also, the objects he failed to name from their definitions were the ones he tended not to recognize visually.

Dennis was good at answering definitions stressing functional knowledge, but poor at answering those stressing visual knowledge. This supports our earlier suggestion that visual and functional knowledge are separated in the brain. Dennis had impaired visual but not functional knowledge. Further, the fact that he had consistent problems with certain objects across all the tasks indicates that the same visual knowledge that we use to recognize objects is also used when we answer visual definitions, when we have to define the appearance of objects, and when we have to draw them from memory. Visual thinking and perceiving seem closely related!

Knowledge for certain categories or visual similarity?

In all of the tests that tapped Dennis's visual knowledge about objects, and for which he was impaired, he tended to perform worst with living things. In fact, his visual recognition of living things was dramatically poor: he was able to identify only a dog and a horse of all the many animals we tested him with, and he could not recognize common animals such as a cat. Though it is undoubtedly true that people differ in their knowledge of different kinds of object, Dennis's degree of impairment with living things was such that it cannot be attributed simply to his previous unfamiliarity with them. His recognition was selectively impaired for living things.

This can be taken to indicate at least one of two things. One possibility is that our knowledge of the world is divided along categorical lines: knowledge of living things being separate from knowledge of inanimate objects, for example. Another is that Dennis found living things particularly difficult because within their categories many living things are visually similar: many animals resemble one another, as do many insects, birds and so forth. Dennis may have difficulty recognizing objects from categories where many of the exemplars are visually similar. We looked at this in various ways. In one simple test, Dennis was asked to point to a named picture placed amongst pictures of other objects. The surrounding 'distractor' objects were always from the same category as the 'target', but in one case they were visually similar and in another they were visually dissimilar. An example would be pointing to a picture of a cabbage surrounded by pictures of a cauliflower, a lettuce and an onion (visually similar), versus pointing to the same picture surrounded by pictures of a carrot, celery and a parsnip (visually dissimilar).[5] Dennis was better able to point to objects in the visually dissimilar condition than in the visually similar condition, even within the 'living' categories for which he was generally impaired. This suggests that, at least for Dennis, it is visual similarity within a category that is crucially important for his visual recognition, rather than whether an object is a living or a non-living thing.

Remediation

Dennis's case illustrates the important point that our ability to recognize objects depends on our stored visual knowledge, which finely differentiates between objects within particular classes. Indeed, if we consider our ability to recognize faces, which as a class are visually very similar, then it becomes clear that our stored visual knowledge for some object classes must be finely differentiated indeed. One of the effects of perceptual expertise may be to develop more and more finely grained visual knowledge, allowing (for example) bird watchers to differentiate between hundreds of different birds. Viewed in this way, most people can be said to be experts in face recognition, though only a few may go on to develop similar abilities for other classes of object. In cases such as Dennis's, we see the breakdown in this finely tuned ability due to the disturbance of stored visual knowledge.

We attempted to help Dennis re-learn to recognize some of the objects he found difficult. In one attempt, we gave him sets of drawings of animals, each with the name of the animal listed at the bottom. Dennis was asked to try to learn the name that went with each animal. He found this very hard to do, though he was able to learn other types of information (e.g. in tests requiring him to associate two names together), so it was not the case that he had a general learning problem. However, over a period of four weeks he was able to learn the names that went with the pictures of six animals. We then gave him the same pictures, along with different pictures of the same animals and pictures of different animals. In this larger set Dennis named only four of the six original pictures correctly, and he failed to name any of the different pictures of the same animals. Thus his re-learning of the pictures was both fragile to interference when placed in a larger set, and it failed to generalize from the particular pictures he had learned to different pictures of the same objects. Perhaps Dennis's poor learning of the pictures reflects the difficulty of trying to re-establish impaired visual memories via visual stimuli. If the stimuli incorrectly remind Dennis of other objects, then re-learning in this way may involve trying to over-rule these inappropriate associations. This may be a particularly difficult task.

We next tried to bypass this problem by building on one of Dennis's strengths – his good functional knowledge about objects. We gave him written definitions that he had to learn to associate to a name. The definitions contained both functional and visual information. For instance, the definition of a bee was: 'a small black and yellow striped flying insect that lives in hives'. He was easily able to learn the definitions for 12 living things. We then tested him with definitions for the same objects that contained only visual information. He named eight of the 12 objects correctly. We then left him to learn just the visual definitions. In a week he was perfect at naming all the visual definitions. Our hope in having Dennis learn such definitions was that it would perhaps help to re-develop his visual memories for objects, using his relatively preserved memory skills. Of course, for this to be useful, the naming ability ought also to generalize to the case where he has visually to recognize the objects. Thus we next tested Dennis's naming of pictures of objects, including the 12 items he had learned visual definitions for and a further 26 that he had not. Dennis named one of the 12 'treated' items, and three out of the 26 'untreated' ones. Unfortunately, having Dennis learn visual definitions did not generalize to improving his picture naming.

These attempts to remediate Dennis's visual recognition problem did not prove successful. There are several possible reasons for this lack of success. One is that Dennis learned the definitions in a purely verbal way, and he did not visualize the objects involved, even when 'visual' definitions were used. Thus there was a lack of transfer to his visual memory. Interestingly, it was not the case that Dennis was unable to visualize. Dennis was able to decide if complex objects could be rotated around to match one another, a task that is usually thought to require active visualization and a form of 'mental rotation'. Perhaps if we had used an active visualization strategy, the learning-via-definitions approach may have been more successful.

A second possible reason for our lack of success is that Dennis had multiple handicaps. Remember that, following his fall, he had had his right frontal lobe removed. Damage to the frontal lobes of the brain can often lead to people having difficulty planning and adopting the most appropriate strategy to carry out tasks. Left to his own devices, Dennis would do little each day, and he found it difficult to initiate behaviour voluntarily. Thus it seems unlikely that Dennis rehearsed the objects we asked him to learn, or that he ever attempted to visualize them spontaneously. These ancillary problems may well have played an important part in the lack of remedial success.

Reading and writing

One further aspect of Dennis's problems is that, after his fall, his reading and writing skills were impaired. Disorders of reading and writing are discussed in detail elsewhere in the book, and we will not attempt to analyse Dennis's problems in great detail here. However, it is interesting to note that his reading and writing were affected in similar ways. In both cases, he tended to use a 'phonological' rather than a 'visual' strategy; in clinical terms, Dennis would be described as having 'surface dyslexia' and 'surface dysgraphia'. For example, whilst he could read most words that follow the spelling-to-sound rules of English (such as 'read'), he would mispronounce words that are irregular in their spelling-sound correspondences (e.g. he would name 'bread' as 'breed', saying that it was to do with having babies). The same also held true for his spelling. It is possible to speculate that these problems in processing the visual aspects of language related in some way to his impaired visual memory of objects. For instance, loss of the visual memory for words might render irregular words particularly problematic. Without a visual memory for words, we might rely on pronunciation by rule, which could be applied to unknown letter strings (e.g. as when we pronounce a non-word such as 'phocks'). However, this would lead to errors with irregular words, which would become regularized. This is exactly what we observed with Dennis. Whether this account of a general visual memory loss is correct or whether it is simply the case that Dennis has multiple but separate deficits, one affecting visual recognition, one affecting reading and one affecting writing, is a question awaiting future research.

Life at home

Following his stay at the rehabilitation hospital, Dennis returned home, where he has lived for the past four years. On two days a week he visits a community centre, but otherwise he is largely confined to his house where he is looked after by his wife. His visual recognition remains very impaired, and he is still unable to recognize his wife or family by sight. Despite his multiple handicaps, he remains a cheerful person, and one of his main daily activities is to keep a diary. His spoken language skills are largely intact, and so his diary capitalizes upon those preserved skills, although the visual expression of his thoughts, as shown in his writing, is quite impaired. We close with an afterword, in Dennis's own words, which helps illustrate both his intact verbal thoughts, and his views on his remaining impairments:

> 'Sometimes I am inclined to write down my present views on my life and its implecations wich are very diferent to those I had a short line ago. If they had been expressed to me then I would have received them with interest and disbeliefe. So perhaps my sanity is a thing of the past or I have at last gained my sences, which ever. I now loke upon life in a very different

manner and I hope the moste recent is the better. brain damage in the past recieved my sumpathed but little else. I am afraid that like many authors I didn't understand much abort it until I received first hand experience. For me it has left my eyes crossed, my right hand with a twitch and my memory of more recent times not very reliable. Unfortunately for me, besides my work, me pastimes, fotograph, riting, reading and drowing all require either gode eyes, good hands or bothe'.

Acknowledgement

Our work with Dennis was supported by a grant from the Medical Research Council of Great Britain.

Notes

1   Damage to both the frontal and occipital lobes can occur with a closed head injury, since (in Dennis's case) the fall can cause the brain to rock back and forth in the skull, injuring both the front and back of the brain. This is known as a 'contra coup' injury. The areas of damage within the brain itself can be determined by computerized tomography (CT scan). X-rays are passed through the brain at a number of different levels, and an X-ray film is produced at each level. This procedure helps to pinpoint the area of damage with quite a high degree of precision.
2   For example, computers can carry out complex calculations in a time span far superior to humans.
3   For instance, in learning to discriminate between different types of bee, the visual knowledge representation may be updated, but functional knowledge may remain unchanged.
4   We do not wish to assert that stored knowledge might not play a part in constructing some visual descriptions; we merely highlight that recognition, by definition, involves contacting stored knowledge.
5   The pictures were all black and white line drawings, so that colour could not be used as a cue.

Further Reading

Ellis, A. W., Young, A. W. (1988) *Human Cognitive Neuropsychology*. London and Hove: Lawrence Erlbaum Associates.
Denes, G., Semenza, C., Bisiacchi, P. (1988) *Perspectives on Cognitive Neuropsychology*. London and Hove: Lawrence Erlbaum Associates.

Eysenck, M. and Keane, M. T. (1990) *Cognitive Psychology: A student's handbook*. London and Hove: Lawrence Erlbaum Associates.

Humphreys, G. W. and Riddoch, M. J. (1987) *To see but not to see: A case study of visual agnosia*. London and Hove: Lawrence Erlbaum Associates.

Humphreys, G. W. and Riddoch, M. J. (1987) *Visual object processing: A Cognitive Neuropsychological approach*. London and Hove: Lawrence Erlbaum Associates.

Shallice, T. (1988) *From Neuropsychology to Mental Structure*. Oxford University Press.

McCarthy, R. A. and Warrington, E. K. (1990) *Cognitive Neurospychology: A Clinical Introduction*. San Diego: Academic Press.

References

Livingstone, M. S. (1988) Art, illusion and the visual system. *Scientific American* (January), 68–75.

Marr, D. (1982) *Vision*. San Francisco: W. H. Freeman.

11

Drawing without meaning?: dissociations in the graphic performance of an agnosic artist

Sue Franklin, Peter van Sommers and David Howard

Drawing ability in normal subjects varies widely. For example, van Sommers (1989) asked undergraduate students to draw a bicylce from memory as accurately as they could. Half the drawings were very bad, and this was attributable as much to a lack of graphic competence as lack of knowledge of bicycles. It is therefore of considerable interest when a person is found who, through brain damage, shows anomalies in graphic performance against a background of known competence. Such is the case with MH who is the subject of this paper.

In broad terms one can identify two categories of input to graphic production processes (figure 11.1 summarizes some of the possible stages employed in various drawing tasks). On the one hand, a drawing may be 'from life'; that is, the task involves direct use of visual input of objects, drawings or photographs (on the left of figure 11.1). On the other, the input can be a spoken word, where the drawer has to 'reconstruct' their drawing from sources not immediately available to the eye. A stroke patient, AB (Grossi et al., 1986) was able to copy accurately, but was unable to draw to verbal instruction. It seems that he was unable to access the appropriate meaning or visual representation from memory,

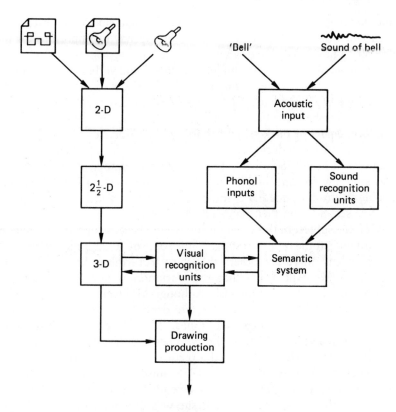

Figure 11.1 A model of graphic processing (van Sommers, 1989).

although his 'eye-to-hand' abilities were not compromised. He seems to have had problems with components on the right of the model in figure 11.1.

How is a good representational drawing achieved? For an artist the graphic production processes will presumably reflect detailed visual representations, but also detailed schema for *planning* graphic productions. To what extent does the successful use of these schema require adequate prior recognition of the item to be drawn? JR, the patient of Wapner et al. (1978), was a skilled amateur artist who became visually agnosic (see Riddoch and Humphreys, chapter 10) following a stroke. Although he was able to make a good attempt at copying pictures he was unable to identify, Wapner et al. demonstrated that his copies were much more poorly executed than they were before his stroke, because they could compare pre- and post-stroke drawings of the same items from life. This patient's impairment suggests that even simple copying and life drawing may make use of components on the right side of figure 11.1. So even when the object being drawn is there, it may be important for the drawer to have recognized what the object is.

When we draw a cup, a cylinder or a cross from verbal instructions we necessarily depend on visual memories, both of how something looks and of how we might draw it (a drawing schema). There is also an important distinction to be made between longer-term visual representations of, for instance, chairs or buckets, and short-term memory for forms presented and then concealed during testing (a procedure also called copying from memory). LB (van Sommers, 1989), a highly competent draughtsman, was still able to copy simple line drawings following a stroke, but was unable to produce adequate line drawings if the model was just shown for five seconds and then removed from view.

MH, the subject of this paper, is interesting because of the anomalies in her drawing at the time of testing. While some of her graphic productions are excellent, there are others that vary from the rudimentary to the abnormal. We will argue that this variation is not unsystematic. It depends on the nature of the task. Although MH was clearly impaired at utilizing visual memories when asked to draw things from a verbal label or in completing drawings, she appeared to be able to utilize visual memories in a very sophisticated way in her high-level drawing from life. In other words, when she copied a picture she did not, like the agnosic artist described by Wapner et al. (1978) misconstrue the significance of the lines and shading that she was reproducing; her drawing from life looked as though she 'knew what she was drawing'. But did she, like Wapner et al.'s patient, have an impairment in *understanding* visually presented material?

Medical history

MH was referred to the neurologist in February 1985 when she was 77 years old. The onset of her cognitive problems was unknown, but she appeared to begin deteriorating around the time of the death of her husband in 1983. A CT scan showed cerebral atrophy, particularly around the left sylvian fissure, and the neurologist diagnosed arteriosclerotic dementia, but suggested that MH may also have had a small stroke. She was also seen by the clinical psychologist who found on testing that her overall level of cognitive functioning was low average/dull normal.

Semantic processing ability

We also assessed MH during the first six months of 1985. During this period there was no obvious further deterioration in her cognitive functioning, although this was to happen subsequently. HM was referred because of her speech difficulties. Investigations centred on her semantic ability and on word finding. Did she understand the meaning of words and pictures?

Word finding

MH's spontaneous speech indicated that she was having word-finding difficulties. She was asked to describe her job as a commercial artist:

> Er, we er, it was er, sometimes painting but more or less doing work – of, of things that had often been sent to me. And they wanted to alter it all or something of that sort. And that's what I did and um as the business grew a bit, long, bigger I got other people to do the things. Actually my husband er he was the one who called on people and got the work and so we went on. Until a time when he had a what is it? A thing that goes round your neck, prevents you from speaking. I can't remember the name of it but that's what it was so we had to give up and er so we changed where we lived, we came up to, where we are now actually. But um he looked after the house and the so forth and I carried on with what I'd done before and so in in that sort of way we went on.
> [*Can you tell me some more actually about the job?*]
> The job? Well I used to quite quite enjoy it. Er because it was . . . was such a quite a good amount of various things that you wanted not tied to too much small stuff . . . and so altogether it was quite interesting. I liked doing people's faces and heads so occasionally I get those to do.

It can be seen from this example that MH on some occasions failed to find the word she wished to use (e.g. her husband had a 'laryngectomy') and on other occasions she used rather general nouns. In order to test her naming she was given the first 20 items of the Boston Picture Naming Test (Goodglass et al., 1983). She was able to name four correctly (bed, house, scissors, bench) and gave no response for 13 of the pictures. Her other three responses were:

tree	→	I just want to say flowers
pencil	→	pen
toothbrush	→	brush

On a subsequent occasion she was asked to produce the written names for these pictures when she was able to name two correctly (bed, house), produced one mis-spelling (bench → bensh), and produced no response to the other 17 items. HM is severely anomic (see Kay, chapter 8). Is this because she knows what word she wants but cannot find it or because of a deeper impairment in which the actual meanings (of words, scenes and pictures) might be compromised: a *semantic* impairment?

Comprehension

In order to establish whether MH had a general semantic impairment, we gave her a number of tests which required her to comprehend words and/or pictures. The British Picture Vocabulary Scale (Dunn et al., 1982) requires the subject to point to a heard word from a choice of four pictures. The words used range from 'car' to 'saltation' and the test is standardized on subjects up to 18 years. MH scored 72/109, which is equivalent to the average 8-year-old performance; she is clearly impaired. Since this test requires MH to understand both the word and the picture, it is important to establish whether her poor performance is due to a specific problem either with words or with pictures, or whether it is truly a general deficit affecting understanding of both words and pictures. So it is important to look at tests which require understanding of pictures or words alone.

To assess picture comprehension, we used the Palm Trees and Pyramids Test (Howard and Patterson, unpublished). This is a test of visual semantic ability where the patient sees, for example, a picture of a pyramid and has to decide which goes with it from a choice of a picture of a palm tree or a pine tree. MH scored 34/52 on this test. Since 50 per cent correct represents chance level, this represents extremely impaired performance. A synonym judgements test (Coltheart, 1980) was used to assess word comprehension. In this test MH had to decide whether two words that she heard had the same meaning or not (e.g. marriage/wedding or marriage/lamp). All the words used could be easily imaged and again chance was 50 per cent. She scored 25/38 which is extremely poor performance. So MH has impairments in word comprehension, picture comprehension and picture naming, which is consistent with her having a central semantic impairment. A summary of test results is given in table 11.1.

The patient described by Wapner et al. (1978) was also unable to derive the meanings of pictures and, although able to copy pictures, was able to do so much less well than before his stroke. So how did MH's semantic problems affect her drawing?

Table 11.1   MH's performance on tests of semantic processing

Boston Picture Naming Test	4/20
British Picture Vocabulary Scale (spoken word/picture matching)	72/109
Pyramids and Palm Trees Test (3-picture version)	26/52
Synonym judgements test (spoken word version)	25/38

Graphic performance

Two sources of evidence indicate MH's high-level drawing ability. The first is circumstantial; she was a commercial artist for her entire working life, running a successful partnership with her husband. The other evidence is direct and comes from graphic productions at the time of testing. MH's drawings from life, and her copies (figures 11.2–4) were rated by two art teachers as characteristic of the top 10–15 per cent of the adult population. MH's graphic performance will be described in five sections: copying; drawing from life; drawing to dictation; drawing and copying from immediate memory; and drawing completion.

Copying

The first tasks required MH either to copy or to draw from life, which will use the procedures shown on the left of figure 11.1. When drawing from life the drawer must solve depiction problems (such as where to draw a line to represent a contour boundary) not demanded when copying a two-dimensional representation. For the first copying task, MH was shown a set of freehand drawings of common objects and asked to copy them. The models and her copies are shown in figure 11.2. The copies are not sophisticated renditions of objects as objects, but they are remarkably faithful to the original drawings (which were poorly executed by one of us, SF!). The copy of the key drawing, for example, reproduces very accurately the succession of serrations. There are, however, several oddities within the set. The asymmetry of the comb is exaggerated. A control study with nine normal subjects (who readily identified the original drawings despite their poor quality) suggests that

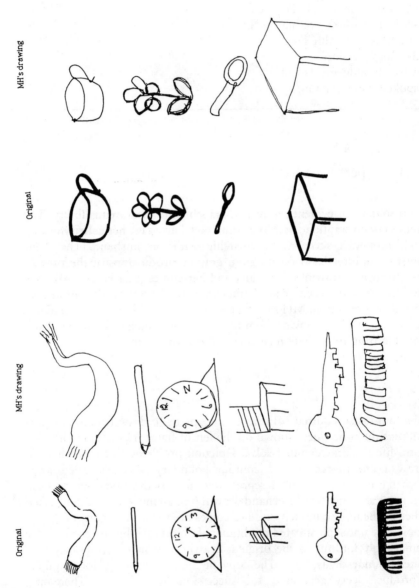

Figure 11.2 MH's copying of (poorly executed) line drawings.

this asymmetry is not normal and points to a mechanical 'geometric' reproduction of the model rather than one driven by recognition of what it represents. The right-hand end in MH's drawing of the key tapers in a way that neither conforms to the original sketch nor represents a typical key. The most obvious aberration in form is found in the copy of the flower drawing. This drawing really does suggest that MH is copying lines without reference to what they portray. The round petal on the left of the original is copied as a circle quite detached from the centre of the flower. It looks as if MH cannot draw on memories of what the original drawings represent when she makes these copies.

The second copying task was to produce in pencil a portrait in oils by Botticelli (figure 11.3). The copy was produced over several weekly sessions of a class taken by an art therapist at the day hospital which MH was attending. The art therapist did not intervene in the drawing process, and all other drawing productions shown in this paper were collected during this same period of weeks. The picture shown in figure 11.4 is, by any standards, an excellent reproduction, and shows virtually no mistakes or misinterpretations. There are, however, several small variations from the model, including the following alterations: the modelling of the lower lip and the right side of the upper lip, the highlight on the left pupil, the changed curvature of the neck, the light above the nostril, and the looseness of the treatment of the hair. All these changes are representationally well-motivated, indicating that unlike the copies of the key, flower, etc. she is acutely responsive to these detailed three- to two-dimensional pictorial conventions.

The disparity in performance between MH's copy of the bad line drawings and the Botticelli is remarkable. Our test of word and picture comprehension demonstrated that MH has impaired semantic ability. The poor quality of the drawings in the copying task may have made them difficult for MH to recognize. So perhaps she succeeds at copying the Botticelli because it is a 'good' likeness, giving access to the sort of semantic detail needed to make a good copyist's rendition. But first we should consider something else; perhaps MH has a single, spared skill. It could be that she has a particularly well-developed ability for drawing faces, because this was important in her job. Is she able to draw things other than faces well?

Drawing from life

Figure 11.5 gives four examples of MH's drawings of real objects: a comb, a fork, an orange and a case. While it could be argued that there are slight flaws in the drawing of the handle and the locks on the case,

Figure 11.3 Botticelli, *Portrait of an unknown man with a medal,* c.1475, Uffizi Gallery, Florence (Photograph: Scala, Florence).

Figure 11.4 MH's copy of Botticelli portrait.

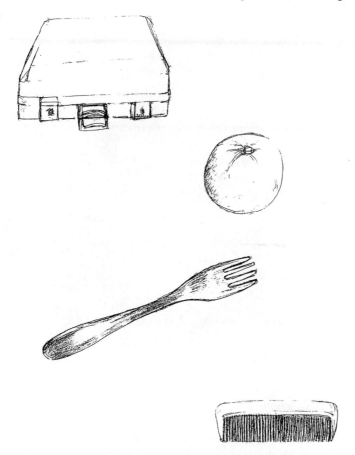

Figure 11.5 Drawing real objects.

there is little doubt that these drawings represent very competent draughting: shape, proportion, perspective and shading are all good. MH's 'good' drawing is not confined to faces.

Figure 11.6 is an unfinished portrait of one of the medical staff at the hospital. Like the copied portrait shown earlier, it was produced in several short sessions. The interruptions to the process are significant, since there is no evidence that MH lost track of the representational significant of her own drawing in the way Wapner et al.'s (1978) agnosic artist did when, halfway through drawing a telephone, he could not see where to put the handset. In contrast MH could 'read' her own drawing in a way she failed to do when copying the sketches of a key, flower, etc.

Figure 11.6   Portrait from life.

Drawing to dictation

We have seen that MH's life drawing skills are very good when she has a richly detailed, meaningful model, but poor for simple, naive drawings. MH has impaired comprehension of scenes and words – can she draw to dictation? It seems probable that subjects drawing from verbal labels or definitions (the right-hand pathways in figure 11.1) must utilize intact or partial visual memory traces of the objects, or memories of representations of them (we may draw a virus or a unicorn without having seen either in the flesh). These visual representations must be accessible from spoken input on the one hand, and on the other must be read out to the graphic production processes.

MH was asked to draw named objects (e.g. 'draw a key'). Her drawings (shown in figure 11.7) were shown unlabelled to a group of 33 judges. Table 11.2 shows how many were able to name each drawing correctly. Because MH's ability to comprehend spoken words is semantically impaired, it is fair to ascribe some of her drawing errors to such a miscomprehension. This certainly applies to the key, pipe and box of matches. In each case she has drawn the wrong object. The *quality* of

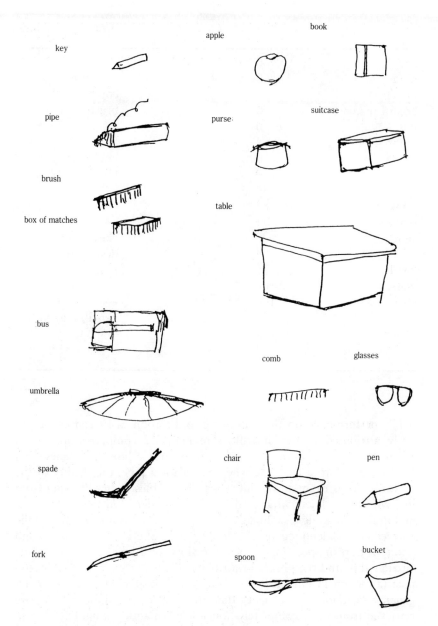

Figure 11.7 Drawing to dictation.

Table 11.2   Naming of MH's drawings by 33 judges

Target	% Correct naming	Alternative names
key	0	—
pipe	0	cigarette, cigar
brush	4	comb
box of matches	0	brush
bus	0	—
umbrella	2	fan
spade	0	hockey stick
fork	0	knife
apple	84	—
book	82	—
purse	1	—
suitcase	0	chest, box
table	4	desk, box
comb	76	—
glasses	100	—
chair	100	—
pen	0	pencil, crayon
spoon	67	—
bucket	94	—

MH's performance on these drawing-to-dictation tasks cannot be entirely attributed to her difficulties in language comprehension. Even when she draws a brush when asked to portray a box of matches, or a pen changed into a cigarette when asked for a pipe, the quality of the performance is dramatically inferior to her copies or her drawing from life. MH either knew what to draw, or misunderstood the instructions and drew something else. In either case she knew *at some level* what the correct or misidentified objects looked like. She knew the shape and juxtaposition of spectacle frames; the slope of a bucket's sides and its circular top; and the profile of a ribbed umbrella canopy. It is conceivable (although in our view exceedingly implausible in the light of her *general* semantic impairment) that the features of these objects are retrieved from some completely non-visual semantic listing, but even so there must be some quasi-visual catalogue, however degraded, that provides the basis for delineating these features and relating their parts within a drawing. MG (Basso et al., 1980), who had a quite comprehensive failure of his phenomenological imagery system, could none the less tack together crude representations of a clock, house, daisy, man and even a recognizable pheasant (Bisiach, personal communication). Wapner et al.'s agnosic artist, JR, had some idea of what to put on the page as he enumerated the functional parts of a telephone: 'It needs a base . . . a place to speak with, something to hear with . . . ' (1978, p. 354). To put it another way, you cannot work out the shape of a spoon simply by inspecting the functional properties of the word, yet in all three cases, MG, JR and MH, the patients' degraded drawings had some visually appropriate aspects.

This realization brings us to the crux of this case: that MH appears to draw on sophisticated memories to add a highlight to an eye or a contour to a lip when copying a painting. When drawing simple objects from memory in the graphic dictation task, she also draws on memories, but the yield is minimal and crudely realized. To this dissociation we have to add another: that when she draws a real comb on the table before her, her attentional analysis and graphic depiction are excellent. When reproducing a poor but recognizable *drawing* of a comb on the table before her she seems to have failed to connect it to her object recognition system.

Drawing and copying from immediate memory

Even when copying drawings she appears not to have recognized, MH is able to produce a fairly accurate, literal copy. Is this true under all circumstances? For example, is she able to produce a good copy of a drawing even when the drawing is no longer in front of her?

MH was given two tasks involving immediate memory for visual material (a task sometimes described as delayed copying). The first involved simple rectilinear forms from the Boston Stick Test (Goodglass and Kaplan, 1972), the second simple sketches of objects like a car, ruler, eye, etc. Figure 11.8 shows the Boston Stick Test geometric forms and MH's attempts to draw them after they had been exposed for approximately two seconds. The pictures were then turned over and MH was required to draw them immediately. MH could reproduce all these designs with 100 per cent accuracy while they remained visible. Under delayed copying conditions she correctly reproduced only two of the 14 designs, both of them letters of the alphabet. In figure 11.8 the designs have been re-ordered according to the type of error made. The majority of errors (nine of 12) consisted of incomplete or incorrectly completed drawings with all the omissions or incorrect elements on the right or at the bottom of the design. This outcome can safely be ascribed to a

192

Incomplete

Correct

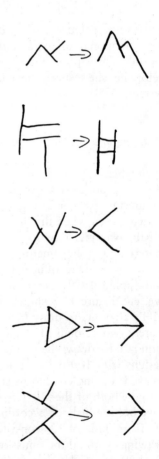

Anomalous

Figure 11.8 Delayed copying: Boston Stick Test.

decaying visual representation or some progressive interference process, since the almost universal pattern or production of such figures (irrespective of handedness) is from left to right and top to bottom (e.g. van Sommers, 1984). The error in copying the arrow symbol is plausibly due to it being recognized as an arrow and being drawn partially from memory, and the drawing beneath it to a perseveration.

Figure 11.9 shows several simple sketches and MH's delayed copies, collected under the same conditions as the abstract designs. These items have also been re-ordered for expository purposes. The first group of errors correspond to the completion errors found with abstract designs. Left-right and top-down sequencing combine with a loss of memory for the form. Like the 'arrow' in the previous test, some items appear to have been reproduced through a recognition and reconstruction process. The drawing-to-dictation task indicated that she had access to certain primitive icons or visual memories that provide a version of a foot, car, sun and chair. The provenance of the six drawings labelled 'anomalous' does tend to strain the analytic imagination, but two are worth comment in connection with MH's deficit: the comb and ruler. First, it is clear that once again MH fails to retain the designs as abstract arrays of lines long enough to get them down on paper. Further, she has failed to identify the objects being portrayed, for had she done so she would hardly represent a comb with semicircular excrescecnes and a ruler with a scalloped edge. It seems possible that in both cases the incomplete geometric features that she *did* retain provided the basis for a sort of graphic confabulation.

It is quite clear that her drawing from memory is rather different from her copies of drawings which remain in full view throughout. They are, in many cases, not even accurate renderings of the visual form with which she was presented. The main conclusions about MH we bring away from this section are (a) confirmation that she has some picture agnosia, (b) confirmation of her ability to use picture recognition, when it occurs, to tap into a crude picture or object memory, and (c) a severe loss of short-term memory for form which allows her to reproduce only the early strokes in a copying sequence. It is not clear whether the limitation is temporal or organized by feature.

Drawing completion

We have suggested that one explanation for MH's good drawing of pictures and real objects is that the model provides rich detail which may aid recognition. In order to maximize the possibility of semantic recognition in another way we gave MH a picture completion task where she was given both auditory and written cues as to the identity of the picture. MH was given a succession of 12 cards each bearing an uncompleted

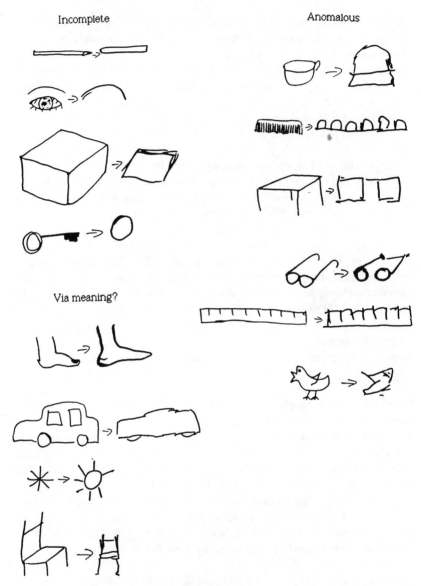

Figure 11.9   Delayed copying: line drawings.

drawing. In each case she was given a short verbal description, which was also given in written form, to maximize the possibility of correct picture identification. For example, a drawing of a cup with the handle and one side missing was accompanied by the instruction 'You drink from a cup. Draw the cup' and a written label 'cup'.

Figure 11.10 shows the stimuli and the stimuli with MH's additions. On six of the 12 drawings (left of figure 11.10) MH appears to have identified the drawing and completed it (although in three cases she could just have been producing a mirror-image, as she does with the igloo). In two cases, the igloo and the star, the completion suggests that MH has failed to identify the drawing and has improvised a solution. The remaining drawings are interesting because in two at least, the broom and the fish, MH has evidently recognized the object, identified the missing part and begun to correct it. These corrections are incomplete, however, and in this regard resemble the failures on the delayed copying tasks in the previous section. What this outcome suggests is that in order to carry out this task successfully, a subject must (a) identify the picture, (b) recognize the nature of the omission, (c) compile a series of strokes that will remedy the omission, these being based on some, albeit primitive, long-term visual representation of the object and (d) store and retain the items in that sequence long enough to complete the drawing. MH's failure to do this both re-affirms her recognition deficit (even in the presence of multiple semantic cues) and the crude nature of the long-term visual stores she draws on in these situations.

General discussion

MH's most remarkable inconsistency in drawing is between the way she can utilize longer-term visual representations while copying detailed pictures and drawing from life, while being unable to use such representations in drawing from memory. A summary of her performance in the drawing tasks is given in table 11.3. Not only can she continue to identify the features of a drawing (as in the portrait of a doctor in figure 11.6) as she progressively completed it, but she was able to add subtle features to her copy of the Botticelli painting (figure 11.4). Unlike Wapner et al.'s patient, MH's drawing under these circumstances indicates no obvious impairment of graphic skill. These and other drawings displayed a considerable graphic virtuosity that was absent from her drawings of common objects and in the drawings from dictation (figure 11.7). In this case she necessarily depended on long-term visual representations in order to traverse the pathway from verbal input to graphic output, but unlike the drawing from life she did not have a rich visual stimulus to maximize the access to long-term representations.

MH's picture recognition impairment meant that when she was presented with drawings of common objects (key, flower, etc.) she reproduced them with reasonable competence, but betrayed an inno-

196

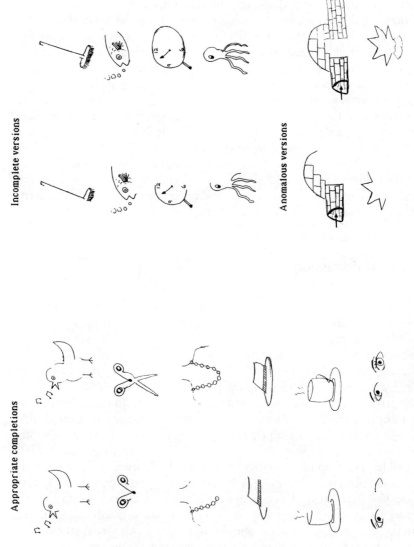

Figure 11.10 Drawing completion.

Table 11.3 Summary of MH's drawing performance

Task	Complex stimulus	Vis. stim. present throughout?	'Good' drawing?
SF's drawings	No	Yes	No
Dictation	No	No	No
Memory	No	No	No
Botticelli	Yes	Yes	Yes
Life	Yes	Yes	Yes

cence of their representational significance. Her actual drawing competence seems to depend on the quality of the recognition; not only are the copies of line drawings and the drawings to dictation often incomplete or inappropriate; they are also executed with little evidence of her considerable motor skill for drawing. Like many of the other patients reported in the literature who have drawing impairments, MH is unable to hold a visual representation in temporary store when the model is removed.

We may close this description with the following general observation: MH performs well when she is presented with a very rich visual display either in a painting or real objects. It is worth noting in this context that during the time of testing MH was still undertaking commissions to do commercial artwork. Yet when she is presented with a minimal visual display such as a simple sketch or an incomplete drawing or with the name of an object without external visual input she is unable to mobilize her evidently still intact and highly sophisticated visual and iconic memories in the service of drawing.

References

Basso, A., Bisiach, E. and Luzzatti, C. (1980) Loss of mental imagery: a case study. *Neuropsychologia*, 18, 435–42.

Coltheart, M. (1980) 'Analysing acquired disorders of reading'. Unpublished manuscript, Birkbeck College, London.

Dunn, L. M., Dunn, L. M., Whetton, C. and Pantilie, D. (1982) *British Picture Vocabulary Scale*. Windsor: NFER-Nelson.

Goodglass, H. and Kaplan, E. (1972) *The Boston Stick Test*. Philadelphia, PA: Lea and Febiger.

Goodglass, H., Kaplan, E. and Weintraub, S. (1983) *The Revised Boston Naming Test*. Philadelphia, PA: Lea and Febiger.

Grossi, D., Orsini, A. and Modafferi, A. (1986) Visuoimaginal constructional apraxia. *Brain and Cognition*, 5, 255–67.

van Sommers, P. (1984) *Drawing and Cognition*. New York: Cambridge University Press.

van Sommers, P. (1989) A system for drawing and drawing-related neuropsychology. *Cognitive Neuropsychology*, 6, 117–64.

Wapner, W., Judd, T. and Gardner, J. (1978) Visual agnosia in an artist. *Cortex*, 14, 343–64.

12

Developmental memory impairment: faces and patterns

Christine M. Temple

Children with developmental dyslexia have selective difficulty in learning to read despite normal intelligence. It could be something unusual about reading itself, which makes it particularly problematic, but it is also possible that these reading difficulties are only one of a range of different types of selective learning problems. Our attention may be particularly attracted to reading difficulties because of their obvious educational implications. Can fluent and articulate people who read well, and pass exams easily, nevertheless have other cognitive weaknesses? The answer to this question is important in understanding the extent to which different systems in the brain are dependent upon each other as the child develops. Is it possible for one system in the brain to function poorly whilst the rest functions well? If different systems are independent this provides information about the brain's underlying organization.

The traditional view is that there can be 'plasticity' in brain development, which means that if a system is not working well the developing brain may have the capacity to reorganize and compensate for the problem. According to this view, selective problems in cognitive skills should not occur in otherwise normal and healthy children and adults. The common existence of developmental dyslexia (see Snowling and Goulandris, chapter 6) suggests that plasticity and compensation fail to correct for potential reading difficulty. Are there comparable non-verbal disorders which show similar resistance to compensation?

Dr S came to our attention because of the life-long difficulty she reported in recognizing people's faces. When I first met her this, of course, was not obvious, as I did not expect her to recognize me. Instead, two other characteristics were instantly apparent. First, she became completely lost trying to find me. Given the complexity of the unversity buildings, this in itself might have been unsurprising but, as we moved between offices and laboratories, it became apparent that she was quite unable to find her way around. Even relatively simple routes appeared to be a mystery, and at the end of the day when I left her by the station I had to ensure that she had actually noted the entrance or she would walk the wrong way down the street, away from the station itself. Secondly, I was struck by the speed and quantity of her speech. She remains the most fluent talker I have ever encountered. So rapid is her speech output, that at times it becomes a challenge to decipher the individual words. The continuous flow of speech, as Dr S herself knows, is tiring for the listener and, because of her capacity to inflict headaches, she carries aspirin with her to hand out in cases of need!

On my second encounter with Dr S, and as I continued to see her, the face recognition problem became obvious. She failed to recognize me as I went to meet her, looking blankly through me until I said her name. She would also report that as she knew I had blonde hair, she had moved expectantly towards several other people before I arrived, thinking them to be me.

Face recognition impairment is documented in the neurological literature; it was given the name *prosopagnosia* by Bodamer in 1947. Prosopagnosia is one of a range of recognition disorders for visually presented material termed visual agnosias. However, in the case of Dr S the difficulty does not result from any neurological injury but has been present since birth.

An intelligent and perceptive lady, Dr S has clear insight about the nature of her difficulties as her own description illustrates:

> There are two problems. I meet somebody who I totally feel I have never seen before, like I told you happened with you, after one or two encounters with you. I had absolutely no idea what you look like and yet know that you are a lovely person, and have the embarrassment of the feeling that I have never seen you before. Also sometimes, I know I have met this person but I do not know where.
>
> I do this game with people to whom I try to explain . . . I say 'Close your eyes', and then I ask them can you see (visualize) my face, and 99 per cent of them say they can. When I close my eyes, I see virtually nothing. In your case, I know that you have blonde hair because I have fixed that verbally. But if asked what do you wear, I haven't got the faintest idea . . . I know that you have lovely blonde hair but the rest I wouldn't have known at all.

Dr S is also aware of her rapid speech:

> I may be overfluent... I talk too much. I overexplain, and all this I'm conscious of. I find it difficult to get out of... Most people complain about me. The most striking thing is she talks to much and too fast.

Dr S was happy to be our guinea-pig and we decided particularly to investigate her face recognition problems but also to explore her intelligence, her verbal fluency and her memory. Before discussing the way in which the studies developed, I shall give a little of Dr S's personal history.

Biographical history

Dr S is now in her sixties and lives in London. She was born in Germany, into a prosperous Jewish family, and lived there and in Austria as a child, coming to the UK at the age of fifteen. In the UK she qualified as a doctor of medicine, in 1945, from the London School of Medicine for Women, at the Royal Free Hospital. Further qualifications included training as a pathologist; a diploma in tropical medicine and hygiene; a diploma in family planning; and a BA in psychology. The latter was taken in evening classes at Birkbeck College, London. For many years, Dr S worked as a family planning specialist in Mauritius. She has also travelled widely.

Dr S speaks fluent German, English, French and some Danish. She reports that she was very good at Latin at school. She has had difficulty in mastering both Russian and Greek, possibly relating to problems in mastering the Cyrillic alphabet. She is highly motivated to learn Hebrew but continues to have difficulty with the script.

Dr S has been married twice. Her first husband was a university professor. Her second husband was a medical doctor. She has four children, three boys and a girl, all of whom have university degrees. None of the children is left-handed. All of the boys are colour blind. Dr S has a first cousin who also has difficulty in recognizing faces.

Dr S is in good health. She has had no major illnesses, has never had an accident with loss of consciousness and has had no seizures. In addition to the difficulties discussed here, Dr S complains of clumsiness; difficulty with figures; excessive anxiety about using machines and appliances; and that she is tone deaf.

Intelligence and verbal fluency

Dr S was obviously intelligent because of the formal qualifications she had attained, and her sharp, alert and thoughtful mind was also apparent in conversation. To assess her intelligence more formally, we used the Weschler Adult Intelligence Scale, in its revised format, and the scores she attained are given in table 12.1. The Weschler contains a range of verbal sub-tests and also non-verbal sub-tests involving puzzles, designs and pictures, which are called performance tests. We were interested in whether Dr S would have much better verbal than non-verbal intelligence. However, the scores revealed that her non-verbal abilities were just as good as her verbal abilities. Thus, any difficulty in face recognition can be attributed neither to a general intellectual problem, nor to a general problem in dealing with pictorial or visual material. Dr S had an exceptionally high IQ. Her scores would be attained by fewer than 1 in a 1000 women in their sixties.

Another feature which struck us about her performance was the exceptionally high score which she attained on the vocabulary sub-test.

Table 12.1   Scores on the intelligence test

Verbal sub-tests		Performance sub-tests	
Information	14	Picture completion	12
Digit span	12	Picture arrangement	13
Vocabulary	19	Block design	10
Arithmetic	13	Object assembly	13
Similarities	16	Digit symbol	17

10 is an average sub-test score. Possible scores are 1–19. The standard deviation is 3, which means that about two-thirds of people score between 7 and 13 on sub-tests.

Verbal IQ	136	Performance IQ	147
Full-scale IQ	147		

100 is an average IQ. Two-thirds of people have an IQ between 85 and 115. Only one in a thousand has an IQ as high as 147.

In fact, her ability to give definitions of words was perfect for all those which we gave to her. This was particularly impressive given that English was not Dr S's first language. However, it was consistent with our informal observations of her extensive speech production.

Another way in which verbal production skills can be measured is to look at the ease with which words in the vocabulary can be found. A standard clinical measure is a fluency task. The subject is asked to generate as many words as possible in one-minute time slots for particular categories. Here we used animals, household objects, words beginning with 'f' and words beginning with 's'. We compared Dr S's performance with that of six other healthy women in their sixties, who acted as normal 'controls'. Results were consistent on all the categories. Dr S generated significantly more items than the other women. For example, the other women generated on average 14 animals in a minute; Dr S generated 35 on one occasion and 42 on another. The animals that she and a typical control subject named are given in table 12.2.

From these investigations, we conclude that Dr S is of exceptionally high intellectual ability and that her vocabulary and verbal fluency are also exceptionally highly developed. If abnormality is defined in terms of distance from the average, then Dr S's fluency is abnormal in its extreme quality. Later, we will examine the difficulty which this extremely highly developed skill creates for Dr S in everyday life. It is not simply impairments which create problems. However, first we will discuss the way in which we explored her face recognition problems.

Table 12.2 Animals generated in the fluency tasks

Subject	Named animals
Typical control	cat dog horse goat sheep elephant leopard lion monkey parrot donkey snake mouse
Dr S	monkey bear walrus whale dog cat hen mouse rat lion tiger leopard wolf hyena eagle owl swan duck goose chicken elephant buffalo cow ox sheep lamb horse donkey sparrow ram dove heron pelican ostrich polar bear

Normal models of visual perception and face recognition

Cognitive neuropsychologists have discussed the recognition disorders, both visual agnosias and prosopagnosias, in relation to information-processing models of object and face recognition. Such models incorporate elements of Marr's theory of visual perception. According to Marr (1976, 1980, 1982), there are at least three levels of description involved in the recognition of objects. The first level is the primal sketch in which texture, gradations of light and discontinuities are coded. The second level is called the '2½-D level'. This incorporates descriptions of the structures of objects but these are said to be *viewer-centred*, in that they are entirely dependent upon the angle of sight of the observer. Thus, if you are looking at a chair from one angle and you get up and move and look at it from a different angle the 2½-D representation changes completely. At the third level in Marr's model, there is a 3-D representation which is said to be *object-centred*, in that it is independent of the view of the observer. At the 3-D level there must be stored descriptions of the variable appearances of objects. The 3-D level is essential for object constancy and in order for us to deal effectively with unusual or partially obscured views of objects.

A functional model for face processing, against which subjects can be interpreted has been proposed by Bruce and Young (1986) (see figure 12.1). This model does not make explicit the distinction between initial representations, viewer-centred representations and object-centred representations. Instead, it describes a general process of *structural encoding*, which includes these processes and which can gain access to *face recognition units*. Each face recognition unit corresponds to a particular person's face and these units are established in the course of our daily life and encounters. In a way analogous to the biologist's discussion of the 'firing' of a nerve cell, face recognition units are said to have thresholds of activation. When a face is seen, there will be an increase in activity in all the units representing faces which resemble it but only the unit which corresponds to the viewed face will be fully activated. This unit will reach threshold and will 'fire'.

Following the structural encoding of a face's appearance, several types of information are extracted simultaneously. Expression is analysed, providing information about the mood and affect of the speaker or his/her message. Facial speech analysis monitors the mouth and tongue movements involved in producing speech. Lip-readers exploit this system which also reduces ambiguity in normal processes of speech comprehen-

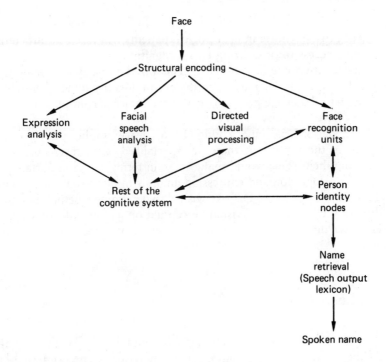

Figure 12.1   Model for face processing (adapted from Bruce and Young, 1986, and reproduced with permission).

sion. Directed visual processing is used, for example, to see the similarities and differences between the faces of unfamiliar people. These inputs all feed into a semantically structured cognitive system. When a face recognition unit fires, it will trigger a corresponding *person identity node* which contains information which specifically identifies an individual, for example, their occupation and their personal characteristics.

In order to retrieve a person's name, it is necessary to first activate a person identity node. Thus, it is an explicit prediction of this model that one should never be able to name a person from their appearance unless one also knows something about the person (i.e. their profession or partner). But one can know something about the person without being able to name him/her.

Face recognition disorders may arise from impairments at several different levels within the face recognition system, and a number of these have been described in patients following neurological injury. In Bodamer's original paper (1947), one patient had a deficit in structural encoding. He appeared to have difficulty perceiving faces and even considered that a dog's face was an unusually hairy human being. Most forms of prosopagnosia in neurological patients will result in difficulties in gaining access to or utilizing face recognition units.

Patients with amnesia, who have generalized memory loss, may have lost or be unable to gain access to the person identity nodes themselves. Patients with language problems may have intact person identity nodes but may have difficulty in generating names.

The model of Bruce and Young (1986) clearly implies that faces are 'special' in the sense that there are specialized brain mechanisms for processing them. This would make sense in terms of the importance of both face recognition and expression analysis in our social interaction.

In our investigation of Dr S we wished to determine whether there was a difficulty with her basic visual perceptual or spatial skills or whether there was a difficulty with a particular component of the face recognition system.

Visual perception

To assess Dr S's basic perceptual skills and her capacity to make judgements about simple components of the visual scene, we tested her ability to make judgements about the orientations of lines. We modified the Benton et al. (1978) line orientation task. Subjects are presented with an array of 31 lines displayed on the lower part of a booklet. On the upper part are two lines of different orientations and varying lengths. The subject must select from the response array, the two lines whose angles match those of the stimulus pair (see figure 12.2).

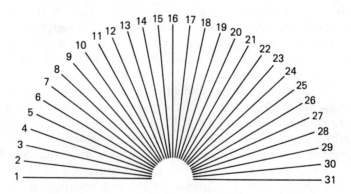

Figure 12.2   Line orientation test.

The performance of Dr S was compared with that of 12 other healthy women in their sixties, who acted as controls. Unless mentioned otherwise, these women acted as controls for all the tests. This line orientation task is not easy, as figure 12.2 may indicate. The control subjects averaged ten correct. Dr S got 12 correct. Thus her performance was normal. She also performed normally on a tactile version of this task. Thus there is no unusual difficulty in making basic perceptual judgements about orientations of lines.

As mentioned above, Marr's model emphasizes the importance of being able to integrate different viewpoints and recognize things from different angles. We tested Dr S's ability mentally to rotate an abstract shape and recognize it in a different angle. The Mental Rotation task used was a shortened version of a task (Vandenburg and Kuse, 1978) requiring the internalized spatial rotation of 3-D structures depicted by 2-D drawings. The drawings appear to represent 3-D structures composed of multiple cubes (see figure 12.3). The subjects are told that they may mentally rotate the structure in any direction and they must then select, two identical structures from an array of four. The score out of 20, represents the number of correct selections.

Once again Dr S's performance was compared with the controls. They averaged nine correct and Dr S averaged 14 correct. Thus Dr S can perform this complex spatial manipulation. She can recognize shapes from different angles. In these tests and others we gave we could find no problem with basic perceptual processes and no reason for difficulty in Marr's terms in establishing either viewer-centred or object-centred representations.

Face processing

In order to recognize that a face is a face it is necessary to integrate its features. Sometimes this must be done in conditions of poor lighting or

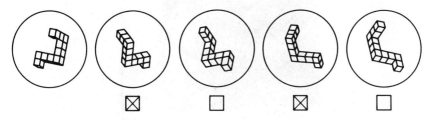

Figure 12.3   Mental rotation.

when the face is partially obscured. Dr S says that she does realize that a face is a face but could she have difficulty with the 'gestalt' processes involved in integrating features? To assess this we tested her with Mooney faces. The Mooney faces (Lansdell, 1968) present patterns of light and shadow in black and white, depicting faces for which sex and appropriate age are judged. The subject is told that all the pictures are faces but she will only be able to assess the face correctly if she can integrate the blocks of black and white (see figure 12.4). Dr S was able to make these judgements as easily as the control subjects. Thus she has intact gestalt integrative skills and she is also able to make correct judgements of age and sex about faces.

We had established that Dr S could match an unfamiliar structure in different rotations but we wanted to see if she could do the same things with faces. We also wanted to see if she could match identical pictures of faces. To test these skills we used Benton's Facial Recognition task (Benton et al., 1983). This involves matching a target face with an identical face in the same or a differing orientation. The faces are black and white and are photographed partially in shadow. Both in comparison to the controls and in comparison to the published test norms Dr S performed normally on these tasks. Although she has difficulty in

Figure 12.4   Mooney face.

recognizing faces in real life, she is able to match unfamiliar faces seen at different angles. The results of the Mooney faces and the Benton task indicate that Dr S's structural encoding of faces and directed visual processing (see figure 12.1) have developed normally. Difficulties in face recognition have a basis elsewhere in the face-processing system.

We decided to investigate Dr S's ability initially to register face recognition units by teaching her some new faces. For this we used the Warrington Recognition Memory Battery (Warrington, 1984). The test is in two matched sections. In the first section, the subject is shown a pack of 50 words. Each word is exposed for three seconds and the subject is required to make a judgement of whether or not the associations of the word are pleasant. This encourages some degree of encoding of meaning or semantics. Immediately after the stimulus cards have all been exposed, the subject is required to make a forced choice judgement between pairs of words, one of which has appeared in the stimulus pack and one of which is novel. The faces section is identical except that the stimulus cards consist of unfamiliar faces of men. The forced choice responses are made to pairs of faces, one of which has been shown in the stimulus pack.

Unsurprisingly, on the word section, Dr S had a perfect score. On the faces section, she was correct on 43/50 items which was slightly better than the controls. Thus Dr S is able to set new face recognition units and gain access to these in a choice situation a few minutes later. Her problems must therefore either lie in a failure of these units to become permanently established in memory or in difficulty in using the units to gain access to person identity information and names.

By this stage we were beginning to wonder what Dr S would be unable to do with faces. She seemed to be able to do all our face tasks yet she still failed to recognize us. We wanted to get another measure of these recognition problems so we tested her on her recognition of famous faces. This would indicate her ability to gain access to person identity information (see figure 12.1) and names.

We showed her two sets of pictures of famous people. There were 45 pictures in total, though a few people appeared on both pictures sets. Dr S was able to identify only 14 pictures (31 per cent). She was significantly poorer than the six healthy women in their sixties with whom we compared her. It appears that she has difficulty in accessing person identity information from faces. One uninteresting interpretation of these results would be that, although these people seem famous, Dr S simply does not know them. We were particularly concerned about this possibility since she had spent time overseas and some of the figures were British. In order to see whether she knew the people and whether there was a genuine difficulty in identifying people from their faces, we gave her the names of 37 of the people who had appeared in the picture sets.

For each name, we asked who they were and what was their occupation to determine whether Dr S had person identity information for these people which was accessible from their spoken name. Dr S could give identifying information for 27 of the 37 people (73 per cent). Thus there were many people whom she knew but whom she had been unable to identify from their faces.

However, we then wondered whether giving somebody's occupation was a less specific task than naming them. You could, after all, identify someone as a politician without knowing exactly who they are. We therefore decided to do a more balanced experiment, with another set of faces. Here we took 40 faces and asked Dr S to give us the occupation of each person from their face. Then, much later, we took the 40 names of these people and spoke them aloud, again asking her to give us their occupations. Dr S could give the occupations for 12 of the faces but 28 of the names. Thus she can gain access to person identity information more easily from spoken names than faces. Many faces failed to elicit the person identity information which we know Dr S possesses.

In terms of the model in figure 12.1, it would appear that there is intact structural encoding and that the initial registration of face recognition units is normal, but we have found that there is a significant impairment in accessing person identity information from faces in order to recognize the face. Either the face recognition units have failed to consolidate and despite their initial registration they are lost over time or there is difficulty in using the units to activate the person identity information.

Recognizing other pictures

As mentioned above, there is a theoretical debate about whether faces are 'special' and have special brain mechanisms devoted to them or whether they are very complex visual stimuli when it comes to identifying individuals. We believed that despite Dr S's difficulty in recognizing faces she did not have generalized recognition difficulties for other visually presented stimuli but we wanted to test this more formally. We therefore gave her the Boston naming test which is a standardized test of object recognition. It consists of a graded set of line drawings of objects: the earlier items are common, e.g. toothbrush, whistle, octopus; the later items are more unusual, e.g. palette, trellis, sphinx. Dr S performed normally on this task.

As another test of object recognition, in comparison to face recognition, we gave her a test constructed by Edward De Haan. It consists of three sets of photographs: familiar (famous) and unfamiliar (novel) faces;

familiar (real) and unfamiliar (novel) objects; and familiar and unfamiliar names of people. The novel objects are actually real but rare objects like specialist hardware tools, unfamiliar to any one except an expert. In each group the subject must indicate whether the items are familiar or not. Thus this test permits a direct comparison of recognition skills for faces, objects and names. There are 16 familiar and 16 unfamiliar items in each set. Results are given in table 12.3. Only with the familiar faces was performance abnormal. Yet on all other sections, performance was good. Dr S can discriminate between familiar and unfamiliar objects. She can also correctly categorize the names of the famous people whose faces she cannot recognize. The deficit is thus specific to faces of people. This supports the view that there are brain mechanisms which are specific to face recognition.

Table 12.3   Scores on familiarity decision

	%
Familiar faces	44
Unfamiliar faces	100
Familiar objects	100
Unfamiliar objects	88
Familiar names	82
Unfamiliar names	94

Visual memory

We had established that the face recognition problems did not generalize to problems in recognizing objects. However, in view of Dr S's difficulty with topographical orientation we decided to explore whether she had other visual memory problems.

We therefore gave her the Weschler Memory Battery which contains a range of different types of memory tasks, including both verbal and visual memory. Her overall score gave a memory quotient of 132, which is in line with her IQ. This result indicated that there was no generalized memory impairment. We did not have control data on the sub-tests from the controls used above, but we had control data from another study we had been doing, which came from 15–16-year-olds. The performance of Dr S is compared to the teenagers in table 12.4. Her logical memory,

Table 12.4   Scores on the Weschler memory battery

	Dr S	Controls (mean ± s.d.)
Personal and current information	6	5.7 ± 0.48
Orientation	5	5.0 ± 0.0
Mental control	7	6.5 ± 2.55
Logical memory (story recall)		
Immediate recall	13.5	9.5 ± 3.08
		[age-matched controls 8.4 ± 2.7]
Delayed recall	10	8.15 ± 2.64
Digits forward and back	10	9.6 ± 1.96
Associate learning (of pairs of words)		
Immediate recall	20	16.9 ± 2.95
Delayed recall	9	9.5 ± 1.08
Visual memory (for designs)[1]		
Immediate recall	4	10.5 ± 1.9
Delayed recall	3	9.9 ± 1.9
Copy of designs	13	12.5 ± 1.27
Overall Memory Quotient	132	

[1] Significant impairment.

which involves the recall of stories, is somewhat better than the teenagers, as is her ability to learn new associations between words in the paired associates sub-test. On other tasks her performance is at approximately the control level except for the visual memory items. On both immediate and delayed recall of simple designs she is significantly impaired. This difficulty in drawing the designs from memory cannot be attributed to any difficulty with the motor control of drawing as her copying is at a normal level.

This impairment in visual memory for designs was confirmed using another, more complex, figure, known as the Figure of Rey. Here, Dr S's recall of the figure was at a 4-year-old level. Thus visual memory is poor.

Memory for faces and patterns

When Dr S had seen something many, many times she may learn to recognize it. She is able to recognize her family and familiar friends and she recognizes the faces of Margaret Thatcher and Princess Anne. She is also able to recognize everyday objects. However, she seems to be unable to register, and gain access to after a few minutes, memories for complex visual information which is novel. Just as she fails to recognize me, she fails to recall designs, and fails to recognize the house in which she lives, which is identified only by number, despite familiarity with the building for several years. In relation to our model of face recognition (see figure 12.1), she cannot gain access to person identity information from faces.

Living with these problems

Dr S has had a career with professional success, has four healthy children and many friends. Nevertheless, her life has often been difficult and her pattern of cognitive strengths and weaknesses have contributed to her problems. In excerpts from our conversations with her she gives these examples from her life.

On faces
There was a very striking example in America [Dr S had just returned from a lengthy visit] of a lady who took me home, when I was trying to find my way home, and I had noticed her in the synagogue every Saturday. I met her in an unexpected place. If I had met her in the synagogue I would have made a probably word-based recognition . . . but by meeting her in the unexpected place I have the feeling dimly that I have seen her a few years ago when I was in the same town and I asked her 'Excuse me, have we met?' which is what I tend to do. I then fish from the conversation. And she couldn't believe it, because the week before she had shown me the way and we had had an intense conversation several times in the synagogue. And I was absolutely totally unable to know who she is. The moment she said 'But we walked home together' I remembered the conversation, I remembered how many children she had, I remembered details which sometimes surprise people, based on verbal memory . . . I have a kind of photographic memory for conversations . . . but as to the visual I was sure that I had perhaps seen her when I was there a year ago and was absolutely unaware that I had seen her every Saturday . . . She thought I was peculiar..

. . . In Cambridge now, I kept on getting lost, and . . . its very embarrassing because I kept on getting lots of lifts and I met lots of people. I had very intense conversations and I didn't recognize them, even though they had been helpful by giving me lifts . . . I look, but the only person I recognize is a lady with a big wart on her nose, that is very striking. It is very embarrassing because they say, you know the fellow with the glasses or whatever they say, I have no idea if they have got glasses. It just doesn't register. People don't like not to be remembered. So I always say, 'You beautiful ladies, I don't recognize you, excuse me, have we met before?'

I warn people now. If we have a wonderful exchange and are going to be friends for life. I say, look if we meet again outside . . . and I wouldn't recognize you, just give me the code word. The code word is something we talked about and then I would recall what we talked of.

People complain, I don't greet them. So I warn them beforehand. It is very embarrassing. I live in this active community . . . and I ask now after four years in the community, 'Who is this?' Now people, cannot understand it. I ask friends of mine who do not know that I have this problem, 'Who is this?' They are amazed. 'Of cource, she is so and so.'

On houses

My own house, I can't recall what it looks like. If I had to draw it, I'm not even sure if it's three storeys. I'm on top so it must be three storeys.
[CMT: You can't conjure up a picture in your own mind of what your own house looks like?]

No, no. I only know its got three storeys because I am in the attic.
[CMT: How long have you known this house?]

Four and a half years, I've been there. First, I lived in the house next door. I rather think it looks similar. It may not be similar.

On talking

I have extremely low self-confidence. I feel very concerned about mutual thoughtfulness. And I feel very upset that I make a lot of effort hoping, wishing, trying, to talk less and even tell people 'give me feedback'. The amazing thing is that people I do talk a lot to don't complain. But the vast majority of people who know me, do complain that I talk too much. They mostly say I am quite interesting but I talk too much. I give more than they want. I overexplain, and all this I'm conscious of. I find it difficult to get out of . . . Most people complain about me. 'The most striking thing is she talks too much and too fast'. I am deeply hurt, not offended because of this valid comment, but I am hurt that I do this to people because I have such a love for people and I want to be mutually constructive and mutually helpful. I don't give others enough chance to get their word in edgeways and I say please interrupt me. I go on too much. I am now talking to you like a psychologist, a psychotherapist, but it is a problem . . . The Jews are a fast-speaking people but I am in the front line of the Jews, I think.

Dr S is eager that problems such as hers should be investigated further and that people should have greater awareness of these types of developmental difficulty. Lack of awareness, in her view, increases the difficulty which people have in tolerating her behaviour. To this end, she has requested from us a written document explaining her problems which she can show to those who become exasperated with her. To her, both this and a copy of this chapter have been of benefit.

Acknowledgements

This research was supported by a research award from the Wolfson Foundation. On sections of data, research assistance was given by Kim Cornish, Joanne Ilsley and Metke Shawe-Taylor.

Further Reading

Bruce, V. (1988) *Recognising Faces*. London: Lawrence Erlbaum.
Stiles-Davis, J., Kritchevsky and Bellugi, U. (ed.) (1988) *Spatial Cognition: Brain Bases and Development*. London: Erlbaum.
Temple, C. M. (1992) Developmental pathologies and developmental disorders. In I. Rapin and S. J. Segalowitz (eds) *Handbook of Neuropsychology: Child Psychology*. Amsterdam: Elsevier.

References

Benton, A. L., Hamsher, K. des, Varney, N. R. and Spreen, O. (1983) *Facial Recognition*. New York: Oxford University Press.
Benton, A. L., Varney, N. R. and Hamsher, K. des (1978) Visuospatial judgement: a clinical test. *Archives of Neurology*, 35, 364–7.
Bodamer, J. (1947) Die Prosopagnosie. *Archiv für Psychiatrie und Nervenkrankheiten*, 179, 6–53.
Bruce, V. and Young, A. (1986) Understanding face recognition. *British Journal of Psychology*, 77, 305–27.
Ellis, A. W. and Young, A. W. (1988) *Human Cognitive Neuropsychology*. Hove, East Sussex: Lawrence Erlbaum.
Lansdell, H. (1968) Effect and extent of temporal lobe ablation on two lateralised deficits. *Physiology and Behaviour*, 3, 271–3.
Marr, D. (1976) Early processing of visual information. *Philosophical Transactions of the Royal Society (London)*, 275B, 483–524.
Marr, D. (1980) Visual information processing: the structure and creation of visual representations. *Philosophical Transactions of the Royal Society (London)*, 290B, 199–218.
Marr, D. (1982) *Vision*. San Francisco: W. H. Freeman.
Vandenburg, S. G. and Kuse, A. R. (1978) Mental rotation, a group test of three dimensional spatial visualization. *Perceptual and Motor Skills*, 47, 599–604.
Warrington, E. K. (1984) *Recognition Memory Battery*. Windsor: NFER-Nelson.

13

Face to face: interpreting a case of developmental prosopagnosia

Ruth Campbell

I had seen her occasionally when I cycled to and from work; she lived in the same street as my family. She dressed younger than her age of about 25 but was not striking to look at. Occasionally I smiled at her but rarely caught a response. She was usually looking at something else in the street. More often we met professionally. The interchanges were a little strange. She did not avoid looking at me, but hesitantly smiled and slowed her walk as I approached. Sometimes she would say hello, but usually it was I who greeted her by name. She always replied, appropriately, but sometimes nervously. We were on friendly terms and respected each other as working academics. When we greeted each other she rarely looked at me as she spoke. Sometimes we arranged to meet in my office or hers, for we had interests in common. Such meetings were always useful, with productive and penetrating discussions that ranged over a number of topics.

Although our conversations were affable and we had a respect and interest in each other, greeting each other was always stilted. We seemed more at ease on the telephone. What could be wrong with this young woman (let us call her AB, not her real initials)? What lay behind these odd interactions? I was intrigued, and about four years ago, after a few casual meetings, I told her I was interested in face processing. She immediately mentioned that she had problems with faces and that she had been examined before by neuropsychologists and would be happy to cooperate in further studies. The earlier investigations had come about as part of a general medical referral through her family, who were concerned (among other things) that her school was not making allowances for her 'clumsiness' and 'untidy writing'. She had always shown these traits, but she was also gifted in languages and very intelligent. We uncovered the earlier reports. This is the gist of them.

Summary of original case description and follow-up

McConachie (1976) gives a report of this case. AB was seen when she was 12 years and 9 months old. She was born at 37 weeks' gestation and she was described by her mother as a normal child, although her milestones were somewhat delayed. AB reported that she had never been able to recognize faces, except the most familiar ones. She recognizes people by their clothing, voice and mannerisms. There were no neurologically abnormal signs except for an EEG recording which showed some small spikes over the posterior part of the right hemisphere. She had no visual field defect. She was not apraxic on clinical tests (that is, she was able to perform a range of actions on command and could pantomime actions adequately), but did not have good fine motor control. AB is right-handed. There was considerable anecdotal evidence for topographical disorientation including problems in discriminating right and left.

On the Weschler Intelligence Scale there was a significant discrepancy between her verbal (IQ = 144) and her performance scale (IQ = 100) scores. Visual perception, as measured with the Ghent Embedded Figures test, which asks the subject to identify the objects shown in a composite line drawing of a number of overlapping objects, was unimpaired, and her reproduction of simple line drawings was untidy but accurate. Her performance on the Benton Visual Retention test, a test of immediate memory for simple shapes, 'suggested a degree of' impairment. Two sub-tests (visual naming and description of use) of the Spreen–Benton aphasia battery, which tests clinical impairments of language use, failed to detect any significant problem in naming or describing objects.

This pattern of deficits is rare. In particular, it is very odd to find someone who, from birth, seems to have been poor at recognizing faces, but has no problem with recognizing other objects and whose visual perceptual abilities, as tested by a range of tasks using drawn stimuli and (for example) by her quick and efficient reading skills, was apparently quite intact. The difference between the two parts of the intelligence test (verbal and performance), for instance, is statistically significant. At the time the report was published, cases of highly specific *acquired* face-processing difficulty were being reported (*prosopagnosia* from the greek *prosopon*: face and *gnosis*: knowledge), and McConachie suggested that here was a case of possible *developmental prosopagnosia*. The diagnosis was tentative: it was difficult to test the specificity of the problem in the teenage years, where norms for different tests, including those for face recognition, are lacking. It was also unique; there were no published reports of such cases and the present report and that of Temple in this volume (chapter 12) are still the only detailed ones available, despite some conference reports of similar cases.

In 1980, AB was seen again for a psychological assessment by a different investigator. The discrepancy in verbal (IQ = 140) and performance (IQ = 102) scores was confirmed. Colour discrimination was unimpaired, and there was no evidence of problems in the estimating of size and distance of objects. This time, speed of performing tasks was noted as well as accuracy. Matching of different perceptual configurations which varied in shape, orientation and number was accurate but slow. Identification of overlapping figures and line drawings of objects was also normal but slow. She needed longer than normal to recognize pictures presented at very short durations in the tachistoscope, that is her 'recognition thresholds for pictorial stimuli were significantly elevated'. AB, it is reported, 'could match and remember photographs of unfamiliar faces, make gender discriminations, and could adequately describe facial characteristics. Very familiar faces could also be recognised.' All this led the second investigator to the conclusion that the face recognition problems may not have been as severe as was originally suspected and that they formed part of a more general visuoperceptual deficit, albeit one that was hard to describe succinctly.

Our investigations

This, then, was the reported clinical background to this young woman: investigators agreed that there was something amiss, but had disagreed about how it could be characterized. One thought that there was something seriously awry in face processing; the other thought that AB could manage faces as well as could be expected given her other perceptual problems. To some extent this discrepancy arises because each investigator may have used different materials. More interestingly, while both agreed that *something* was more generally wrong, they could not decide *precisely* what it was that was odd about her perceptual skills.

Could I do any better? In the ten years since AB was last formally investigated some different approaches and techniques have come into practice; perceptual function is tested in a number of new ways; new ideas from cognitive science inform our theories about visual recognition, and new perspectives on face processing have developed in cognitive psychology. I wanted to see whether these could shed new light on AB. Could one get closer to what might be functionally amiss? With colleagues Edward De Haan and Charles Heywood, I sought answers to three questions: (a) could we find anything wrong with AB's vision using tests that had not been used before?; (b) what might be askew in AB's visual-object processing? and (c) what would a *systematic* study of her face-processing skills tell us?

Vision

Although we all know that visual acuity is important in perceptual skills (it is what is tested, primarily, by routine optician's tests), it is only recently that we have realized that a defect in sensitivity can be seen for different 'grains' of visual texture, that is for areas of different spatial frequency. One might be good at seeing the contrast between light and dark bar patterns (contrast sensitivity) when the bars are wide (low spatial frequency, few bars per unit area), but not when they are narrow (high spatial frequency, many bars per unit area). Norms are now available for testing contrast sensitivity at different spatial frequencies. This is important because it has been claimed that there may be a link between the development of *low* spatial frequency contrast sensitivity (coarse visual textures, few changes in contrast per unit area) and right cerebral hemisphere function. Since, in most people, the right hemisphere is important for face processing, we should find out if AB has problems in contrast sensitivity at low spatial frequencies. We have now tested this and, as far as we can tell, she has no such problems.

We also repeated the tests of line and simple shape recognition and those of recognizing line drawings of some shapes when they overlapped. We found she was fast and perfect at these tasks. But we did find one anomaly while testing her colour vision. The test includes a part where the subject has to order shades of grey in sequence from black to white. AB made some small errors in the middle of this range. These were not accidental; they happened on repeat testing. There may be something anomalous (not clinically impaired) in her ability to grade monochrome shades of light and dark.

Visual object processing

There is quite a leap to be made, conceptually and computationally, in moving from tests of visual function and simple line and shape perception and recognition, to those that tap the ability to perceive and recognize the complex visual world that we inhabit. Two aspects, in particular, are important. One is the ability to interpret objects in scenes despite different viewpoints, lighting conditions and so forth (the invariance aspect) and the other is the ability to recognize objects 'for what they are': the ability to discriminate a giraffe from a camel requires that we have a detailed, relevant structural representation to which we match the perceived input (object recognition). These two aspects need not necessarily be independent and one of the many insights of computer science approaches to these problems has been to show ways in which one of these aspects may be informed by and affect the other. These approaches make explicit the types of possible operation needed to bring about recognition, a goal that cannot be achieved either by older psychological theories (which sought descriptive 'rules' that determined the criterial aspects of the visual world) nor, yet, by neurophysiological and anatomical theories of vision, which can describe but not yet fully explain neural activity that coincides with 'seeing'.

In one of the first and most brilliant of these computational schemes, David Marr outlined how the visual system might go about extracting a full and stable representation of the three-dimensionsal visual scene from the flat, noisy retinal array and how such a representation might contain within it the necessary information for object discrimination and recognition. The ways in which such schemes work, and alternative approaches, are described by Humphreys and Bruce (1989). For our purposes we want to know whether AB has any problems that indicate that this perceptual leap is not properly attained.

We examined this in several ways. First, we tried to see how well she could recognize silhouettes of familiar objects presented at unfamiliar orientations and also as they were rotated through different angles. Professor Elizabeth Warrington tested this on AB. Although the items were very familiar (rabbits, guns) AB was very poor, significantly worse that others of her age. Then we set about testing her object recognition through photographs. Warrington also developed a test of recognition of objects photographed from unfamiliar views that is very sensitive in adult patients to right brain damage. AB was very poor at this. But she was also poor at discriminating and naming *within* object categories. For instance, although she has a garden she was not reliably able to name flower pictures and even sometimes chose the wrong picture when given a picture of a flower and asked, for instance, 'Is it a tulip or a crocus?' It did not seem that living categories were worse affected than non-living (occasionally patients with recognition problems following brain damage show problems specific to such very high-level distinctions) for she was completely unable to recognize any make of automobile.

This quite marked debility sent us back to standardized naming tasks which are routinely given to neurological patients. These present simple line drawings of objects for naming. AB was not good at this; certainly she was abnormal for her age. Age-related norms are very important for tests of visual recognition; this is one skill that deteriorates in the elderly. Her problems were not just in naming unfamiliar objects (such as gyroscopes) but also in misnaming fairly common objects that resemble others ('violin' for a picture of a guitar).

So, while AB can 'unpack' embedded line drawings into their constituent parts her object recognition abilities are not normal. She is poor at recognizing pictures that demand the construction of a three-dimensional representation to be named and she can be poor at identifying particular objects within more general categories. Even the naming of simple line drawings may present problems when the pictures are of relatively unfamiliar objects or are of visually confusable objects. In all these tasks her errors were not random or slapdash. She often made errors that seemed to respect some aspects of the picture but did not quite focus on the requisite aspect. For instance, a picture of a donkey might be named as 'a horse'. This was not because she did not know what the differences were between these animals: she did, though often her descriptions of their visual appearance were very thin. It was as if AB had had little visual experience of the world; these are the sorts of error a child might make to whom the difference between a horse and a donkey had not yet been pointed out. The difference is that the child, after that one experience, knows the difference. AB does not always do so. Nevertheless, it should be pointed out that AB's early environment may not have been entirely normal. As a child she had a debilitating medical condition (unrelated to any cognitive or neurological debility) and was kept at home a great deal through her school years.

Face processing

IN the past ten years or so systematic models have developed in cognitive psychology that give us insights into how the remarkable adult skill of identifying people by small differences in facial features might arise. One of these is shown in figure 13.1. This is a simple stage model, familiar to

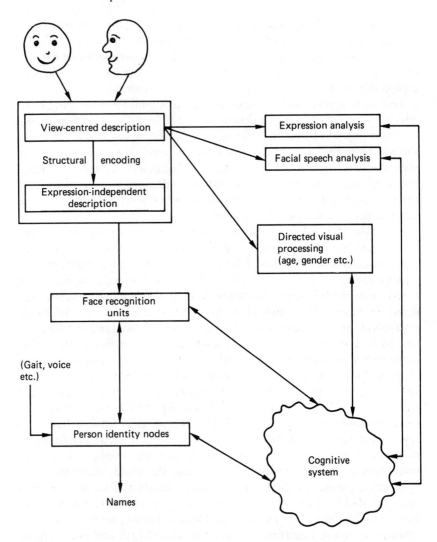

Figure 13.1   A model of face processing (from Bruce and Young, 1986).

students of cognitive psychology. It was proposed by Bruce and Young (1986). The idea is that it identifies the various functional components of a cognitive skill in such a way that one can clearly identify which are necessary to which processes. It is based on evidence from studies with normal populations (see Bruce, 1988) and from neuropsychological impairments acquired after brain lesion. Since AB has a *developmental* anomaly, we can ask whether she fits this sort of framework. We will start with the assumption that the framework is roughly accurate and see what happens.

Testing Stage 1: structural encoding

The first requirement for processing a face is that it be adequately encoded for further cognitive processing; this is needed in order to identify expression, age and gender reliably across different faces; to extract some speech from faces (lip-shape differs for different vowels and closed and open lip consonants can be distinguished easily) as well as to 'pass information up the system' to processes that deal with specific identification.

So one of the first things to establish is whether AB is normal at these tasks. In brief, she is not. Her ability to match and to label facial expression on photographs is worse than that of others of her age, and she made some mistakes in judging age and sex, again in comparison to age-matched controls. We tested lip-reading by seeing if she showed the 'McGurk' illusion, when one hears one sound (for instance 'bait') while one sees another (for instance 'gate') and one perceives a 'fusion' of the two ('date'). While AB could report silently lip-read material quite well, she was abnormal in showing no sign of the McGurk illusion. She always reported the auditory input. One this basis, it seems that there may be something wrong with structural encoding. But this is not conclusive: it is possible that it is not this box, but the decision processes for emotion, age-judgement etc. that are compromised. To test this we should see if she can identify expression, gender· and age from sources other than faces. She can; AB is good at judging voices for all these things – *only* faces are compromised. This implicates structural encoding more closely.

When we recall how she managed the various visual recognition tasks this should not be too surprising; they all showed signs of *underspecified* knowledge, as if the structural representation were formed, but not well enough to support these various other tasks. In faces she showed a similar propensity; for example, she would mistake a beardless, long-haired man's face for that of a woman and sometimes confused expressions of surprise and disgust. These errors do respect something of the face meaning, but fail to take all aspects into account in the requisite way.

Testing stage 2: FRUs and face familiarity

The notion of a face recognition unit (FRU) stage came about by analogy with processes in word recognition. Speed and accuracy of word recognition is affected by the familiarity and recency of presentation of that word in a lexical decision task (is it a word or not?). This suggests that *individual* words have a *distinct* representational locus that is sensitive to these effects. This locus is called the logogen system by Morton (1969) and a recognition or input lexicon in other schemes (see, for instance, Patterson, 1981). Similarly for faces; Bruce (1988) reports several studies that suggest that in recognizing faces we are sensitive to face familiarity and recency, and that these factors can, to some extent, be separated from other aspects of processing faces, such as knowing who the person is, or whether they look angry or happy. In essence, *judgements of face familiarity* should tap the integrity of this part of the system. Even *un*familiar faces could use the system: when one decides whether a just-seen face has been seen before one may make use of a newly established FRU that has just been activated and so will inform the decision 'yes; this is a familiar face.'

While AB has underspecified structural encoding, we did not know whether it may, nevertheless, be sufficient to drive a FRU-system. Could she make familiarity decisions reliably? We found that she could not: not only is she completely at chance at deciding whether photographs of people are famous or not she is also unable to discriminate whether photographs of people she knows are of familiar people or not. As for *unfamiliar* face photographs, she is at chance on a simple test of old–new recognition devised by Elizabeth Warrington. In this test 50 photographs of unknown faces are inspected and then half of them are seen again with 25 new faces. AB was quite unable to do this. Note that Dr S, the patient described by Temple in chapter 12, was able to recognize immediately re-shown unfamiliar face pictures. Dr S and AB have problems in different parts of the face-recognition system. Dr S seems to have particular problems in making output from the FRUs available to the person identity node (PIN) or semantic system; she cannot put an identity to a famous face and cannot tell one anything about the person portrayed, though she can recognize the face if she sees it again. Recognizing a person and knowing who it could be are separate processes.

It is worth stressing that at no time were we able to get AB to name *any* famous face picture reliably (unlike the 1980 investigator who reported that she could name one or two very familiar faces). Even such familiar faces as Mrs Thatcher were identified very tentatively and not always correctly; it made no difference whether these were cartoons or coloured or black and white photographs.

Testing stage 3: knowledge of people

In order to identify and name people one needs knowledge of them (there is no direct face recognition unit to name link). Does AB have such knowledge or are all her deficits to do with simply 'ignoring people'? AB does know who famous people are. When she is tested with famous names she is fast and accurate at discriminating them from non-familiar names (Elvis Presley but not Joseph Dean). She accurately classifies famous names by profession. Similarly for familiar but not famous people. She was able, for instance, to give full descriptions of the work done by colleagues when she was shown their names and was able to discriminate familiar names from made-up unfamiliar ones.

Access to different stages impaired: covert face recognition?

Since AB does know about these people, perhaps she has face recognition skills that may show themselves in a *covert* face recognition task. Face recognition skills may possibly use a normal face-processing system, which could become isolated from the ability to report on these processes; that is, while *access* to the system may be impaired, the system itself may be functioning normally.

One robust covert recognition effect involving faces occurs when subjects are asked to decide as quickly as possible whether or not a written name is familiar. They are reliably speeded by prior presentation of a face associated with that name (for instance, a picture of Princess Diana would speed familiarity responses to the written name: Prince Charles; see Bruce and Valentine, 1986). The effect is specific to the particular association, because a picture of another famous but unassociated individual will not speed familiarity decisions to the names. Perhaps AB will show such effects which ask her about the *name* and not the face. However, she does not. Indeed, on a range of tasks which can all show intact covert face recognition skills in other people, AB shows none (De Haan and Campbell, 1991). In terms of speed and general ability to recognize familiar names, however, she is completely normal. Altogether, it seems that AB shows no activity in the components of the model that specifically concern a unitary, modular face recognition system. The model allows us to see which processes are and are not impaired. She does not seem to have effective face recognition units and cannot reach semantic knowledge about individuals when she sees their face, though she can by other means. Similarly, knowledge about what faces in general can mean (directed visual processing) is poor. Impaired structural encoding for faces seems to be the reason for this. However, two apparent paradoxes remain to be explained.

AB *can do some face tasks normally*

We tested AB with Benton and Van Allen's (1973b) face matching task. This is a clinical task (i.e. norms from clinical populations are the yardstick for performance) that requires the 'patient' to match a small black and white photograph of a face to six other face photographs some of which are of the same person, but changed through viewpoint or lighting so that the photographs are not identical. This task clearly requires the ability to construct a 'view-independent' representation and this is a crucial aspect of structural encoding. AB, we have seen, is poor at tasks that demand this for object recognition. But on this face-matching task, although she was abnormally slow, she was not in the clinically disordered range described by Benton and Van Allen (1973a) for patients with acquired right hemisphere lesions.

On another task, we asked AB to decide if a set of features constituted a face or not: a face-decision task (see figure 13.2). One aspect of structural encoding must be concerned with knowing which features go where. But AB was normal at this; that is, she was as fast and as accurate as age-matched controls.

How are we to interpret her performance on these two tasks in contrast to her very marked impairment on all other face-photo and face-drawing tasks? Some of the Benton pictures might be matched by looking for an *unchanging face feature* (such as a skin-feature like a mole or wrinkle) across the array of photographs. The face/no-face decision can be made by checking the order of identified features ('two eyes above a nose above a mouth'), and we assume that face *features*, as such, are not too much of a problem for AB. Furthermore, the ability to detect face-like-configurations (even three dark blobs arranged in the positions of the eyes and mouth in an upright face frame) could be based on a separate process than that which is used for identifying faces. For instance, such schematic faces are extremely powerful in attracting babies' attention. Some research in infant perception and behaviour suggests that this may reflect a basic, innate and *independent* system for responding to members of our own species; a *conspecific* detection system (Johnson, 1988; de Schonen and Mathivet, 1989).

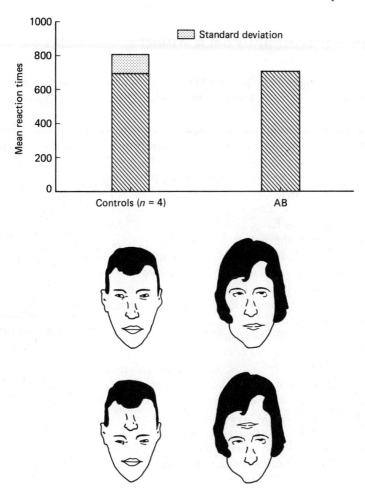

Figure 13.2   Face decision task.

In other words, we think that the tasks that AB *can* do with faces reflect two things: (a) an *idiosyncratic* use of face feature information, without much regard to spatial integration of features and (b) reliance on a quite separate face-processing system: the native, coarse, ability to recognize a human being on just the simplest symmetrical pattern of a darker T-shape or three dark triangularly arrayed blobs in a lighter oval frame. The point is that neither task demands the use of a fully functional face-processing system with all the components of the model sketched for normal function. I shall return to this point in concluding the chapter.

Faces or objects: just what is wrong?

Has this investigation helped answer the questions I posed in introducing this study: do we now know more about AB than earlier reports had revealed?

She has good vision, but with a possible anomaly in grey vision. This might have something to do with a more pronounced problem in her defective visual object processing. How is this problem best characterized and does it relate to her face-processing problems? I think it might: in other words a *single* functional defect may underlie both sets of deficit, but because faces demand more of the 'missing process' than much object recognition, it is in faces, and in particular the identification of different individuals, that the deficit is most clearly seen. What exactly is the deficit? First of all, it is pretty clear what it is not. Features, in the sense of local, simple, two-dimensional attributes of a figure or scene are well perceived and well recognized. Critical features can even be extracted from deformed or noisy displays: for example, she is very fast and accurate at recognizing letter forms with many parts missing or obscured by visual noise (Warrington's Letter Recognition test). With object depictions, the impressive contrast is that her ability to handle silhouettes and highly tonal depictions, as well as unfamiliar views of familiar objects, is very poor, while she is good at identifying line drawings of objects when these all overlap. So it seems that she has more of a problem with the global and spatial aspects than the local, line-feature aspect of object recognition. Furthermore, her errors of misidentification, while often respecting local salient information (flower colour, number of florets in flower naming) seem to be most pronounced where spatial or conjoint properties might have helped make the correct decision. One example might be the ability to distinguish relative length and shape of different parts (she could not distinguish a parsnip and a carrot).

Another test we made may indicate the same thing. AB was unable reliably to discriminate direction of eye-gaze in photographs ('tell me which of the faces in these photographs is looking straight at you': see Campbell et al., 1990). Yet when she was asked to indicate the 'odd one out' of three sets of concentric circles in which one set had an inner circle in a different orientation than the others she was accurate and fast. She can distinguish the local (relative orientation) visual features that are required to perform the gaze task when these are presented as two-dimensional line drawings, out of a face context, but cannot incorporate them into a judgement on the face as a whole three-dimensional pattern.

So AB may have particular problems in establishing a *spatial frame-work* into which salient feature information might fit. Her problems with facial expressions fit this account, too. For example, in identifying surprise on a face, it is the distance between the eyes and eyebrows, as much as the shape of the features themselves, that signals the expression. And the difference between a surprised face and a disgusted or a happy one is not signalled by any one feature but rather by the attributes of a spatially defined *set* of features. So while AB's deficit in face processing is indeed severe compared with her deficit in object recognition, this severity could be explained in terms of a disruption of some *general* perceptual processes, rather than a deficit in a *specific* 'face-processing module'. But these general perceptual processes are at a high level and concern the ways in which two- and three-dimensional knowledge of objects in the world is integrated and represented. AB is impaired at tasks that require spatial, rather than 'purely' visual, two-dimensional analysis: face processing may be particularly demanding of both, so that a weakness in the former, or in linking the two (hypothesized) types of analysis, will be particularly debilitating in trying to identify people and making sense, generally, of their appearance.

Since AB has such dense problems we could infer that such a spatial framework is needed for all good face processing to develop because without such an underpinning it may be difficult to integrate the specific values of features in order to identify an individual or their facial expression, or even gender. To test this assertion, try to make any sort of judgement about a face when you inspect it upside down or in a photographic negative. Faces, much more than other sorts of visual stimulus, are particularly affected by manipulations that impair the construction of a spatial representation which is independent of view-point and lighting (see Yin, 1969; Galper, 1970; Phillips, 1972).

AB and models of normal face processing

The other side of the question 'what is wrong here?' is 'what does this tell us about normal function?' I have suggested that, because her structural encoding skills failed to develop to the normal level, AB did not develop a functional face-processing system; none of the 'purely facial' components in figure 13.1 work for her. Now it should be possible to make use of some of her *spared* capacities to indicate some possible refinements to the cognitive stages model.

*Some of the things AB can do with faces: a reminder and
extension to the model*

AB can make fast and accurate face decision judgements on stimulus
arrays like those in figure 13.2. She can do the Benton face-matching
task, albeit slowly. She can also, again slowly, do *some* expression and
age judgements. When I gave her the name of a colleague and asked her
to point to one of a page of photographs she was slightly better than
chance. An earlier investigation suggested that there were some (very
few) famous faces that she could name.

One way to accommodate these facts is to extend the stages model of
face processing as shown in figure 13.3, so that those things that AB can
do with faces are made explicit. The extended model suggests that there
may be two ways to perform some tasks with faces. One way is to use the
face-processing system. However, additional or alternative systems may
be used, particularly when structural representations are not very well
specified. These are shown as separate extrinsic routes in figure 13.3 and
I suggest that these *are* available to AB. Thus she can make face–non-face
decisions using an intact 'conspec' (conspecific-species member) system
of identification, which has developed from the infant's innate skill at
discriminating face-like configurations. This should be independent of
the ability to identify a given individual or to identify expression or age;
it serves the purpose of early (infantile) adaptation to the caretaker and
could be the basis for orientating oneself to others in the world
(discriminating between front and back views, for instance). Also, the
fact that AB could make use of face *feature* information reasonably well
(for instance in the Benton and Van Allen matching task) suggests
another extrinsic route, that of feature-by-feature analysis. She can even
use stored semantic knowledge about the person to inform her search for
particular face features (choosing the right face, given the name). This
particular extrinsic route seems to work idiosyncratically and is not very
reliable, nevertheless it is probably what is used when AB attempts to
recognize people whom she knows. Eye colour, hair texture, face hair,
spectacles are all such features that are more or less reliable indicators of
identity which do not require the level of integration with other face
features and a spatial face frame that may be needed for the 'dedicated'
face-processing system. Are these special extrinsic processes developed
only by AB? I think not: consider what happens when a telephone call
tells us to 'look out for a fat guy, balding with glasses'. We can use
feature information well without necessarily implicating the face-
processing system. Whether AB is *better* than normal at discriminating
people from descriptions of their features is another matter, and one to

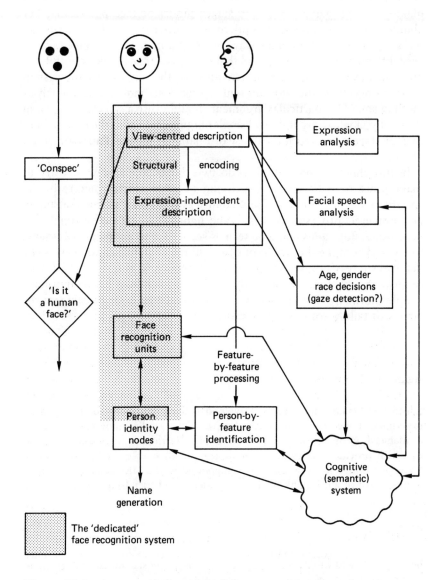

Figure 13.3 An extended model of face processing (based on Bruce and Young, 1986). Note that feature-by-feature processing enables face *matching* to occur (Benton and Van Allen task).

be experimentally decided. By interpreting AB's deficits in this way I am making strong claims about the stages model of face processing; her abilities and weaknesses do not prove or disprove the 'truth' of the model but she does suggest different ways of extending it. I could have taken a very different tack and suggested that the things that AB does with faces are evidence of a low level of activation in the face-processing system itself, rather than the workings of a separate, 'indirect' face-analysis mechanism. (This particular argument should cause a sense of *déja vu* in those of you who have followed similar arguments about the number and type of stages required for visual word naming; see e.g. Patterson et al., 1985.)

In this chapter I have tried to do two things: the first was to try to make sense of AB's debility by trying to get a clearer picture of the specificity of the problem. The second was to use her pattern of spared and impaired processes to cast some light on models of normal face processing. Both aims could be seen as secondary to another goal; that is to try to determine the conditions for optimal cognitive functioning. The detailed study of AB, set in a functional framework, gives us several hints on how this goal may be achieved. They may not help her to recognize people 'normally' but can show us what might be done to mitigate the effects of failures of normal development.

Acknowledgements

Edward De Haan and Charles Heywood actively collaborated in the many experimental investigations of AB. Dr M. Wyke kindly made clinical details available. I am most grateful to Professor E. Warrington for testing AB, tests of which provided the evidence for the (personal) interpretation offered here. Some of the time spent in testing was supported by the MRC on various project grants. Most of all, I thank AB for her patience and friendship.

References

Benton, A. L. and van Allen, M. W. (1972) Prosopagnosia and facial discrimination. *Journal of the Neurological Sciences*, 15, 167–72.
Benton, A. L. and van Allen, M. W. (1973a) *Tests of Visual Function*. Department of Neurology, Iowa, USA.
Benton, A. L. and van Allen, M. W. (1973b) *Test of Face Recognition Manual*. Neurosensory Center Publication no. 287, Department of Neurology, Iowa, USA.
Bruce, V. (1988) *Recognising Faces*. Hove, East Sussex: Lawrence Erlbaum.

Bruce, V. & Valentine, T. (1986) Semantic priming of familiar faces. *Quarterly Journal of Experimental Psychology*, 38A, 125–50.

Bruce, V. and Young, A. (1986) Understanding face recognition. *British Journal of Psychology*, 77, 305–27.

Campbell, R., Heywood, C., Cowey, A., Regard, M. & Landis, T. (1990) The detection of eye-gaze direction in Macaque and prosopagnosic subjects. *Neuropsychologia*, 28, 1123–42.

De Haan, E. D. F. and Campbell, R. (1991) A fifteen year follow-up of a case of development prosopagnosia. *Cortex*, 27, 000–000.

de Schonen, S. and Mathivet, E. (1989) First come, first served; a scenario about the development of hemispheric specialization in face recognition during infancy. *Cahiers de Psychologie Cognitive*, 9, 3–46.

Ellis, A. W. and Young, A. W. (1988) *Human Cognitive Neuropsychology*. Hove, East Sussex: Lawrence Erlbaum.

Galper, R. E. (1970) Recognition of faces in photographic negative. *Psychonomic Science*, 19, 207–8.

Humphreys, G. W. and Bruce, V. (1989) *Visual Cognition*. Hove, East Sussex: Lawrence Erlbaum.

Johnson, M. (1988) Memories of Mother. *New Scientist*, 18 February, 60–62.

McConachie, H. R. (1976) Developmental prosopagnosia. A single case report. *Cortex*, 12, 76–82.

Morton, J. (1969) The interaction of information in word recognition. *Psychological Review*, 76, 165–78.

Patterson, K. E. (1981) Neuropsychological approaches to the study of reading. *British Journal of Psychology*, 72, 151–74.

Patterson, K. E., Marshall, J. C. and Coltheart, M. (1985) *Surface Dyslexia: Cognitive and Neuropsychological Studies of Phonological Reading*. London: Lawrence Erlbaum.

Phillips, R. (1972) Why are faces hard to recognise in photographic negative? *Perception and Psychophysics*, 12, 425–6.

Warrington, E. (1984) *Recognition Memory Battery*. Windsor: NFER-Nelson.

Yin, R. (1969) Looking at upside-down faces. *Journal of Experimental Psychology*, 81, 141–5.

Afterword: failing with faces, comparing cases

Developmental prosopagnosia has not been reported before the two cases discussed here in chapters 12 and 13; it is worth considering the similarities and differences between them, in particular since the two women were tested using some similar tests and were investigated with very similar aims in mind.

But first, why should they have turned up now, and not before? Are difficulties with faces as common as difficulties with reading or writing, but have just been ignored? We do not know the answer to this and it is a difficult question to pose experimentally. Face recognition is not a schooled skill, with a 'set curriculum' and tests every year! But there are plenty of anecdotes about people with face-recognition problems. I suspect that, just as there are degrees of reading weakness and strength, so too with face-recognition skills, and there may be many people with problems roughly as severe as those of AB and Dr S. The reason that these two women are only now being investigated is because it is only recently that interesting models of the possible components in face processing have been proposed in any detail, so that cases of anomalous face processing could shed light on the viability of such models as well as enable us to understand such anomalies more clearly.

Although these two women were, it seems, always bad with faces, there is one reported study of a child who, after an attack of meningitis at 14 months followed by another 18 months of medical complications, became prosopagnosic. This child was first investigated when she was nearly nine years old by Young and Ellis (1989) who tried without success over three years to improve her face recognition skills by a series of rote-learning tasks (Ellis and Young, 1988). KD, at nine years, had far worse vision than AB, and indeed attended a school unit for visually handicapped children, but in other ways she was surprisingly similar: she showed poorish object recognition (especially when presented with unusual views) and was poor on tasks of expression analysis, gender discrimination and unfamiliar face matching (although, like AB, she was not completely unable to do these tests). Like AB, KD was completely unable to recognize familiar faces, both in overt and covert tests. But, also like AB, her dense visual recognition problems did not affect her reading; she learned to read at a normal age and was within normal range for reading, despite her visual handicap. (Her visual acuity was only 6/18; normal vision is 18/18 or 20.20.)

This pattern of similarity between AB, who has never recognized faces, and KD, who could recognize faces until illness intervened, suggests that the brain does not show much plasticity for the skill of face recognition and that if the necessary components are missing or damaged before the age of three years, then face recognition will fail, although other visual skills may develop reasonably well. It is unlikely that KD's severe visual problems caused the prosopagnosia since children with visual problems (acuity, colour) as severe as KD's do not seem to develop problems in face processing to anything like this extent (Ellis et al., 1987).

But how do AB and Dr S compare? Although the two women were not given precisely the same tests, sufficient similar tests were given for some firm conclusions to be drawn. The first and most important difference is that while Dr S 'passed' Warrington's unfamiliar face test, correctly recognizing as 'old faces' 43 out of 50 photographs of those she had just seen, AB was at chance on this task. This failure of AB to register a face photograph sufficiently well to recognize it again when it was presented immediately afterwards, occurs despite very similar 'pure vision' test scores by the two women. A complementary and important difference, though not established by formal test, is that whereas AB can recognize people by their gait and voice, in Dr S recognition is not improved when the 'unknown person' speaks or moves. In terms of the face recognition model of Bruce and Young, this different pattern of impairment indicates damage to different stages in the model. AB's problems are in structural encoding; Dr S's concern the person identification node, particularly, suggests Temple, in accessing that node from the face recognition units. There is supportive evidence for this dissociation: AB is poor or odd at all tasks involving structural encoding of faces; Dr S is not. AB is good at all tasks to do with knowledge of people, other than those that depend on the face. Dr S can certainly identify people better from their name than their face; nevertheless she was not very good even at identification from the name (28/40), suggesting a possible problem with the PIN itself, which is concerned with processing (coordinating) all sorts of specific information about a person: their face, voice, detailed knowledge about them as individuals.

In turn, these problems with faces seem to be nested in other, but milder, problems. I made a case for considering AB's face-processing failure to be connected with a mild problem in using three-dimensional information; in establishing the $2\frac{1}{2}$–3D step (in Marr's terms), so that all the small feature distance differences between faces are respected. It is just that faces are more demanding of such processes than are other sorts of stimuli. Similarly, Temple shows that Dr S does not only have problems in remembering people (by face or other identificatory detail), she also has some mild problems in remembering other things that need to be discriminated by stored small details (for instance, in the memory for simple designs test).

So these two women show us that a separate stages model of face processing can work well to describe developmental as well as acquired face-processing problems and they confirm the possibility that there may be little or no plasticity for this set of cognitive functions which comprise, in Fodor's terms (1983), a cognitive *module*. But in confirming this picture they do not show us that the face-processing module is completely isolated from all other cognitive components; rather, it relies on or is connected with inputs from other systems – underspecified structural processes in object perception (AB), and specifically detailed (visual) memory representations (impaired in Dr S). Faces may be more demanding of these cognitive components than are other sorts of identification tasks. The demands they make cannot, however, be easily equated with simple perceptual or memory skills; they have a different character which is still elusive.

References

Ellis, H. D., Young, A. W. and Markham, B. (1987) The ability of visually impaired children to read expressions and recognize faces. *Journal of Visual Impairment and Blindness*, 485–6.

Ellis, H. D. and Young, A. W. (1988) Training in face processing skills for a child with acquired prosopagnosia. *Developmental Neuropsychology*, 4, 283–94.

Fodor, J. (1983) *The Modularity of Mind*. Cambridge, Mass.: MIT Press.

Young, A. W. and Ellis, H. D. (1989) Childhood prosopagnosia. *Brain and Cognition*, 9, 16–47.

14

Transient global amnesia

John R. Hodges

You have to begin to lose your memory, if only in bits and pieces, to realise that memory is what makes our lives. Life without memory is no life at all, just as intelligence without the possibility of expression is not really an intelligence. Our memory is our coherence, our reason, our feeling even our action. Without it, we are nothing . . . (Luis Bunuel, 1982)

The syndrome of transient global amnesia (TGA) offers fascinating and unparalleled insights into the workings of the human mind. It allows a glimpse into the void of human existence without normal memory, and sheds light on several controversial issues concerning memory function.

This condition, which was first recognized about 25 years ago by two American neurologists (Fisher and Adams, 1964), usually afflicts previously healthy middle-aged and elderly people. There is a sudden and apparently complete cessation of the ability to lay down new memories; learning capacity is limited to seconds only. Subjects appear disorientated and confused and in an attempt to understand what is happening they characteristically ask a repetitive series of questions ('where am I?', 'what day is it?', etc.) only to forget the answers within minutes and thus begin the cycle again. The continuing, or anterograde, memory deficit is accompanied by a more variable deficit in the recall of old memories (i.e. retrograde amnesia) which may extend back over months, years or even decades. But despite this devastating memory loss other aspects of higher cognitive function (e.g. language, visuospatial abilities) remain intact. Indeed, many subjects continue to perform quite complex tasks, such as driving a car, although later have no memory of having done so.

Thankfully, this state is temporary, and after a few hours the ability to register new memories gradually returns. There is shrinkage of the retrograde amnesia and patients return to normal except that there remains a complete and permanent gap for everything that happened during the attack (see Miller et al., 1987; Hodges and Ward, 1989). To 'come to' in an unfamiliar environment, such as a hospital ward, with no recollection of the past six or so hours, is clearly extremely worrying; as is the fear of recurrence, and that the next time it might not be temporary. Such fears are in fact groundless since further attacks are the exception.

Although TGA is not a very rare condition – most neurologists will see several cases each year – its cause remains a mystery. Most medical authorities have favoured a cerebrovascular origin, that is to say, a temporary disturbance in the blood supply to part of the brain due to a small blood clot or cholesterol debris passing through the cerebral circulation (for review, see Logan and Sherman, 1983; Caplan, 1985; Hinge et al., 1986; Miller et al., 1987; Hodges and Warlow, 1990a). Others have refuted this suggestion, and have argued in favour of epilepsy (Fisher, 1982) or possibly migraine as the pathological basis (Crowell et al., 1984). The fact that most attacks are singular, whilst reassuring for patients and relatives, has been one of the facts most difficult to accommodate into any aetiological theory. My own studies show that the outlook following TGA is excellent: there is no circumstantial evidence, from the study of risk factors usually associated with stroke (such as high blood pressure, heart disease, smoking etc.), to support a cerebrovascular causation; and, furthermore, the risk of subsequent stroke is no greater than to be expected in a similarly aged population (Hodges and Warlow, 1990a). A very small proportion of patients do go on to develop epilepsy. There is also an association with migraine in about a quarter of cases, but in the remaining majority the cause for the attacks still remains an enigma (Hodges and Warlow, 1990b).

My interest in TGA began when I had just started training in neurology in the early 1980s. At that time I had little knowledge of the condition but my orientation towards higher cognitive function was already primed by my experience in psychiatry. One day a general practitioner referred to the ward an elderly woman in the throes of a typical attack of TGA. I was able to perform only elementary 'bedside' tests of memory – recall of a name and address, digit span, orientation in time and place – and to question her about recent personal and public events. Even within the limits of this assessment, it was obvious that various aspects of memory warranted further systematic evaluation and that this might have a bearing on more fundamental aspects of human memory. However, I did not realize that this chance encounter would lead to several years of research into the nature and causation of TGA.

Eventually I managed to see over 100 patients who had experienced attacks of transient memory loss. Of course, the majority were assessed some time after the event and details had to be gleaned from eye-witnesses: such evidence was invaluable for epidemiological studies of the aetiology but was of limited neuropsychological value. I was also fortunate enough to observe and test a smaller but substantial group of patients actually in the throes of an attack. By that time I had assembled a battery of neuropsychological tests designed to dissect the nature of the amnesic deficit and to answer several specific questions. Since there have been very few reports in the literature of patients being tested during attacks of TGA, severl questions remained unanswered (Wilson et al., 1980; Caffarra et al., 1981; Regard and Landis, 1984; Gallassi et al., 1986). These will be addressed in more detail following the case descriptions below. Briefly stated, the major issues are these: (a) is it a pure amnesic syndrome or are other aspects of cognition also impaired?; (b) is the anterograde deficit (i.e. memory for continuing events) truly global, in other words involving both verbal and non-verbal memory?; (c) what is the extent and pattern of the retrograde deficit (i.e. memory for events *before* the attack)?

Case Reports

Case 1

ES, a 58-year-old council worker, was seen on 19 August 1985 in the early stages of his first episode of TGA. He was in excellent general health with no past history of vascular disease, psychiatric illness or migraine. He had not smoked for many years and was a non-drinker. On the day of the attack he and his wife had been out shopping, on their return home at 13.00 he was quite normal. He went into the garden only to return minutes later in a perplexed and bewildered state saying 'something's gone wrong', 'I don't know what has happened.' He was clearly amnesic for recent events and asked repetitively why he was not at work, what day it was and what they had been doing. After seeing his general practitioner he was brought to the Radcliffe Infirmary.

On arrival, at 15.00, he was fully conscious and alert, but had no idea why he was at the hospital. His speech and language were normal, although in contrast to his normal personality he volunteered little spontaneous information. He was disorientated in time, believing that it was 1984. When asked the season he attempted to work it out by observing that the trees were in full leaf so if must be summer. The degree of anterograde amnesia was profound; his wife had been present during the first hour of the examination, but within a few minutes of her departure he was unable to recall that she had been present. When given a simple name and address, he was able to repeat it immediately after presentation, but moments later had no memory of the task – let alone the address!

Informal assessment suggested a dense retrograde amnesia of around six months. For example, he had no memory of his brother's death a few months before and was genuinely distressed when told of this event. He had also forgotten visiting his brother-in-law in hospital a week before. However, recollection of earlier life events appeared to be preserved (e.g. schooling, military service) and he could recall a change of job following redundancy some two years before. His general world knowledge was also excellent. For instance, in addition to recalling that his wife was on regular home haemodialysis for renal disease, he could give an accurate account of the procedure and its attendant problems.

From these observations it can be seen that there was a striking discrepancy between the severity of his anterograde amnesia (for new information) and the limited extent of his retrograde amnesia (for past events). This was also dramatically illustrated during his performance on the famous faces test (described below); he could accurately and fluently name the previously famous personalities, but during the test frequently stopped to ask what he was supposed to be doing, why he was at the hospital and where his wife was. In addition, half an hour later when re-presented with some of the photographs from the famous faces test he had no recollection of having been previously shown any photographs. This clearly illustrates that some aspects of his memory were intact whilst others were severely impaired.

The dense anterograde amnesia persisted until 20.00 (seven hours post-onset) when he gradually began to recover the ability to lay down new memories. The retrograde amnesia had shrunk by that stage to a few days and he could recall details of his brother's recent death. He was admitted to the ward for overnight observation. The following day he was clearly much improved. The qualitative difference was striking, for instance when given the test of past autobiographical memory during the attack (see below), he produced memories that were curiously empty and lacking in colour, as if reduced to the 'bare bones' of the memory. The following day he had no recollection of having done this test, but when prompted to produce the same memories did so with all the usual colour and detail of personal memories.

He was reassessed at one week and again at six months post-attack. Detailed investigation of brain anatomy (using computerized brain scanning) and of physiology (by electroencephalography) were, as is usual in TGA, normal.

Case 2

LV, a 67-year-old retired telephonist, was observed during his first episode of TGA on 15 July 1985. He was generally fit, did not suffer from high blood pressure and had no other recognized risk factors for cerebrovascular disease. Ten years before he had suffered a depressive illness and had remained on lithium since then without further psychiatric problems. Interestingly, he was a lifelong migraine sufferer. After retiring from full-time work in the post office at the age of 60, he had worked as a part-time gardener and handyman at a local convent.

On the day of his attack he had arranged to meet a nun at Oxford railway station and to drive her to the convent. This he did quite normally. He returned home at around 15.30 and went out again, without seeing his wife, to mend a broken window in their garage. At 16.45 he came into the house in a confused state; he could not remember what he had been doing that day and said that he did not know if he was 'coming or going'. His wife rang the convent to confirm that he had safely delivered the sister and, after consulting their general practitioner, he was transferred to the Radcliffe Infirmary.

On arrival, at 21.00, he appeared quiet and perplexed. His speech and language were normal. He was orientated in place but did not know the day, month or year. After prompting he guessed the year inaccurately to be 1983. He repeated every few minutes a remarkably stereotyped phrase: 'by the way, let me tell you, there is a slight pressure on top of my head.' As in the former case, his anterograde amnesia was profound; when given a simple eight-item name and address to recall he repeated it immediately. After two minutes he had no recollection whatsoever of the task.

Unlike Case 1, however, informal assessment suggested an extensive retrograde amnesia of around 30 years. He was unable to furnish details about his early life, war service and immediate post-war occupation. The general framework of his subsequent life appeared preserved but he could provide virtually no specific details and was particularly confused about the sequence of events over the past two decades. There was no consistent or sharp cut-off point to his retrograde amnesia. For instance, he was able to recall his son's wedding 12 months before but not the assassination of President Kennedy. He had forgotten the birth of his grandchild one month earlier and was unaware of an impending prostate operation. In general, his recall of public events was considerably more impaired than his autobiographical memory.

By 23.30 (seven hours post-onset) the retrograde amneisa had shrunk, he was able to remember his grandson's recent birth and that he had been due to meet someone from the train that day. Although there appeared to be no dense retrograde amnesia at this stage, his chronological sequencing of past public and personal events was still very poor. When given a list of nine post-war Prime Ministers, he was unable to place them in anything approaching the correct order. By 02.30 the following morning his memory was clearly improving and was able to lay down new memories.

The following day his family felt that he had returned to 'normal'. He recalled events of the preceding day, up until 13.30. The two-hour permanent retrograde gap for events before the onset of the attack did not subsequently decrease. All other investigations were, as in Case 1, entirely normal. Repeat neuropsychological assessment was performed at 24 hours, one week, four weeks and six months post-attack.

Neuropsychological testing

The bedside assessment of memory and cognition show that memory is severely impaired during TGA, and suggest that retrograde memory may be affected to very different degrees in patients, while anterograde amnesia is always very profound. These informal tests do not, however, explore the various recognized sub-components (such as immediate, verbal and non-verbal) of memory. Nor do they establish the pattern of the remote memory loss. In order to assess these aspects formally, a battery of tests was given to the patients.

Anterograde Memory

Immediate (short-term) memory: recall over very short periods is mediated by brain systems that are distinct from, but clearly related to, longer-term memory (Baddeley and Warrington, 1970). It is traditionally measured by digit span, in which a progressively lengthening series of numbers (like telephone numbers) is presented verbally. This was within normal limits in both ES (five digits) and LV (six digits). They were also given a similar test designed to assess short-term spatial memory, the Corsi block tapping test. In this, subjects are presented with an array of nine small black blocks fixed in a random fashion to a black board. The examiner taps the blocks in a prearranged sequence and the subject must then copy the sequence. By adding one tap to each successive sequence, the examiner assesses the subject's memory span. Normal subjects achieve a block-tapping span equivalent to their digit span (i.e. 6 ± 1); both ES and LV managed a sequence of five blocks.

Longer-term memory for verbal and non-verbal memory was profoundly impaired in both patients. They were first read two short stories, each containing 21 distinct items, after being told that they would be asked at the end to recall as much detail as possible. ES and LV could recall only the last one or two details and had lost the normal primacy effect (i.e. the tendency to recall selectively the first items). Half an hour later they had no recollection of having been given any such stories, even after cueing with the most essential details (e.g. 'it was about a ship sinking at sea'). Normal subjects of their age would recall at least ten parts of the stories immediately after presentation, and would retain the vast majority for at least an hour.

Their performance on a word list learning task (Weintraub and Mesulam, 1985) illustrated an extremely rapid rate of forgetting. In this test, subjects are presented with a short list of words, just above span, which is repeated until they can successfully recall all items on three trials. This technique of so-called 'learning to criterion' ensures that the list has entered long-term memory. Recall is then tested, without warning, at various time intervals. Normal subjects are able to retain such a short list for at least 15 minutes. In contrast, ES and LV showed rapid forgetting, so that after three minutes retention was below 50 per cent.

It was important to assess non-verbal memory because, as I shall discuss below, memory function is lateralized within the brain; right-sided structures being more important for non-verbal memory. In both of the patients memory for non-verbal material appeared devastated. In order to test this, they were given a test of incidental spatial recall developed at the Montreal Neurological Institute (Smith and Milner, 1981). In this test, subjects are shown an array of 16 toys arranged in an apparently random fashion on a large board. They are asked to name each item in turn, and to assess the price of the real item represented by the toy (e.g. washing machine, watering can, comb, purse etc.). The naming and pricing task is used to ensure that subjects attend equally to each item and to distract them from the real objectives of the test. After finishing the price estimation, subjects are taken away from the board and occupied with another unrelated task. Meanwhile the examiner removes the toys from the board. After four minutes the subject is asked to recall as many items as possible, then after being given all 16 toys he is asked to replace them on the board in exactly their original positions. Scores can be derived for the number of items recalled and their displacement from the original position. Both ES and LV performed the pricing part of the test normally, although they frequently had to be reminded what to do. After four minutes, however, they had forgotten the test. With prompting, LV recalled two items but ES could recall none (normal subjects recall at least eight). Their replacement was entirely random and bore no relationship to the original positions. The measured mean displacements were in excess of 20 cm, whereas normal subjects achieve a mean of around 8 cm per item.

In another test of non-verbal memory, they were asked to copy a complex abstract design, the Rey–Osterreith Figure (Osterreith, 1944), which they did very well thus demonstrating preserved visuospatial skills. However, 30 minutes later no elements of the picture could be recalled by ES or LV; normal age-matched controls produce at least a third of the total of 36 elements after a similar delay.

Thus, there was a striking dissociation between the patients' immediate (short-term) memory, as measured by digit span or block-tapping span, and their longer-term recall of verbal and non-verbal material. This could be due either to a difficulty transferring material from short-term (working) memory into a longer-term store (encoding), rapid disappearance from the store or a deficit in retrieval. The results of the rate of forgetting test suggest that rapid loss of information plays an important role in TGA, although further research is required to clarify the nature of the deficit.

Retrograde memory

The quantitative measurement of remote memory remains a difficult methodological issue. A number of tests using famous events or famous faces have been devised in which knowledge of such events arranged by decade is assessed (e.g. Albert et al., 1979; Cohen and Squire, 1981; Hodges and Ward, 1989). In patients with permanent amnesia it is necessary to compare the performance of the patient with that of matched controls. But individual variation on such tests is clearly very wide, and it is never possible to be sure whether the patient ever knew the famous face or event. In TGA this is not the case. Because of the transient nature of the condition, the patient can act as his own control by comparing performance during the attack with that after recovery. Three measures of remote memory were used: two tests of remote public knowledge (famous faces and events) and one test of remote autobiographical memory (Hodges and Ward, 1989). For each of the tests control data were also obtained from a group of 40 normal volunteers, aged 50–75, recruited from local general practitioners, who were screened to exclude anyone with brain disease.

In the *famous faces test*, portrait photographs of people who had come to prominence between 1930 and 1980 and had remained in the public eye for a limited time were used. They were arranged so that each decade contained photographs from each of the main categories (i.e. politicians and statesmen, stars of the stage and screen, members of the Royal Family and sports people). Subjects were asked to name the famous person represented. The pattern of results in the two patients ES and LV was very different and fitted with the informal estimate of the retrograde amnesia: ES's performance fell within the normal range for his age in that he correctly named 59 of the faces with an even distribution across the decades. More importantly, when retested at one month there had been no significant improvement in his scores. By contrast, LV was clearly impaired naming only 32 faces which were unevenly distributed with a clear temporal gradient across the decades (i.e. progressive worsening from 1930s to 1970s). This was confirmed on retesting when his performance had improved to within the normal range and with a loss of the previous temporal gradient.

In the *famous events test*, 50 clearly datable events from the period 1930–1980 were selected using a variety of published news reviews. These were mixed in with 50 fictitious items made up to sound like real news events (e.g. 'The Harrow train disaster', 'The Jin-Jin', 'Vienna Airlift' etc.). Subjects were read each item in turn and then asked to signify those items remembered as real events. They were told beforehand that the list contained a mixture of real news items from the past 50 years, together with fictitious items. Whenever they identified an event as real they were asked to date it by assigning the event to a single decade. The result on the recognition part of the test were similar to those on the famous faces; ES performed normally across all decades and showed no improvement when retested after the attack; LV was impaired on events from the 1960s and 1970s but improved to within the normal range after the attack. On the dating task, however, a different pattern emerged: both subjects showed a marked impairment in their ability to date events from recent decades although the deficit was, as one would predict, more extensive in the case of LV. Their dating accuracy returned to normal when retested at an interval after the attack. The significance of this finding will be discussed later.

To test remote personal memory the *Crovitz Test of cued autobiographical memory* was used (Zola-Morgan et al., 1983; Sagar et al., 1988). As its name suggests, this test attempts to quantify autobiographical memory. Subjects are asked to relate personally experienced events from any remote time period, evoked by each of ten noun cues (bird, flag, tree, car etc.) and then to estimate when that event occurred.

The cued personal autobiography test was performed on both subjects during TGA and was repeated at 24 hours and six months using the same word list. Normal controls find this test extremely easy, they are usually able to produce specific memories rich in detail which are then consistently reproduced and dated 24 hours later. The pattern of results differed between subjects: ES found the test difficult. He produced memories which were temporally specific, but devoid of the normal richness and detail with which the same memories were subsequently related. He also consistently overestimated the age of the memories during TGA by around six years. In contrast, LV produced a reasonable number of specific episodes only after extensive cueing the age of which he systematically underestimated by around seven years. Neither patient produced any memories from the most recent five years, whereas in normal subjects at least a quarter of memories come from this era. Table 15.1 summarizes the results of the neuropsychological tests in the two patients.

Table 14.1   Neuropsychological test results in two patients tested during TGA

| | Patient | |
Test	ES	LV
Anterograde memory		
Immediate memory	Normal	Normal
Long-term memory		
Verbal material	Severely impaired	Severely impaired
Non-verbal material	Severely impaired	Severely impaired
Retrograde memory		
Famous faces	Normal	Impaired with TG
Famous events		
Recognition	Normal	Impaired with TG
Dating	Impaired	Impaired
Autobiographical	Defective and misdating	Defective and misdating

TG, temporal gradient.

Implications

Having described the two patients and their neuropsychological test results I shall try to relate these findings to the theoretical issues briefly mentioned in the introduction.

Is TGA purely an amnesic state?

Reports of 'confusion' during TGA have suggested that aspects of cognitive function other than memory – such as attention, concentration, problem-solving, language – may be impaired. ES and LV were disorientated during the attack because of the profound degree of amnesia, but there was no clouding of consciousness; they attempted to orientate themselves with respect to time and place by using environmental cues, remained capable of manipulating complex information, reasoned coherently and all aspects of language and visuospatial function (that were tested) appeared intact.

This remarkable dissociation of memory from other aspects of cognition is a striking illustration of the modularity of processing within the brain. The finding of a pure amnesic state also tells us that the pathological process in TGA is confined to those areas of the brain which specifically subserve memory, i.e. the medial temporal lobe structures (notably the hippocampus) and the deep midline nuclei surrounding the third ventricle (known collectively as the diencephalon). The hippocampus and diencephalon are bilateral structures (i.e. in the left and right hemispheres) connected by complex circuitry and collectively form the limbic system. Damage to any part of this circuit will produce a measurable memory deficit but it appears that a severe amnesic state only occurs after bilateral damage (for review see, Parkin 1984; Squire, 1986; Oxbury and Oxbury, 1989).

The nature of the anterograde amnesia

The degree of the new learning deficit was clearly very severe during TGA. This is apparent from both the performance on the memory tests and from the completeness of the permanent amnesic gap for the attack. Interestingly, the patients seemed to have awareness of which memories ought to be readily recallable: so-called metamemory (Hirst, 1982; Shimamura and Squire, 1986). For example, when asked to name the current Prime Minister they would initially appear to answer with confidence and would then be surprised at themselves for not knowing the name ('now I really should know that'), as if a familiar drawer had been opened but the normal contents were found to be unexpectedly missing.

Despite the profound deficit in laying down any new memories, immediate verbal (digit) and non-verbal (block-tapping) span was unimpaired in these patients. The dissociation between immediate (short-term) and longer-term memory has previously been observed during TGA (Wilson et al., 1980; Regard and Landis, 1984). It is also characteristic of permanent amnesic syndromes, whether due to diencephalic damage, as in Korsakoff's disease (Baddeley and Warrington, 1970) or bitemporal damage (Milner et al., 1968). These findings strongly support the idea that immediate and longer-term memory are localized to functionally independent brain areas.

It is clear even from informal testing that verbal memory (e.g. recall of a name and address etc.) is profoundly impaired during TGA. But non-verbal memory, for material such as faces, designs and routes is less easily tested at the bedside. Whether non-verbal memory is involved is an important question because memory function is, at least in part, lateralized within the limbic system: the left medial temporal structures being more important for verbal memory and the right for non-verbal memory (Milner, 1971). In the patients described, non-verbal memory was as severely impaired as verbal memory. For instance, despite performing adequate copies of the Rey figure, which illustrates their excellent visuospatial abilities, after a delay the patients recalled no element of the figure. Also, on a task which is considered more selective for right hemisphere memory function – the incidental spatial recall test (Smith and Milner, 1981) – both patients showed profound impairment. These findings also imply that limbic structures are bilaterally impaired during TGA as previously suggested by other workers (Wilson et al., 1980; Caffarra et al., 1981; Regard and Landis, 1984; Gallassi et al., 1986).

The extent and pattern of retrograde amnesia

The phenomenon of retrograde amnesia has been of particular importance to theories of human memory. It has also been the subject of considerable controversy because of the uncertainty about the pattern of remote memory loss in patients with permanent amnesia. This is largely because the interpretation of remote memory tests is much more difficult than the interpretation of anterograde memory tests. The major problem results from the fact that the content of memory before the onset of permanent amnesia can never be firmly established; non-recognition or recall of an event could result from ignorance or amnesia. To measure remote memory, in such cases, comparisons are generally made between patients and normal controls. But this poses problems due to the great inter-individual variation in knowledge of test material (e.g. famous faces, famous events etc.). TGA provides the opportunity to compare patients' performance during an episode of dense amnesia with their own performance after the attack.

The formal tests of remote memory confirmed the clinical impression that, in contrast to their universally severe anterograde amnesia, the extent of retrograde amnesia was very different in the two patients: while LV had an extensive retrograde amnesia for famous faces and events, ES performed normally on the famous faces and on the recognition part of the famous events test. They also revealed that in LV the retrograde deficit showed a characteristic temporal gradient in that more distant memories were spared. In both cases there was a more subtle problem with the dating of recent personal memories and public events. The qualitative difference in the memories produced during TGA, which lacked the normal richness and detail of personally experienced episodes, was also striking.

These findings have relevance to the debate about the nature of the memory deficit in permanent amnesia. There have been two major schools of thought concerning the basic cognitive deficit. One school has sought to explain both anterograde and retrograde amnesia in terms of a defect in the storage of memories (Milner et al., 1968; Cohen and Squire, 1981); the other school favours an underlying problem in the retrieval of memories (see Weiskrantz, 1985). Central to distinguishing between these theories is the way in which they account for retrograde amnesia, particularly since the extent of the deficit may depend upon the cause of the amnesic syndrome (Hirst, 1982; Weiskrantz, 1985; Parkin, 1984). Damage to midline structures in the temporal lobe, as in the celebrated patient HM who underwent bilateral temporal lobectomy in an attempt to treat his intractable epilepsy (before the importance of these areas was realized), produces a retrograde amnesia limited to a short period before the damage (Milner et al., 1968). By contrast, patients with diencephalic damage, as in alcoholic Korsakoff's disease, have an extensive amnesia covering many decades of their lives and particularly affecting the recall of more recent memories (Albert et al., 1979; Cohen and Squire, 1981; Butters, 1985). Those in favour of a storage defect argue that the temporally graded pattern in Korsakoff's disease is not an inherent feature of the amnesic syndrome, but that it must be due either to a progressive defect in laying down (encoding) of new memories during the

20 or so years of alcohol abuse that precede the onset of the amnesic syndrome (Butters and Albert, 1982; Squire and Cohen, 1982) or that it results from additional alcohol-induced brain damage (Squire, 1986). Those in favour of a retrieval hypothesis have argued that the temporally graded loss reflects a fundamental property of memory storage such that older memories are, by nature, more resistant to retrieval deficits. Elucidation of the extent and pattern of remote memory deficit in other conditions is clearly important to this debate.

The retrograde amnesia in TGA, which may be extensive – as in patient LV – must be due to a temporary retrieval deficit since memory for past events recovers as the TGA attack recedes. This finding supports the idea that the age of memories is an important property, which under certain circumstances is functionally relevant to their retrieval, as originally suggested by Ribot (1882).

It is interesting to speculate that a defect in dating and ordering past events may underlie the retrieval deficit in TGA. Other authors have commented upon defective chronological judgement during and immediately after TGA (Caffarra et al., 1981; Regard and Landis, 1984; Gallassi et al., 1986). In my two patients it was the most consistent abnormality on the famous events test; they were able to distinguish real from fictitious events but were severely impaired when dating these events. Moreover, they showed a similar difficulty in estimating the age of personal memories. It is at present unclear whether temporal disorganization is merely a more sensitive and therefore easily detected indicator of a general disorder of retrieval, or whether a primary defect in memory sequencing could radically impair other aspects of retrieval.

Can the combination of neuropsychological deficits observed during TGA be brought together under a single unifying 'core deficit'? The normal immediate memory in these patients shows that material can be registered normally. The permanent amnesic gap indicates a defect in the process required for the acquisition of memory, and the reversible retrograde amnesia implies a retrieval deficit. One unifying possibility is that the transfer of data into and out of long-term storage from working (short-term) memory is interrupted by TGA. The relationship between anterograde and retrograde amnesia is clearly important in this regard. These two features are always present during the attack, but whereas the patients had an equally profound anterograde deficit the extent of retrograde loss varied considerably. This finding is not easily reconciled with the view that a single cognitive deficit underlies both anterograde and retrograde amnesia. Rather, the processes of laying down new and retrieving memories, while functionally and even anatomically closely related, appear dissociable. Clinical studies of patients with permanent memory disorders have also suggested that anterograde and retrograde amnesia may occasionally occur independently of each other (Goldberg et al., 1982; Kapur et al., 1986).

Recovery from TGA

During the recovery phase there is progressive return of distant memories followed by more recent ones. This pattern of 'shrinking retrograde' has been observed following closed head injury (Benson and Beschwind, 1967; Russell, 1971) and must provide an important clue about the brain's storage of remote memories.

Following recovery from TGA, patients are left with a dense amnesic gap for the duration of the attack. In addition, there is a short permanent retrograde amnesia of between one half and two hours covering the period before the apparent onset of the attack. Fisher (1982), who was one of the first authors to describe the syndrome, has also noted that patients often have a permanent but brief retrograde memory loss. This permanent loss of memory for events before TGA suggests that after memories are first laid down there is a period of active remodelling (or consolidation) which lasts for some hours when they are susceptible to erasure.

Recovery of anterograde memory function after TGA superficially appears to be rapid with a subjective return to normality within 24 hours. However, it is clear that sub-clinical impairment persists for some time (Caffarra et al., 1981; Regard and Landis, 1984; Hodges and Ward, 1989). Deficits in both verbal and non-verbal anterograde memory can be consistently detected at 24 hours and some patients are still clearly impaired at seven days. Non-verbal memory appears to recover more rapidly than verbal memory. In a few patients mild deficits in the latter have been detected for several weeks post-attack.

Finally, we should not neglect the humanistic implications of these observations. The sudden and profound cessation of memory function during TGA illustrates the point made, much more eloquently, by Luis Bunuel about the essential role of normal memory for the integrity of human cognition and personality. We are, after all, largely what our memory makes us.

References

Albert, M. S., Butters, N. and Levin, J. (1979) Temporal gradients in the retrograde amnesia of patients with alcoholic Korsakoff's disease. *Archives of Neurology*, 36, 211–16.

Baddeley, A. D. and Warrington, E. K. (1970) Amnesia and the distinction between long- and short-term memory. *Journal of Verbal Learning and Verbal Behaviour*, 9, 176–89.

Benson, D. F. and Geschwind, N. (1967) Shrinking retrograde amnesia. *Journal of Neurology, Neurosurgery and Psychiatry*, 30, 539–44.

Butters, N. (1985) Korsakoff's syndrome: some unresolved issues concerning aetiology, neuropathology and cognitive deficits. *Journal of Clinical and Experimental Neuropsychology*, 7, 181–210.

Butters, N. and Albert, M. S. (1982) Processes underlying failures to recall remote events. In L. S. Cermak (ed.) *Human Memory and Amnesia*, pp. 257–74. Hillsdale, NJ: Lawrence Erlbaum.

Caffarra, P., Moretti, G., Mazzucchi, A. and Parma, M. (1981) Neuropsychological testing during a transient global amnesia episode and its follow-up. *Acta Neurologica Scandinavica*, 63, 44–50.

Caplan, L. R. (1985) Transient global amnesia. In P. J. Vinken, G. W. Bruyn and H. L. Klawans (eds) *Handbook of Clinical Neurology*, vol. 1 (45), pp. 205–18. Amsterdam: Elsevier.

Cohen, N. J. and Squire, L. R. (1981) Retrograde amnesia and remote memory impairment. *Neuropsychologia*, 19, 337–56.

Crowell, G. F., Stump, D. A., Biller, J., McHenry, L. C. and Toole, J. F. (1984) The transient global amnesia-migraine connection. *Archives of Neurology*, 41, 75–9.

Fisher, C. M. (1982) Transient global amnesia. Precipitating activities and other observations. *Archives of Neurology*, 39, 605–8.

Fisher, C. M. and Adams, R. D. (1964) Transient global amnesia. *Acta Neurologica Scandinavica*, 40 (suppl. 9), 1–83.

Gallassi, R., Lorusso, S. and Stracciari, A. (1986) Neuropsychological findings during a transient global amensia attack and its follow-up. *Italian Journal of Neurological Science*, 7, 45–9.

Goldberg, E., Hughes, J. E. O., Mattis, S. and Antin, S. P. (1982) Isolated retrograde amnesia: different aetiologies, same mechanism? *Cortex*, 18, 459–62.

Hinge, H. H., Jensen, T. S., Kjaer, M., Marquardsen, J. and Olivarius, B. de F (1986) The prognosis of transient global amnesia: results of a multicenter study. *Archives of Neurology*, 43, 673–6.

Hirst, W. (1982) The amnesic syndrome: descriptions and explanations. *Psychological Bulletin*, 91, 435–60.

Hodges, J. R. (1991) *Transient Amnesia, Clinical and Neuropsychological Aspects*. London: Baillière Tindall.

Hodges, J. R. and Ward, C. D. (1989) Observations during transient global amnesia: a behavioural and neuropsychological study of five cases. *Brain*, 112, 595–620.

Hodges, J. R. and Warlow, C. P. (1990a) The aetiology of transient global amnesia: a case-control study of 114 cases with prospective follow-up. *Brain*, 113, 639–57.

Hodges, J. R. and Warlow, C. P. (1990b) Transient amnesia: towards a classification. A study of 153 cases. *Journal of Neurology, Neurosurgery and Psychiatry*, 53, 834–43.

Kapur, N., Heath, P., Meudell, P. and Kennedy, P. (1986) Amnesia can facilitate memory performance: evidence from a patient with dissociated retrograde amnesia. *Neuropsychologia*, 24, 215–22.

Kritchevsky, M., Squire, L. R. and Zouzounis, J. A. (1988) The amnesia of transient global amnesia. *Neurology*, 38, 213–19.

Logan, W. and Sherman, D. G. (1983) Transient global amnesia. *Stroke*, 14, 1005–7.

Markowitsch, H. J. (1990) *Transient Global Amnesia and Related Disorders*. Bern: Hogrefe and Huber.

Miller, J. W., Petersen, R. C., Metter, E. J., Millikan, C. H. and Yanagihara, T. (1987) Transient global amnesia: clinical characteristics and prognosis. *Neurology*, 37, 733–7.

Milner, B. (1971) Interhemispheric differences in the localization of psychological processes in man. *British Medical Bulletin*, 27, 272–7.

Milner, B., Corkin, S. and Teuber, H-L. (1968) Further analysis of the hippocampal amnesic syndrome – 14 year follow-up study of HM. *Neuropsychologia*, 6, 215–34.

Osterrieth, P. (1944) Le test de copie d'une figure complexe. *Archives de Psychologie*, 30, 205–20.

Oxbury, J. M. and Oxbury, S. M. (1989) Neuropsychology, memory and hippocampal pathology. In E. H. Reynolds and M. R. Trimble (eds) *The Bridge between Neurology and Psychiatry*. Edinburgh: Churchill Livingstone.

Parkin, A. J. (1984) Amnesic syndrome: a lesion-specific disorder? *Cortex*, 20, 479–508.

Regard, M. and Landis, T. (1984) Transient global amnesia: neuropsychological dysfunction during attack and recovery in two 'pure' cases. *Journal of Neurology, Neurosurgery and Psychiatry*, 47, 668–72.

Ribot, T. (1882) *Diseases of Memory*. New York: Appleton-Century-Crofts.

Russell, W. R. (1971) *The Traumatic Amnesias*. Oxford: Oxford University Press.

Sagar, H. J., Cohen, N. J., Sullivan, E. V., Corkin, S. and Growden, J. H. (1988) Remote memory function in Alzheimer's disease and Parkinson's disease. *Brain*, 111, 185–206.

Shimamura, A. P. and Squire, L. R. (1986) Memory and metamemory: a study of feeling-of-knowing-phenomenon in amnesic patients. *Journal of Experimental Psychology: Learning Memory and Cognition*, 12, 452–60.

Smith, M. L. and Milner, B. (1981) The role of the right hippocampus in the recall of spatial location. *Neuropsychologia*, 19, 781–93.

Squire, L. R. (1986) Mechanisms of memory. *Science*, 232, 1612–19.

Squire, L. R. and Cohen, N. J. (1982) Remote memory retrograde amnesia and the neuropsychology of memory. In L. S. Cermak (ed.) *Human Memory and Amnesia*. Hillside, NJ: Lawrence Erlbaum.

Weintraub, S. and Mesulam, M. M. (1985) Mental state assessment of young and elderly adults in behavioural neurology. In M. M. Mesulam (ed.) *Principles of*

Behavioural Neurology, pp. 71–123. Philadelphia: FA Davis.

Weiskrantz, L. (1985) On issues and theories of the human amnesic syndrome. In N. M. Weinberger, J. L. McGaugh and G. Lynch (eds) *Memory Systems of the Brain*, pp. 380–415. New York: The Guildford Press.

Wilson, R. S., Koller, W. and Kelly, M. P. (1980) The amnesia of transient global amnesia. *Journal of Clinical Neuropsychology*, 2, 259–66.

Zola-Morgan, S., Cohen, J. J. and Squire, L. R. (1983) Recall of remote episodic memory in amnesia. *Neuropsychologia*, 21, 487–500.

15

Adult commissurotomy: separating the left from the right side of the brain

Dahlia W. Zaidel

One bright summer day, during the Depression years in the American south-west, James, a normal, happy 14-year-old, was on his way home with a bundle of dirty clothes tucked under his right arm. Patiently he waited for the traffic light to change before he crossed the street. But just then an elderly man, oblivious of the traffic signal, drove straight through; the car hit James in the legs, and he fell down on the hot asphalt road. This was a hit-and-run accident. He lost consciousness but strangers took him to a nearby clinic where he received treatment for injuries, including a head wound. When he recovered someone took him home by car. He was able to resume normal activities a few days afterwards. Unfortunately, his brain suffered irreversible damage at that time, although the serious consequences of this would not become obvious until four years later. Because of it he would undergo a dramatic type of neurosurgery and would serve as an important subject in some of the most intriguing studies ever conducted in the annals of brain research. They would shed light on the workings of the left and right hemispheres of the brain and would have far-reaching implications for psychology, education, the arts, philosophy and medicine.

The left and right sides of the brain

One of the most fascinating areas in brain research is hemispheric specialization. Why the thinking part of the human brain, the cerebrum, or cortex, is made up of structurally similar but functionally different left and right hemispheres, each with its own unique cognitive abilities, and why language is specialized mainly in the left and visuospatial abilities in the right hemisphere, are questions which have intrigued neurologists and neuropsychologists for the last hundred years. There is evidence for some functional asymmetry even in certain non-human species, including songbirds, rats, chicks and monkeys, but the highest and most developed range of hemispheric specialization of functions is seen only in humans (Glick, 1985). Thus, hemispheric specialization is part and parcel of what it means to be human. The ability to speak, to write poetry or to paint pictures reflects this cognitive specialization within each hemisphere and yet, at the same time, the two hemispheres are designed by mother nature to maintain easy communication: they are anatomically richly connected to each other with the largest neuroanatomical tracts of fibres in the entire brain (Sperry, 1961). The largest of these tracts is called the corpus callosum and it features prominently in our story.

Although hemispheric specialization occurs in some lower animals, no animal besides man has the capacity to control much of the range of organismic behaviours from either side of the brain. In other words, each hemisphere by itself is distinctly and distinctively human. Indeed, our behaviour reflects the fact that each hemisphere has its own sensations, perceptions and problem-solving strategies and, most importantly, each has its own unique organization of long-term semantic memory or knowledge of the world (Zaidel, D. W., 1990b). This duality is illustrated most dramatically in the split-brain syndrome described below but it is also likely to be present in each one of us. Functional hemispheric asymmetry may account for many human conflicts, ambivalences and contradictions. It may eventually explain how we can believe something and its opposite at one and the same time: each belief may be anchored in cognitive representations of an opposite hemisphere.

Until the mid-1960s scientists did not have a good experimental human preparation for studying the dynamics of hemispheric specialization, that is, for teasing apart the components of cognitive specialization of each hemisphere from the components of cooperation between them. A unique opportunity to tackle these questions was provided when two California neurosurgeons, Joseph Bogen and Philip Vogel, surgically separated the two hemispheres of selected patients in order to alleviate otherwise intractable epilepsy (Bogen and Vogel, 1962). Following surgery, these commissurotomy, or so-called split-brain, patients were studied intensively in Roger Sperry's psychobiology laboratory at Caltech, the famous scientific institute in Southern California (Sperry et al., 1969). The investigations confirmed what was known about the cognitive specialization of each hemisphere from studies of patients with unilateral brain damage due to stroke, gunshot wounds or tumour (Paterson and Zangwill, 1944; Warrington, 1975; Hecaen and Albert, 1978; De Renzi, 1982), but also enhanced and added much new knowledge that could not have been determined from the study of unilaterally brain-damaged patients alone.

Some of the scientific areas to which the split-brain studies added the most new knowledge are perhaps language, memory, spatial perception and motor control (Bogen and Gazzaniga, 1965; Preilowski, 1972; Levy, 1974; Nebes, 1974; Zaidel and Sperry, 1974; Plourde and Sperry, 1982). The most important neuroanatomical contribution of these studies was the elucidation of the function of the forebrain commissures, and particularly the corpus callosum (see figure 15.1), namely, that they serve as communication channels for sensory and cognitive information between the two hemispheres (Sperry and Stamm, 1957). The investigations confirmed that in right-handers the main functional representation for speech, writing, reading or language comprehension are still in the left hemisphere, as has been known since Paul Broca's discoveries in the mid-nineteenth century. But left hemisphere specialization for language was not as exclusive as had been presupposed. The extent to which the right hemisphere was capable of such language functions was now mapped out in detail for the first time (Zaidel, E., 1977, 1978, 1979). With memory, it became clear that sectioning of the commissures did not significantly impair what was already long-term memory, that is, for engrams laid down before surgery. But for the newly laid engram the two hemispheres must be completely connected on a cortical level if memory functions are to be carried out normally. Memory for some new materials ranging from words to stories appeared especially dependent on such cortical connections (Zaidel, D. W., 1990a).

The story of James

The young teenager described above had grammar school education and most likely had average intelligence. Because money was scarce then, boys as young as he had to work, so they left school at an early age. But they found time to play. He was one of the leading baseball players on the city's junior team. Before the accident and even afterwards, he had

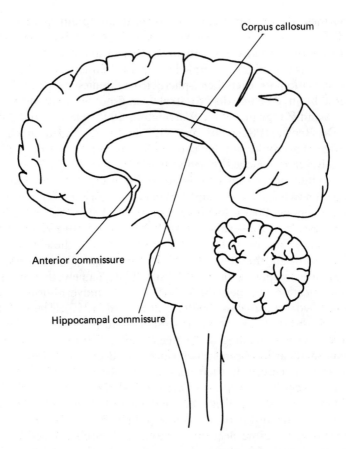

Figure 15.1 Schematic medial section of the human brain showing the three forebrain commissures. In complete commissurotomy all three are sectioned to alleviate drug-resistant epilepsy.

several home runs to his credit and was known for being a left-handed batter. He was and remains right-handed for writing, eating and all other major activities. His team won a local tournament and the prize was a coveted all-expenses-paid trip to the Yellowstone National Park.

Quite suddenly, when he was 18 he suffered his first epileptic seizure. 'I'll never forget the day on which I had my first fit', he recalls now:

> I was sitting in the kitchen one morning with my mother and two nephews. They were sitting drinking coffee and I was sitting there too. All of a sudden everything started going back and forth. I was scared, I didn't know what had happened. And then I keeled over, and that's when I had my first

epileptic seizure. They told me afterwards I was shaking all over. It took me several hours to get back to normal. I couldn't remember very clearly and I had an awful headache on the left side of my head.

This was the beginning of habitual epilepsy and, according to medical opinion, the cause was the brain damage suffered four years earlier in the car accident.

Medication was prescribed to control seizures and for a few years afterwards it helped and he suffered only about one seizure per week. He was able to work and was even drafted into the army when the United States entered the Second World War, but he was discharged when officers witnessed a convulsion soon after he was enlisted. Then, gradually, the rate with which the seizures occurred increased to a couple per week. Medication was altered but relief was minimal. By then he had moved to Los Angeles where two well-known neurosurgeons J. Bogen and P. Vogel were eventually to perform radical surgery on his brain.

Life as an epileptic with *grand mal* seizures was 'not easy to say the least.' In the morning he could predict that he would have a convulsion later on in the day. 'I just did not feel right,' he says. He stayed indoors on such days. On good days, he worked in a lumber yard, lifting and hauling wood. However, even this activity was heavily curtailed when the level of medication was increased to control the ever more frequent seizures.

His family reports that the epilepsy did not affect his verbal skills, and that reasoning and problem-solving went unchanged. This would include such diverse abilities as counting change at the store and following a conversation. Finding his way around his neighbourhood did not pose a serious problem either and this memory for continuing or past events remained normal. Unfortunately, no formal record of his cognitive or memory abilities by way of standardized neuropsychological tests is available. At the same time, he did become short-tempered and had frequent nightmares. He became increasingly dependent and needed the personal attention of family members. With each seizure he lost several hours of normal daily living because when one was over he needed time to recover physical, cognitive and emotional balance. His interaction with women was minimal and he never married, but as far as can be determined this was not due to sexual dysfunction.

With the years, seizures became so frequent – there were several a day, everyday – that they were dangerous, indeed life-threatening. Finally, at the age of 38, a last resort procedure was applied, namely, a surgical intervention called complete cerebral commissurotomy. This consisted of separating the left and right cerebral hemispheres of the brain by sectioning longitudinally the forebrain commissures, those large tracts of fibres that connect the two hemispheres. The rationale for the surgery was to restrict the spread of abnormal electrical activity from one side to the other. Otherwise, epileptic foci on one side activated foci on the other through the forebrain commissures and the foci reinforced each other until *grand mal* seizures occurred (Bogen, 1969). It was hoped that following the surgery epilepsy within each hemisphere could be controlled with medication. This, in fact, is what happened. He has been virtually seizure-free for 25 years now and for many years off medication altogether.

What is epilepsy?

Epilepsy is a neurological condition which reflects a long-known type of brain dysfunction. 'Fits', convulsions or seizures are the result of abnormal bioelectrical or biochemical neuronal discharges which interfere with normal brain activity and may lead to disturbance in movement, sensation and even consciousness. The range of normal interruption may be very brief or quite prolonged and may result in a life-threatening medical condition. About one in 20 people experience an epileptic seisure in their lifetime but only about 1 in 200 or 300 (estimates vary) may have several seizures.

In some cases, anti-convulsant drugs alone do not control the seizures and surgery must be considered as a therapeutic alternative. Clinicians look for a 'focus' or the source of diseased tissue in the brain whence the abnormal bioelectrical activity emanates. If both the clinical and physiological evidence point to a consistent focus then it is possible to excise the part surgically. If, on the other hand, there is no clear-cut localization of the source and the patient is diagnosed as having generalized convulsions, another type of surgery must be considered. The commissurotomy surgery in which the two hemispheres of the brain are disconnected is one such procedure.

The surgery

The commissurotomy operation is a last resort step in cases where the patient reaches a state of *status epilepticus*, suffering from as many as 50 seizures a day. The surgery that James underwent – he was one of a group of 20 operated on by the same neurosurgical team – is called complete commissurotomy because the surgical section includes the corpus callosum, an anatomical structure containing about 200 million fibres, as well as the hippocampal and the anterior commissures (see figure 15.1). The surgery effectively separates the thinking part of the brain into two halves, the left and the right hemispheres, and makes it possible to study directly the competence of each in various tasks as well as the performance of the two hemispheres together now that the cortical connections between them is severed. The latter allows us to learn about subcortical functional integration. What is most important is that each half serves as an experimental control or baseline for the other. Thus, unlike any other neurological preparation, here the two are equated for age, sex, education, economic status, and so on.

Those abilities which are now considered to be specialized in the left hemisphere include reading, speaking, writing, logical and analytic problem-solving strategies, whereas those in the right include face recognition, spatial perception, figural unification and global or wholistic thinking strategies. Yet, while we have learned quite a lot about the functional asymmetries themselves, from split-brain patients and normal subjects, the dynamics of hemispheric cooperation in the normal brain still elude us, despite widespread scientific effort in many laboratories throughout the world. At the same time, from the split-brain patients we have learned that certain material, for instance memory for stories and knowledge of where one is, is dependent on normal cortical connections between the two hemispheres (Zaidel, D. W., 1990a).

The aftermath

Immediately after surgery

As soon as the effects of the anaesthesia wore off, a period of mutism followed and it lasted for three days. James could not talk to the nurses, family members or the surgeons. There were no seizures. He could walk and eat. Language comprehension appeared intact as well. Recognition of family members was normal. In fact, he did not report feeling strange in any way (Bogen, 1976).

Complete section of the forebrain commissures sometimes leads to short-term mutism which may last from three days to four months. At the same time, comprehension seems to remain normal. The reasons for this are not well understood. It may or may not be associated with the commissures themselves but it may be aggravated in patients with discordant dominance for manual control and speech. James is most probably not one of those. The mutism may be the first example of the dependence of language functions in the intact brain on the integrity of the commissures and on right hemisphere contribution to language. Yet,

James's left hemisphere, and that of the other split-brain patients, does not appear to be linguistically deficient in any way, at least as measured by various clinical tests. It would appear then that the surgery renders the left hemisphere linguistically isolated whereas in the normal brain the left side may interact continuously with the right. For example, there is a suggestion, based on studies of neurological patients with unilateral hemispheric damage, but not confirmed at all in split-brain patients, that humour appreciation is a right-hemisphere function.

Daily life

The surgery was successful; it alleviated seizures and saved James's life. He resumed daily activities as soon as it was medically safe to do so. At night, he no longer suffered nightmares and, in fact, reported that he stopped dreaming altogether. This was noticeable because before surgery he could usually recount the contents of his dreams. Verifying James's assertion that he was not dreaming at night has always been difficult without rigorous scientific observation. He was never studied under the careful conditions used in a sleep laboratory. But there were no reports by family members or by himself that he felt tired in the morning or that he did not sleep throughout the night. And we do not know whether or not James really did not dream or just could not report the content of dreams verbally. This is quite interesting. For a while, in some scientific circles, there was a debate about whether or not dreaming is lateralized in the brain, whether it takes place in the right hemisphere alone. The fact that James was unable to report having dreams was taken to support this hypothesis. Otherwise, with speaking lateralized to the left hemisphere, he should have been able to do so. In fact, however, there is no conclusive evidence as of now on what role hemispheric specialization plays in dreaming. James can still provide critical clues to this scientific puzzle.

Formal testing

After surgery James's intelligence was measured formally and his IQ was recorded as 90, ten points below the average IQ in the general population. By comparison, formal testing of his memory was 30 points below the average memory level in the population, and 20 points below his IQ. These results supported informal observations, namely, intelligence was unchanged but memory was.

Considering what was cut

From anatomical considerations alone, one would expect that sectioning these particular large tracts of nerve fibres in the brain would result in major disruption of motor coordination, personality, old memories and daily activities even if seizures ceased or decreased in frequency. In fact, the most remarkable outcome of the surgery is that it does not appear to affect personality, habits, sense of humour, motor coordination or old skills. James can still ride a bike, swim and play the piano, all skills learned in childhood. The only time that the two halves of the brain are seen to have their own unique cognitive styles is when the patients are examined in the laboratory under special testing conditions designed specifically to tease hemispheric differences apart. Otherwise, old and established modes of behaviour are assumed to be either carried out by one hemisphere or are coordinated by structures which are located in deeper, unseparated, parts of the brain (Sperry, 1990).

The changes

What became impaired in daily life

Following the surgery, topographical orientation appeared impaired. James now has difficulty in finding his way around, even in a familiar environment. He can be hopelessly lost in the laboratory area where he has been studied for years, for instance. 'I am always going in one door and coming out of another. What makes it worse is that I know I've been there before and yet I still turn the wrong way. If you put me in a new place, I forget it. I'll never find my way out, like those corridors over there at UCLA.' But this never compares with gross deficits in topographical orientation observed in some patients with unilateral damage in the posterior part of the right hemisphere (spatial agnosia) (De Renzi, 1982).

Memory in daily life is affected as well but is not severe enough to be considered amnesia (Huppert, 1981). Family members observe frequent inability to find objects, remember appointments or recall events. Over and over again, scientists have noticed that James and the other patients tell the same anecdotes many times to the same audience, including the same punch lines and jokes. Some have exceptional difficulty in relocating a parked car, an ability which requires both memory and topographical orientation. The latter is an ability specialized in the right hemisphere. The fact that split-brain patients have a deficit in a spatial orientation may be taken to mean that either the surgery disrupts the functional routes by which the right hemisphere normally conveys information to the left hemisphere regarding this function, or that during normal activity both hemispheres are involved in spatial orientation. This may be a good example of bihemispheric cooperation in the normal brain.

Recalling the argument made above regarding linguistic independence gained by the left hemisphere after disconnection from the right, we may infer that when there is a strong hemispheric specialization for a particular ability, as in the case for spatial perception or orientation, the disconnection itself would not lead to competence for the task in the other hemisphere. Indeed, we have observed repeatedly James's poor performance in free right-hand execution of skills that require memory for visual figures, e.g. for drawing two-dimensional shapes representing three-dimensional shapes, and so on (Bogen and Gazzaniga, 1965; Bogen, 1990). The disconnected left hemisphere has never acquired spatial skills that are comparable so that of the right, just as the right hemisphere has never acquired language skills comparable to that of the left.

An interesting phenomenon

'My left hand has a life of its own sometimes. The left hand comes out and slaps my right hand. I may turn the water on with my right hand and then the left comes out and turns it off. Or when I smoke, the left hand would take the cigarette out of my mouth and put it out. Sometimes, I have no control over it and I don't understand why this happens.' This was true only for a few months after surgery but milder aspects of the manual conflict can last longer, in some cases as long as several years. In traditional neurology, what James was complaining about is called the 'strange hand syndrome', and it is usually observed following strokes in several parts of the cortex, including part of the corpus callosum. There is no ready explanation for the phenomenon. It is noteworthy that here it is the non-dominant left, not the right, hand that 'perpetrates' these 'undesirable' acts. Split-brain patients report that on occasion they had the intention and purpose in mind when their normally dominant right hand executed an act but that the left hand was not behaving in accordance with their intention. This implies that when they describe the intentions in their mind, the patients actually refer to the mind in the left hemisphere. But this dramatic illustration of a motoric conflict need not truly reflect a conflict between two personalities, one in the left and one in the right hemisphere. Given that the dramatic features are transient, the conflict probably reflects some imbalance in motor coordination (Zaidel, P. and Sperry, 1977). At the same time, it also incorporates an element that can be observed many years after surgery, namely, left hemisphere dominance in ordinary behaviour in these patients.

Laboratory tests: dual semantic systems

To a casual, or even an astute, observer walking into the psychobiology laboratory at Caltech (California Institute of Technology, Pasadena) or the psychology laboratory at UCLA (University of California, Los Angeles), where a commissurotomy patient is being tested, the man talking to the examiner would appear normal in every way. His verbal discourse is fluent, his gestures are appropriate, his jokes are to the point. When he stands up his gait is normal, his eyes are focused and hardly anything seems to be amiss. But if the observer were to linger on through a testing session what is in store for him is a most fascinating example of the working of the mind.

Naming objects via the tactual modality When a small toy cup is placed in his left hand out of sight, James is unable to name it correctly. But if it is placed in the right hand, it is named immediately. The anatomical connections are such that sensory neuroanatomical projections from the left hand are represented contralaterally in the right hemisphere, where there is no speech specialization and consequently no way to show knowledge through a linguistic output. The main control for the right hand is in the left hemisphere, where language is specialized. If the same object is palpated by the left hand of a normal right-hander, then correct naming of the object is immediate and fluent because the corpus callosum is intact and allows a transfer from the area of sensory representation of the left hand in the right hemisphere to the speech centre in the left hemisphere. With James, however, there is no communication between sensory centres in the right hemisphere and speech and language centres in the left hemisphere, hence the incorrect or absent verbal label for the toy cup (Sperry, 1974).

The inability to provide verbal labels does not mean that there is no semantic or knowledge system in the right hemisphere. Failure to name correctly does not mean that the right hemisphere lacks knowledge of the meaning of objects in the world. In fact, the existence of such a store of knowledge in the right hemisphere can be demonstrated in several ways (Zaidel, D. W., 1986, 1990b).

The same experimental paradigm described above for the left hand feeling objects out of view still applies: first, he can show that he can recognize the very same object in an array of other objects also hidden from view. This shows that perception is intact. Then, he can recognize by touch which other objects belong to the same category as the cup, and which ones do not. Thus, he has knowledge of concepts. Similarly, he can match one cup with another cup having a different shape. And along the same lines, he shows his semantic knowledge by demonstrating the use of the cup by holding it correctly. And under special viewing conditions, in lateralized vision, his episodic memory can be demonstrated when he recognizes which cup of several shown is his very own. (Knowledge or sense of history is described below, in the visual modality.) Yet, throughout these tests, he is unable to name the cup correctly even once. This latter point, by the way, is one important piece of evidence that the left hemisphere is not involved in the performance, that the information did not somehow 'leak' over to the left hemisphere through subcortical pathways.

Another important demonstration for semantic knowledge in the right hemisphere: with his hand still out of view, James can signal with his fingers the sum of two numerals which had been placed in his hand one at a time. So he puts four fingers up to show the sum of a plastic numeral three and a plastic numeral one. In this fashion he can go on to show his right hemisphere knowledge for sums under ten (Sperry, 1974).

Naming pictures or words presented visually   The anatomical connections between the eyes and the brain are such that the left visual half-field is represented in the right hemisphere and the right visual half-field is represented in the left hemisphere (see figure 15.2). This is true for either eye. Thus, when a picture of a bird is shown quickly in the left half of visual space of split-brain patients, they would be unable to name it or they would name it incorrectly. But the same picture shown in the patient's right half of visual space is named correctly and immediately. A normal person would have no problem in naming the picture in either visual field. When the forebrain commissures are intact, what the right hemisphere sees is transferred to the left hemisphere where the production of the name is controlled, but when the commissures are absent, each hemisphere is on its own. The same applies to words printed in the two visual half-fields. However, with the information restricted to the right hemisphere alone, a split-brain patient may still be able to recognize the correct written name of the picture which he has been unable to name out loud. He will still be unable to name it but may be able to indicate its meaning non-verbally with the left hand out of view. This indicates that there is some language representation in the right hemisphere as well, although the main language centres are represented in the left.

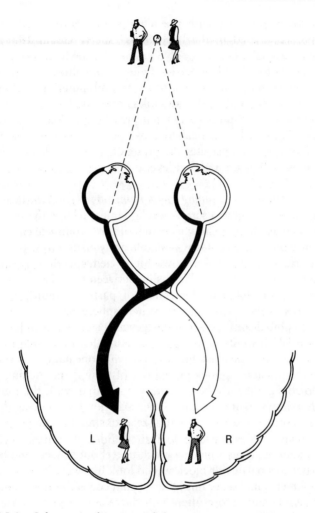

Figure 15.2 Schematic diagram of the primary visual system. With the eyes focused on a central fixation point, a figure shown in the left visual half-field, the man, is processed initially in the visual areas of the right hemisphere (R). Similarly, a figure shown in the right visual half-field, the woman, is processed initially in the left hemisphere (L).

To know the past is to know oneself Knowledge of history and the past in his right hemisphere can be tested with non-verbal responses. This can be done by first showing him historical figures, configurations used as cultural symbols, and pictures of family members or of himself, and then asking him to show preference. This is done by restricting the picture to only one hemisphere at a time and by requiring a 'thumbs up' or a 'thumbs down' response with the left thumb. Thus, in an important experiment conducted in the late 1970s (Sperry et al., 1979), James responded positively to pictures of Churchill, Kennedy, Roosevelt, family members, and other highly valued individuals or cultural symbols. At the same time he indicated negative attitude (thumb pointing downward) to pictures of Hitler, Stalin, the swastika, and similar negative images. When the same visual information was presented to the left hemisphere, responses were nearly identical to those provided for the right hemisphere. All of this demonstrates the presence of knowledge of one's past on a local as well as on a global level.

Special cognitive tests showing right hemisphere specialization   If we place a plastic arc behind a screen and let James feel it with one hand at a time and then ask him to show us which of three complete circles the arc was taken from, he would do so significantly better with the left than with the right hand. This shows right hemisphere superiority for knowing the correct spatial relationship between the arc and the circle or for knowing the global configuration of parts belonging to a whole (Nebes, 1974, 1990). The same right hemisphere superiority for apprehending the global configuration (the 'gestalt') can be shown for different types of stimuli. If we show James a symmetrical visual design with a part missing from it, and then ask him to show with one hand at a time which one of three possible options placed out of view is the missing part, he would do so significantly better with the left than with the right hand. Again, this shows right hemisphere specialization for knowing the global design and understanding the spatial relations among the parts but this time the relationships are also logical! (Zaidel, P. and Sperry, 1973). Another example: if he is given a block to feel out of view and he has to decide what this particular block would look like were it to be displayed as a two-dimensional diagram, James would correctly choose the correct diagram significantly more often with the left than with the right hand (Levy, 1974, 1990).

A fine point   All of the tasks described above rely on non-verbal input and responses. Otherwise we would not be able to gain access to the right hemisphere and its non-verbal cognitive system. These illustrate the fine art of testing split-brain patients. The credit for inspiring and guiding the design of appropriate tests for the right kind of questions was provided by Roger Sperry of Caltech. Indeed, in 1981 Sperry shared the Nobel Prize in physiology and medicine for this work.

Summary of essential features of the hemispheric disconnection syndrome   Section of the forebrain commissures in higher mammals, both animals and humans, results in multiple deficits of interhemispheric integration. The split-brain patients have displayed what has come to be known as the syndrome of hemispheric disconnection. This includes an inability to name verbally, or in writing, while blindfolded, the names of objects felt in the left hand, and pictures projected to the left visual half-field. Similarly, patients are unable to compare pictures flashed simultaneously to the two visual half-fields. In short, the patients show absence of sensory transfer of information from one hemisphere to the other, symptoms which can be observed dramatically even 25 years after surgery.

Traditional conceptualization of the hemispheres and the split-brain lesson

Up until the time of the split-brain studies, hemispheric specialization was viewed as an either/or state of affairs, with certain functions specialized only in the left hemisphere and certain other functions only in the right. Conclusions were based on studies of patients with unilateral focal damage with all the limitations that go with such patients. Functional representation in the two hemispheres came to be viewed as complementary, that is, the mind as a whole comprised left plus right functions but without offering deeper evolutionary reasons for the particular pattern of functional segregation (Milner, 1958, 1980). The prevalent common characterization was, and still is to some extent, 'verbal' = left hemisphere, while 'non-verbal' = right hemisphere. This normally referred to the material used as stimuli so that processing verbal stimuli, words or stories was shown to be impaired following damage to the left hemisphere whereas non-verbal, meaningless shapes or hard-to-visualize patterns were impaired with damage to the right hemisphere (Newcombe and Ratcliffe, 1975; Warrington, 1975). This material-specificity approach eventually gave way to process-specificity, an approach which stressed the kind of mental strategy specialized in each side, that is, 'analytic, logical' = left and 'global, gestalt' = right (Levy, 1990). The lesson of the split-brain studies has led the way to another heuristic conceptualization of the two hemispheres, namely, as separate semantic systems: each hemisphere has its own internal organization of long-term knowledge with which to interpret reality whether of everyday life or of problem-solving tasks in the laboratory (Zaidel, D. W., 1983, 1990b).

New conceptualization of the two hemispheres

In order for the mind-in-the-brain to give meaning to sensory information, a memory store of previous experiences must be available and accessible. Otherwise, sensory visual information is nothing but patches of light or colour and a collection of contours and changes, and auditory sensory information is nothing but a jumble of pitches and loudness. Psychologists believe that the past interacts with the present, and that actions or responses reflect what was stored earlier, that is, that perception is partly recognition.

The view proposed here is that each hemisphere has its own long-term memory store with which to interpret incoming information so that meaning can be achieved. Otherwise, how would we explain James's right hemisphere knowledge of what a cup is? Surely, knowing how to hold a cup correctly implies knowledge about the use of objects. Similarly, producing the sum of two plastic numerals, without even the help of a multiple-choice array where the correct answer is present, clearly indicates semantic knowledge (although some would argue that numerals are a separate system altogether).

The implication is that the left and right hemispheres, though they may be exposed to the same external experiences, form differently organized memory stores or deploy different retrieval strategies from these stores. And each is capable of extracting different information from the environment. Most importantly, this account applies not only to split-brain patients but to normal subjects as well.

Conclusion: duality in the normal brain

How can we show that the normal brain has two different systems of internal conceptual organization with which to understand reality, one in the left hemisphere and one in the right? James's brother is Paul. He is ten years younger, has never had epilepsy, has a family and leads a normal productive life. Like James, Paul is right-handed and he could serve as a useful control against which to compare the pattern of hemispheric specialization observed in James. This can be done by restricting sensory information and motor response to one hemisphere and measuring reaction time to quick tasks.

Concepts of natural categories   In effect we can 'split' Paul's brain with reaction time. Here is how we would do it: Paul sits in front of a screen, his chin resting on a chin-rest, his eyes fixed on a red dot in the centre of the screen. Behind the screen there is a projector operated by the experimenter. The experimenter (E) says, 'I am going to show you pictures, one at a time, and I want you to tell me by pressing a button whether or not each one is an example of a predesignated category.' Then E says, 'Ready.' Paul stabilizes his gaze on the dot, E says 'furniture' and a picture of an object is flashed briefly either to the left or the right of his fixation dot. The picture is quick, no more than 150 ms long, too quick to initiate an involuntary eye movement towards it. Because of the way the visual system works, if the picture of the object is flashed to the left of Paul's fixation, it will reach the right hemisphere first; if it is flashed to the right of the fixation dot, it will reach the left hemisphere first. This method is called tachistoscopic presentation, from the Greek 'quick view'. On the first trial, the category is 'furniture', the picture is of a chair, and the visual half-field of stimulation is the left. It takes Paul 600 ms to press the 'yes' button with his left index finger. A few trials later, E again says, 'furniture', and the picture is of a stove flashed quickly to the left visual half-field. This time it takes Paul 900 ms to press the 'yes' button.

The trials keep coming with E saying the names of five different categories, one per trial. Sometimes the answer is 'no' and sometimes 'yes'. When the results are analysed, the pattern of hemispheric responses reveals a right-hemisphere sensitivity to whether the picture represented common (typical) or rare (atypical) members of the designated category, while the left hemisphere shows no sensitivity to the level of typicality at all. Moreover, the right is quicker than the left to make decisions regarding typical members but slower than the left on the atypical members. The accuracy level reveals that each hemisphere knows the correct answer but the reaction time pattern suggests that they do so differently (Zaidel, D. W., 1987).

What kind of conceptual organization would be more sensitive to common than to rare members of natural categories? Would other types of stimuli show differences in hemispheric processing of that which is common as opposed to that which is unusual? What is the evolutionary advantage for having such separate systems? The answers lie in more experiments conducted in normal people with tachistoscopic presentations (Zaidel, D. W., 1988; Zaidel, D. W. and Frederick, 1988).

Paintings as stimuli   One set of experiments (Zaidel, D. W. and Kasher, 1989) capitalizes on naturalistic stimuli, namely, art works. Twenty-four paintings of which 12 were surrealistic (they portrayed impossible representations of objects in the known world) and 12 were realistic (they represented the known world correctly) were shown to art-naive normal subjects to remember. Then, the same 24 targets were combined with an equal number of decoys into one series of trials in which single pictures were flashed quickly either left or right of a fixation point. The task was to indicate by pressing a button whether the picture on the screen was seen before or not, and both accuracy and reaction time were measured.

The results revealed a dramatic pattern. Visual field of stimulation interacted statistically with type of painting so that surrealistic ones were remembered significantly faster and better in the right visual half-field, the left hemisphere, while there was no difference between the two half-fields on the realistic paintings. Moreover, within the right visual half-field surrealistic paintings were remembered better than realistic ones. No such dissociation was seen in the left visual half-field.

Art and brain These results not only show that 'art' cannot be viewed as a single entity as far as hemispheric specialization is concerned, it also cannot be viewed as a right hemisphere function alone, something that has been suggested in the non-scientific literature. Instead, they show that art is multifaceted and, at least in the mind of the observer, has a left hemisphere component or a right hemisphere component. More importantly, with regard to the hemispheric organization of knowledge, the fact that there was a left hemisphere superiority for the surrealistic paintings but no hemispheric difference for realistic paintings suggests asymmetries in interpreting perceptual reality.

In sum By now, several experiments in my laboratory have led to the following conceptualization of differential hemispheric representation of long-term memory: the left is not sensitive to familiarity, it provides multiple possibilities for processing the environment, and is better suited than the right for processing *novel* aspects of reality whether in words or pictures. Conversely, the right can provide quick effective processing strategies for common, familiar stereotypical stimuli. They complement each other with the one, the left hemisphere, providing cognitive processes that process the new in reality, and the other, the right hemisphere, providing stability by processing that which is already known. These dual representations may exist in all of us and which one dominates in a given circumstance depends on the task, the context and on our own internal state.

Further reading

Segalowitz, S. J. (1983) *Two Sides of the Brain: Brain Lateralization Explored.* Englewood Cliffs, NJ: Prentice-Hall.

Trevarthen, C. (ed.) (1990) *Brain Circuits and Functions of the Mind.* Cambridge: Cambridge University Press.
Zaidel, E. (1990) Language functions in the two hemispheres following complete commissurotomy and hemispherectomy. In R. D. Nebes and S. Corkin (eds), *Handbook of Neuropsychology.* Amsterdam: Elsevier.

References

Bogen, J. E. (1969) The other side of the brain. I: Dysgraphia and dyscopia following cerebral commissurotomy. *Bulletin of the Los Angeles Neurological Society,* 34, 73–105.
Bogen, J. E. (1976) Language function in the short term following cerebral commissurotomy. In A. Avakian-Whitaker and H. A. Whitaker (eds) *Current Trends in Neurolinguistics.* New York: Academic Press.
Bogen, J. E. (1990) Partial hemispheric independence with the neocommissures intact. In C. Trevarthen (ed.) *Brain Circuits and Functions of the Mind.* Cambridge: Cambridge University Press.
Bogen, J. E. and Gazzaniga, M. S. (1965) Cerebral commissurotomy in man: minor hemisphere dominance for certain visuospatial functions. *Journal of Neurosurgery,* 23, 394–9.
Bogen, J. E. and Vogel, P. J. (1962) Cerebral commissurotomy in man. *Bulletin of the Los Angeles Neurological Society,* 27, 269–72.
De Renzi, E. (1982) *Disorders of Space Exploration and Cognition.* New York: Wiley.
Glick, S. (ed.) (1985) *Cerebral Lateralization in Nonhuman Species.* New York: Academic Press.
Hecaen, H. and Albert, M. L. (1978) *Human Neuropsychology.* New York: Wiley.
Huppert, E. A. (1981) Memory in split-brain patients: a comparison with organic amnesic syndromes. *Cortex,* 17, 303–12.
Levy, J. (1974) Psychological implications of bilateral asymmetry. In Dimond S. J. and Beaumont, J. G. (eds) *Hemispheric Function in the Human Brain.* London: Elek Science.
Levy, J. (1990) Regulation and generation of perception in the asymmetric brain. In C. Trevarthen (ed.) *Brain Circuits and Functions of the Mind.* Cambridge: Cambridge University Press.
Milner, B. (1958) Psychological defects produced by temporal lobe excision. *Proceedings of the Association for Research of Nervous and Mental Diseases (ARNMD),* 36, 244–57.
Milner, B. (1980) Complementary functional specializations of the human cerebral hemispheres. In R. Levi-Montalcini (ed.) *Nerve Cells, Transmitters and Behavior.* Rome: Pontifica Academia Scientarium.
Nebes, R. D. (1974) Hemispheric specialization in commissurotomized man. *Psychological Bulletin,* 81, 1–14.
Nebes, R. D. (1990) The commissurotomized brain: introduction. In R. D. Nebes and S. Corkin (eds) *Handbook of Neurpspychology.* Amsterdam: Elsevier.

Newcombe, F. and Ratcliff, G. (1975) Agnosia: a disorder of object recognition. In F. Michel and B. Schott (eds) *Les Syndromes de Disconnexion calleuse chez l'Homme*. Lyon: Hôpital Neurologique de Lyon.

Paterson, A. and Zangwill, O. L. (1944) Disorders of visual space perception associated with lesions of the right cerebral hemisphere. *Brain*, 67, 331–58.

Plourde, G. and Sperry, R. W. (1982) Left hemisphere involvement in left spatial neglect from right-sided lesions: a commissurotomy study. *Brain*, 107, 95–106.

Preilowski, B. F. B. (1972) Possible contribution of the anterior forebrain commissures to bilateral motor coordination. *Neuropsychologia*, 10, 267–77.

Sperry, R. W. (1961) Cerebral organization and behavior. *Science*, 133, 1749–57.

Sperry, R. W. (1974) Lateral specialization in the surgically separated hemispheres. In F. O. Schmitt and F. G. Worden (eds) *The Neurosciences Third Study Program*. Cambridge, Mass.: MIT Press.

Sperry, R. W. (1990) Forebrain commissurotomy and conscious awareness. In C. Trevarthen (ed.) *Brain Circuits and Functions of the Mind*. Cambridge: Cambridge University Press.

Sperry, R. W., Gazzaniga, M. S. and Bogen, J. E. (1969) Interhemispheric relationships: the neocortical commissures; syndromes of hemispheric disconnection. In P. J. Vinken and G. W. Bruyn (eds) *Handbook of Clinical Neurology*. Amsterdam: North-Holland.

Sperry, R. W. and Stamm, J. S. (1957) Function of corpus callosum in contralateral transfer of somesthetic discrimination in cats. *Journal of Comparative and Physiological Psychology*, 50, 138–43.

Sperry, R. W., Zaidel, E. and Zaidel, D. W. (1979) Self-recognition and social awareness in the deconnected minor hemisphere. *Neuropsychologia*, 17, 153–66.

Warrington, E. K. (1975) The selective impairment of semantic memory. *Quarterly Journal of Experimental Psychology*, 27, 635–57.

Zaidel, D. W. (1983) Specialized hemispheric retrieval from long-term semantic memory: convergent evidence from normal and commissurotomy subjects. *Society for Neuroscience Abstracts*, 9, 527.

Zaidel, D. W. (1986) Memory for scenes in stroke patients: hemispheric processing of semantic organization in pictures. *Brain*, 109, 547–60.

Zaidel, D. W. (1987) Hemispheric asymmetry in long-term semantic relationships. *Cognitive Neuropsychology*, 4, 321–32.

Zaidel, D. W. (1988) Hemi-field asymmetries in memory for incongruous scenes. *Cortex*, 24, 231–44.

Zaidel, D. W. (1990a) Memory and spatial cognition following commissurotomy. In F. Boller (ed.) *Handbook of Neuropsychology*. Amsterdam: Elsevier.

Zaidel, D. W. (1990b) Long-term semantic memory in the two cerebral hemispheres. In C. B. Trevarthen (ed.) *Brain Circuits and Functions of the Mind: Essays in Honor of Roger Sperry*. Cambridge: Cambridge University Press.

Zaidel, D. W. and Frederick, K. (1988) Hemispheric asymmetries in logical categories: convergent evidence from normal and split-brain subjects. *Society for Neurosicence Abstracts*, 14, 1138.

Zaidel, D. W. and Kasher, A. (1989) Hemispheric memory for surrealistic versus realistic paintings. *Cortex*, 25, 617–41.

Zaidel, D. and Sperry, R. W. (1973) Performance on the Raven's Colored Progressive Matrices Test by subjects with cerebral commissurotomy. *Cortex*, 9, 34–39.

Zaidel, D. and Sperry, R. W. (1974) Memory impairment after commissurotomy in man. *Brain*, 97, 263–72.

Zaidel, D. W. and Sperry, R. W. (1977) Some long-term motor effects following commissurotomy in man. *Neuropsychologia*, 15, 193–204.

Zaidel, E. (1977) Unilateral auditory language comprehension on the token test following cerebral commissurotomy and hemispherectomy. *Neurospychologia*, 15, 1–18.

Zaidel, E. (1978) Concepts of cerebral dominance in the split brain. In Buser, P. A. (ed.) *Cerebral Correlates of Conscious Experience*, pp. 263–84. Amsterdam: Elsevier North Holland Biomedical Press.

Zaidel, E. (1979) Performance on the ITPA following cerebral commissurotomy and hemispherectomy. *Neuropsychologia*, 17, 259–80.

Zaidel, E. (1987) Hemispheric monitoring. In D. Ottoson (ed.) *Duality and Unity of the Brain*. New York: Macmillan Press.

Glossary

agnosia   Impairment or inability to recognize events or objects.

agraphia   An impairment or loss of the ability to write words or letter strings.

alphabetic stage   A posited second stage in learning to read in which children begin to understand the relationship between graphemes and phonemes reliably. This enables them to decode words phonetically.

amnesia   A partial or total inability to remember.

angular gyrus   A gyrus, or convolution of the cortex, in the parietal lobe. The left angular gyrus is important for language functions.

anomia   A difficulty in retrieving words, particularly those naming objects.

anomic aphasia   An impairment in which word-retrieval difficulties occur as a relatively selective deficit in the context of normal sentence formation.

anterograde amnesia   The inability to recall or recognize events which have occurred since the onset of the amnesic condition.

aphasia   Impairment of language abilities. In British usage aphasia implies a more widespread and profound deficit than dysphasia.

apraxia   Loss of intentional movement which may occur in the absence of paralysis or impairment by sensory or motor functions.

auditory lexicon   A set of recognition units for individual spoken words. If the incoming acoustic code is one for a familiar word it will activate its particular recognition unit.

autism   A developmental disorder whose features include a lack of interest in other people, various language abnormalities and an intense desire to preserve sameness in the environment. It shows in childhood.

autobiographical memory   *See* episodic memory.

commissure   A bundle of fibres connecting corresponding parts on the two sides of the brain.

commissurotomy   Surgical disconnection of the two hemispheres by sectioning the corpus callosum (the cerebral commissures).

corpus callosum   The large sets of axons that connect the left and right hemispheres of the cerebral cortex.

cortical blindness   Visual loss following damage to the occipital lobe, even though the peripheral visual system (the retina, optic nerve and subcortical structures) is intact.

CT scan   Computerized tomography. An X-ray based procedure in which a computer draws a map from the measured densities of the brain.

diencephalon   The posterior part of the forebrain, including the thalamus and hypothalamus.

double dissociation   When a patient is impaired in one ability but not in a second, and another patient is impaired in the second ability but not in the first. This implies that the two abilities are mediated by different modules since they can be independently disrupted.

dysarthria   Difficulty in speech productions caused by motor impairments of the speech apparatus (the cortical control of the tongue, larynx and mouth).

dyslexia   A group of disorders manifested by difficulty in reading. In the USA dyslexia implies developmental reading disorder, while alexia is the term often reserved for reading problems subsequent to brain damage in literate adults.

dysphasia   A specific language impairment in speaking or understanding speech.

dyspraxia   The loss of intentional movements associated with speech production. It may be less profound than apraxia and may involve errors in action rather than action loss.

echolalia   The repetition of other people's words, phrases or sentences verbatim.

egocentrism   The inability of a person to perceive situations from the perspective of others.

electroencephalography   (EEG). Electrical brain potentials recorded by placing electrodes on the scalp.

episodic memory   An internal store of personal experiences and events which are tied to a specific context; it is autobiographical in nature.

face recognition unit   Recognition units containing stored representations of particular faces. A familiar face will activate its particular recognition unit.

forebrain   The most anterior part of the brain, including the cerebral cortex and other structures.

frontal lobes   The most frontal of the cortical lobes: there is one on the left and one on the right.

gestalt processes   Where pattern recognition processes are thought to depend on the relations among the elements of a stimulus, rather than on its component features.

graphemes   Individual elements of writing: single letters in English can be graphemes, but so, too, can larger units of writing, such as SH or TT, when they map onto specific phonemes.

hemianopia   Loss of vision in the left or right visual field. It can affect one eye or both eyes.

hemiparesis   Muscular weakness affecting one side of the body.

hippocampus   A large forebrain structure situated between the thalamus and the cortex.

infarct   An area of tissue that dies because of impaired blood supply to it.

Korsakoff's disease   A medical condition including memory deficits and other disorders caused by a thiamine disorder; usually secondary to chronic alcoholism.

lexical agraphia (surface agraphia)   Loss of the ability to retrieve word-specific spelling patterns, which consequently means reliance on the phoneme to grapheme conversion system when trying to spell.

limbic system   A set of subcortical structures in the forebrain, including the hypothalamus, hippocampus, amygdala, and parts of the thalamus and cerebral cortex.

lobectomy   Surgical removal of a lobe of the brain.

logogen model   A model of the processes involved in word recognition in which each logogen, or word recognition unit, has a threshold which determines the amount of activation which must be present in that logogen before it will 'fire' and provide access to the word's meaning and pronunciation.

logographic phase   A posited stage in learning to read in which children appear to encode the words to be remembered in terms of idiosyncratic salient visual features, such as particular letter shapes.

metamemory   The faculty of knowing what we know and knowing about our memories.

mind-blindness   A lack of awareness of the mental states of others. The world appears to be viewed purely in physical terms. Autists may be mind-blind.

modularity   The belief that mental faculties are composed of distinct components or modules. These modules are thought to be relatively independent of each other in their functions, so damage to one module does not directly affect the functioning of other modules.

morphemes   Meaningful units of language that are larger than the phoneme but smaller than the word. Morphemes carry meaning but in a variety of ways: they can be affixes, like -ing or de- or -er, which may serve a grammatical purpose (inflexions), or a semantic one (derivations). They can be root-morphemes which form the bases to which affixes adhere (-here in adhere is a root morpheme).

occipital lobe   The most posterior of the four lobes of the cerebral cortex. There are right and left occipital lobes.

oral dyspraxia   Loss of intentional oral and thoracic movements.

orthographic stage   The final posited stage in learning to read in which the skilled reader can reliably use the large visual segments in a word (e.g. embedded words, morphemes, etc.) in order to assemble a candidate pronunciation as a phonemic form.

parietal lobe   The lobe of the cerebral cortex which lies between the occipital and frontal lobes. There are two; one on the left and one on the right.

person identity node   Nodes containing semantic representations of particular individuals. These representations provide detailed information about the person's occupation or about prior associations with them.

phenomenological   Concerned with subjective experience. The individual's personal view of the world and interpretation of events.

phonemes   The minimal meaning unit of spoken language. In English the sounds 'r' and 'l' are different phonemes because 'row' and 'low' mean different things. In other languages this phonemic contrast may be absent, just as, in English, we fail to distinguish the 'p-sound' in 'pea' from that in 'hip' – though they are different.

phonological agraphia   Loss of the ability to spell by phoneme to grapheme conversion which consequently means spelling is dependent on the established spelling vocabulary.

prosopagnosia   Difficulty in recognising familiar faces while the ability to recognize objects is relatively unimpaired.

retrograde amnesia   The inability to recall information about events which occurred prior to the onset of the amnesic condition.

schema   A high level mental representation which encapsulates knowledge about everything connected with a class of objects and events.

semantic memory   A store of general world knowledge which has been abstracted from individual experience. It is not dependent on individualized, specific context as is episodic memory.

spatial agnosia   An inability to recognize spatial relationships between objects in the environment.

spatial frequency   Changes in light energy per unit distance. This metric is useful for describing properties of a visual scene in physical (optical) terms.

speech output lexicon   A hypothesised internal word-store from which spoken word forms are retrieved for speech production.

spelling lexicon   A hypothesised internal store from which the correct spelling of a word can be retrieved.

split-brain patients   Patients whose chronic epilepsy has been treated surgically by cutting the major commissures between the two cerebral hemispheres.

surface dysgraphia   *See* lexical agraphia.

surface dyslexia   An inability to read words correctly on the basis of their visual appearance, while still possessing the ability to read phonemically: surface dyslexics can read nonwords like 'filk' but not irregularly spelled words like 'yacht'.

sylvian fissure   A groove on the surface of the cerebral cortex separating the temporal and parietal lobes.

temporal lobe   The lateral lobe of the cerebral cortex. There is one on the right and one on the left.

topographical memory   An internal material-specific store of information used in the recall or recognition of routes and buildings.

verbal dyspraxia   Loss of intentional movements associated with speech production in conjunction with more extensive language problems.

visual agnosia   Impairment or inability to recognize objects presented to vision.

Author Index

Aaron, P. G., 115
Abel, G. L., 38, 45
Adams, R. D., 237, 252
Albert, M. L., 154, 160, 257, 273
Albert, M. S., 244, 249, 250, 251, 252
Allport, D. A., 136, 148, 154, 160
Antin, S. P., 251, 252
Apkarian-Stielan, P., 37, 44
Aram, D. M., 97
Auger, E., 82

Baddeley, A. D., 242, 248, 252
Baker, E., 51, 60
Baraitser, M., 82
Baron-Cohen, S., 23
Basso, A., 190, 197
Baxter, D. M., 141, 148
Beauvois, M. F., 141, 148
Bellugi, U., 215
Benson, D. F., 251, 252
Benton, A. L., 206, 208, 215, 226, 232
Berndt, R., 138, 149

Bertelson, P., 38, 45
Biederman, I., 44
Biller, J., 238, 252
Bishop, D. V. M., 7, 9
Bisiacchi, P., 176
Bisiach, E., 190, 197
Bloom, P., 83
Bodamer, J., 200, 205, 215
Bogen, J. E., 256, 257, 260, 261, 264, 273, 274
Bowlby, M., 117
Bradley, L., 38, 40, 44, 94, 98, 115, 116
Bramwell, B., 118, 133
Bridgeman, E., 95, 98
Bruce, V., 204, 206, 215, 220, 222, 224, 225, 232, 233
Bryant, P., 38, 44, 94, 98, 115, 116
Bub, D., 142, 148
Butters, N., 244, 249, 250, 251, 252
Butterworth, B., 116
Byng, S., 116

Caffarra, P., 239, 248, 250, 251, 252
Campbell, R., 58, 60, 116, 225, 228, 233
Caplan, L. R., 238, 252
Caramazza, A., 138, 141, 149
Carey, P., 154, 160
Carr, T. H., 44
Chapman, E. K., 44
Clahsen, H., 82
Cohen, D., 23
Cohen, J. J., 246, 254
Cohen, N. J., 244, 246, 249, 250, 252, 253
Collins, A. M., 153, 160
Coltheart, M., 116, 126, 133, 136, 142, 146, 149, 182, 197, 232, 233
Conners, F., 116
Corkin, S., 246, 248, 249, 253
Cowey, A., 228, 233
Crago, M., 82
Crary, M. A., 97
Crowell, G. F., 238, 252
Curtiss, S., 81, 83

Davidoff, J. B., 153, 160
De Haan, E. D. F., 225, 233
De Renzi, E., 257, 263, 273
de Schonen, S., 226, 233
Denes, G., 176
Derousne, J., 141, 148
Desberg, P., 38, 42, 45, 116
Diedrich, W. M., 85, 98
Diesfeldt, H. F. A., 153, 160
Diringer, D., 34, 44
Dodd, B., 58, 60
Dunn, L. M., 182, 197

Edwards, M., 84, 98
Ehri, L., 115, 116
Ekelman, B. L., 97
Elder, L., 39, 46
Ellis, A. W., 136, 138, 148, 149, 176, 215, 233, 234, 236
Eysenck, M., 177

Farah, M. J., 159, 160
Fein, D., 8, 9
Fisher, C. M., 237, 238, 251, 252
Fodor, J., 3, 9, 235, 236
Foulke, E., 38, 44
Fraiberg, S., 35, 43, 44
Franklin, S., 118, 123, 133, 138, 148, 233
Frederick, K., 271, 274
Fredman, G., 117
Friedman, M., 38, 42, 45, 116
Friedman, R., 118, 133
Frith, C. D., 116
Frith, U., 23, 38, 44, 116, 117
Fulker, D., 116
Funnell, E., 136, 149

Gallassi, R., 239, 248, 250, 252
Galper, R. E., 229, 233
Gardner, J., 179, 180, 182, 187, 191, 198
Garnham, A., 115, 116
Garwood, J., 233
Gazzaniga, M. S., 257, 264, 273, 274
Geschwind, N., 251, 252
Giusteolisi, L., 138, 149
Glick, S., 256, 273
Goldberg, E., 251, 252
Goldstein, M., 118, 133
Goodglass, H., 51, 60, 154, 160, 181, 191, 197
Goodman, R. A., 141, 149
Gopnik, M., 81, 82
Gordon, N., 97
Goswami, U., 115, 116
Goulandris, N., 116, 117
Graham, A., 117
Graham, F., 82
Grodzinsky, Y., 82
Grossi, D., 178, 198
Growden, J. H., 246, 253
Grunwell, P., 85, 98
Guyette, T. W., 85, 98

Hall, A. D., 38, 44
Hamsher, K., 206, 208, 215

Hatfield, F. M., 141, 149
Hatlen, P. H., 38, 45
Heath, P., 251, 253
Hecaen, H., 257, 273
Heilman, K. M., 141, 149
Hermelin, B., 37, 38, 45
Heywood, C., 228, 233
Hinde, R. A., 35, 44
Hinge, H. H., 238, 252
Hirst, W., 247, 249, 252
Hobson, R. P., 35, 44
Hodges, J. R., 238, 244, 245, 251, 252
Holgate, D., 159, 160
Howard, D., 118, 133, 233
Howell, P., 117
Howes, D., 136, 149
Huey, E. B., 37, 44
Hughes, J. E. O., 251, 252
Hulme, C., 115, 116, 117
Humphreys, G. W., 8, 9, 27, 45, 136, 149, 177, 220, 233
Huppert, F. A., 263, 273
Hurst, J. A., 82

Ingham, R. J., 85, 98

James, K. J., 154, 160
Jensen, T. S., 238, 252
Johnson, M., 226, 233
Judd, T., 179, 180, 182, 187, 191, 198

Kanner, L., 13, 23
Kaplan, E., 181, 191, 197
Kapur, N., 251, 253
Kasher, A., 271, 275
Kay, J., 126, 133, 136, 138, 142, 146, 148, 149
Keane, M. T., 177
Kelly, M. P., 239, 248, 254
Kennedy, J. M., 27, 45
Kennedy, P., 251, 253
Kertesz, A., 142, 148
Kjaer, M., 238, 252
Klein, B., 154, 160
Kohn, S., 118, 133

Kolb, B., 9
Koller, W., 239, 248, 254
Kritchevsky, M., 215, 253
Kuse, A. R., 207, 215

Landis, T., 228, 233, 239, 248, 250, 251, 253
Lansdell, H., 208, 215
Leonard, L. B., 82
Leslie, A. M., 23
Lesser, R., 126, 133, 142, 146, 149
Levin, J., 244, 249, 251
Levy, B. A., 44
Levy, J., 257, 268, 269, 273
Lewis, V., 43, 45
Livingstone, M. S., 166, 177
Loftus, E. F., 153, 160
Logan, W., 238, 253
Loomis, J. M. A., 37, 44
Lorusso, S., 239, 248, 250, 252
Lovegrove, W. 116
Lowenfeld, B., 38, 45
Luzzatti, C., 190, 197

McCarthy, R., 153, 160, 177
McConachie, H. R., 217, 233
McHenry, L. C., 238, 252
McKinlay, I., 97
McLoughlin, V., 117
Markham, B., 234, 236
Markowitsch, H. J., 253
Marquardsen, J., 238, 252
Marr, D., 27, 45, 165, 177, 204, 215
Marsh, G., 38, 42, 45, 116
Marshall, J. C., 232, 233
Martin, F., 116
Masterson, J., 116
Mathivet, E., 226, 233
Mattis, S., 251, 252
Mazzucchi, A., 239, 248, 250, 251, 252
Mesulam, M. M., 243, 253
Metter, E. J., 238, 253
Meudell, P., 251, 253
Miceli, G., 138, 149

Millar, S.,   38, 45
Miller, D.,   148, 149
Miller, J. W.,   238, 253
Millikan, C. H.,   238, 253
Mills, A. E.,   35, 45
Milner, B.,   243, 248, 249, 253,
    269, 273
Modafferi, A.,   178, 198
Moretti, G.,   239, 248, 250, 251,
    252
Morley, M.,   84, 98
Morton, J.,   132, 133, 224, 233
Mousty, P.,   38, 45
Muma, D.,   51, 54, 60
Muma, J.,   51, 54, 60
Myklebust, H.,   60

Nebes, R. D.,   257, 268, 273
Newcombe, F.,   269, 274
Newman, S. E.,   38, 44
Nielsen, J. M.,   154, 160
Norell, S.,   82

O'Connor, N.,   37, 38, 45
Oakhill, J.,   115, 116
Obler, L. K.,   8, 9
Olivarious, B. de F.,   238, 252
Olson, R.,   116
Orsini, A.,   178, 198
Osterreith, P.,   244, 253
Oxbury, J. M.,   247, 253
Oxbury, S. M.,   247, 253

Pantilie, D.   182, 197
Parkin, A. J.,   247, 249, 253
Parma, M.,   239, 248, 250, 251,
    252
Paterson, A.,   257, 274
Pathak, K.,   27, 45
Patterson, K. E.,   141, 148, 149,
    224, 232, 233
Pennington, B. F.,   115, 116
Perin, D.,   91, 98
Peterson, R. C.,   238, 253
Phillips, R.,   229, 233
Pinker, S.,   83
Plourde, G.,   257, 274

Potts, C. S.,   135, 149
Preilowski, B. F. B.,   257, 274
Pring, L.,   27, 28, 29, 37, 41, 42,
    45, 116
Prior, M.,   116

Quinlan, P. T.,   45

Rack, J.,   116
Ratcliff, G.,   269, 274
Regard, M.,   228, 233, 239, 248,
    250, 251, 253
Reynell, J.,   86, 98
Ribot, T.,   250, 253
Riddoch, J.,   116
Riddoch, M. J.,   8, 9, 27, 45, 136,
    149, 177
Robson, J.,   7, 9
Rochford, G.,.   136, 149
Roeltgen, D. P.,   141, 149
Rosch, E.,   153, 160
Rosenthal, J.,   85, 98
Ross, R.,   81, 83
Russell, W. R.,   251, 253
Rusted, J.,   27, 28, 45
Rutter, M.,   115, 117

Sacks, O.,   3, 9, 56, 57, 60
Sagar, H. J.,   246, 253
Scraggs, D. G.,   140, 149
Segalowitz, S. J.,   272
Semenza, C.,   133, 176
Seymour, P. H. K.,   38, 39, 46,
    115, 116
Shallice, T.,   4, 7, 9, 141, 142,
    149, 153, 154, 160, 177
Sherman, D. G.,   238, 253
Shewell, C.,   148, 149
Shimamura, A. P.,   247, 253
Sin, G.,   148, 149
Slaghuis, W.,   116
Smith, M. L.,   243, 248, 253
Snowling, M. J.,   41, 45, 95, 98,
    115, 116, 117
Sperry, R. W.,   256, 257, 263, 265,
    266, 268, 274, 275
Spreen, O.,   208, 215

Squire, L. R.,   244, 246, 247, 249, 250, 252, 253, 254
Stackhouse, J.,   94, 95, 97, 98
Stamm, J. S.,   257, 274
Stevenson, J.,   117
Stiles-Davis, J.,   215
Stone, J. M.,   44
Stracciari, A.,   239, 248, 250, 252
Strang, B. M. H.,   140, 149
Stump, D. A.,   238, 252
Sullivan, E. V.,   246, 253

Tager-Flusberg, H.,   23
Tallal, P.,   81, 83
Temple, C. M.,   215
Teuber, H. L.,   248, 249, 253
Tomblin, J. B.,   82, 83
Toole, J. F.,   238, 252
Torgesen, J.,   117
Trevarthen, C.,   273

Valentine, T.,   225, 233
van Allen, M. W.,   226, 232
van Sommers, P.,   178, 179, 180, 193, 198
Vandenburg, S. G.,   207, 215
Varney, N. R.,   206, 208, 215
Vogel, P. J.,   256, 273

Wagenar, R.,   117
Wapner, W.,   179, 180, 182, 187, 191, 198
Ward, C. D.,   238, 244, 245, 251, 252

Warlow, C. P.,   238, 252
Warrington, E. K.,   141, 148, 153, 154, 155, 160, 177, 209, 215, 233, 242, 248, 252, 257, 269, 274
Weintraub, S.,   181, 197, 243, 253
Weiskrantz, L.,   249, 254
Welch, V.,   38, 42, 45, 116
Wells, B.,   97
Whetton, C.,   182, 197
Whishaw, I. Q.,   9
Williams, M.,   136, 149
Williams, R.,   85, 98
Wilson, R. S.,   239, 248, 254
Wise, B.,   116
Wyke, M.,   159, 160

Yamadori, A.,   154, 160
Yanagihara, T.,   238, 253
Yin, R.,   229, 233
Young, A. W.,   176, 204, 206, 215, 222, 233, 234, 236
Yule, W.,   115, 117

Zaidel, D. W.,   256, 257, 261, 265, 268, 269, 271, 274, 275
Zaidel, E.,   257, 268, 273, 274, 275
Zangwill, O. L.,   257, 274
Zettin, M.,   133
Ziehl, F.,   118, 133
Zingeser, L. B.,   138, 149
Zola-Morgan, S.,   246, 254
Zouzounis, J. A.,   253

Patient Index

AB   An adult woman who has experienced difficulty   216–36
throughout her life in recognizing people's faces.

Becky   A young blind girl who is learning to read Braille.   24–46

David   A young dyslexic boy whose impaired visual   99–117
memory and perceptual weaknesses led to
difficulties with both reading and spelling.

Dennis   An adult man whose brain damage has led to a   161–77
profound impairment in visual recognition.

Derek   A dysphasic adult who, following a stroke, cannot   118–33
comprehend the meaning of abstract words.

ES   An adult man who experienced global amnesia for   237–54
a relatively short period.

EST   An anomic adult man who, in addition to a   134–49
profound naming disorder, has difficulties in
reading and spelling.

James   An adult man who, because of severe epilepsy, had   255–75
his left and right cerebral hemispheres surgically
separated.

Jane   A young autistic girl who appears to view the   11–23
world in purely physical terms.

Keith	A young dyspraxic boy whose impaired speech production affected other areas of his development such as literacy skills.	84–98
LV	An adult man who experienced global amnesia for a relatively short period.	237–54
Margaret	A young girl who, despite her profound hearing loss, has exceptional spoken and written abilities.	47–60
MH	An agnosic artist whose access to visual and graphic knowledge appears to be limited to just one type of input.	178–98
NB	A young woman whose brain damage has led to impaired visual and functional knowledge.	150–60
Paul	A young boy who appears to lack the ability to use grammatical structures in understanding and producing language.	61–83
Dr. S.	An adult woman who has experienced difficulty throughout her life in recognizing people's faces.	199–215
Sally	A young blind girl who has exceptional drawing abilities.	24–46
Stephen	A young dyslexic boy whose impaired visual and phonological abilities led to difficulties with both reading and spelling.	99–117

Subject Index

agnosia 150–60
  and graphic processing 8,
    178–98
alphabetic phase 38, 40, 41, 113,
  114
amnesia 206, 263
  see also Transient Global
    Amnesia
angular gyrus 1
anomia 133, 135, 181–3
anomic aphasia 6, 134–49
  and lexical agraphia 139–49
anterograde amnesia
  and short-term memory 242–3
  and long-term memory 243–4
  memory-stores,
    dissociations 247–8
aphasia 63, 217
  see also dysphasia
apraxia 217
  see also developmental verbal
    dyspraxia
auditory comprehension
  model of 122–4

and word repetition 124,
  128–30
auditory memory 94
autism 5, 9, 11–23, 35
  and IQ 14
  and face recognition 14–15
  and egocentrism 15–20
  and mind-blindness 21–3
autobiographical memory 151,
  267–68
  see also retrograde amnesia

blindness 5, 24–46
  perceptual v. semantic
    processes 33–4, 41–3
  reading by Braille 36–42
  tactual object recognition 26–34
Braille *see* reading by Braille

cascade processes 28
categories 153–4
  animate v. inanimate 154–60,
    170–1, 172, 221
  cuing 29, 34, 42

faces v. objects 211
in word comprehension 125–7, 133
commissurotomy *see* split-brain.
conspecific detection 226, 227, 230–1
corpus callosum 5, 256, 257, 259, 260, 265
cortical blindness 8, 162
CT scan 119, 134, 150, 180, 241
cued speech 47

deafness 4, 7, 47–60
  cognitive strategies 54–5, 56
  iconic v. semantic processes 53, 56, 58
  rule abstraction 52
  semantic organization 53–4, 56, 58
  linguistic knowledge 55–6

developmental dyslexia 5, 6, 99–117, 199
  v. acquired dyslexia 114–15
  phonic strategy, reading 101–2, 104, 109
  phonic strategy, spelling 102–3, 104–6, 109–11, 112
  theories of 111–15
  and verbal memory 101, 107, 112
  and visual memory 101, 107, 110, 112, 113, 114
  and visual perception 100, 101, 102, 107, 112, 113
developmental dysphasia 4, 6–7, 61–83
  and genetic influences 72–81
  grammatical deficits 63–81
  syntax 69–70, 81
developmental prosopagnosia 6, 199–215, 216–36
  v. acquired disorder 233–6
  conspecific detection 226, 227, 230–1
  covert recognition 225–6
  face recognition units 204, 206,

209, 210, 224–5
  feature-by-feature analysis 226, 227, 230–1
  and object recognition 210–11, 217–19, 220–1, 226
  person identity nodes 205, 206, 209–10, 213, 224–5, 226, 235
  structural encoding 204, 205, 207–9, 210, 223, 224, 226, 228–9, 235
  and visual memory 211–12
  and visual perception 206, 207, 217–19, 219
developmental v. acquired disorders 4–6, 84–5, 114–15, 233–6
developmental verbal dyspraxia 5, 7, 84–98
  v. acquired dyspraxia 84–5
  defining characteristics 84–5, 92–7
  and reading 89, 90, 91, 95
  and spelling 7–8, 89, 90, 91, 95
diencephalon 247, 248, 249
divided visual field studies 270–2
double dissociation 4, 142
drawing *see* graphic processing
dysarthria 150
dysphasia 118–33
  word-form deafness 118, 123
  word-meaning deafness 118, 123, 125–33
  word-sound deafness 118, 123, 124–5
dyslexia 2, 94, 114
dyspraxia 84

echolalia 35
egocentrism
  conceptual-perspective 16–20
  visual-perspective 15–16
electroencephalography 217, 241
episodic memory 266

face recognition 173
  and autism 14–15
  model of 204–6, 221–3

face recognition (*cont'd*)
  see also developmental
    prosopagnosia
face recognition units   204, 206,
  209, 210, 224–5
feature-by-feature analysis   226,
  227, 230–1
figure-ground separation   167
frontal lobe   162, 174

genetic influences   7, 72–81, 107,
  226, 231
Gestalt   208, 268, 269
grammatical structures   4, 5
  plurality   52, 63–7, 71, 73–5, 87
  progressive-aspect   68–9, 71
  subject-pronoun omission   69,
    71
  syntax   69–70, 81, 87, 89, 94,
    107
  tense   67–8, 71, 73, 75–7
graphemes   40
graphic processing
  agnosia   178–98
  model of   179–80
  visual agnosia   163, 167–71
  without sight   26–34

handedness   85, 94, 201, 217
hemianopia   162, 163
hemiparesis   162
hemisphere specialization   38, 217,
  219, 220, 243, 248, 255–75
hippocampus   247
homophones   104, 112

iconic processes/memory   53, 193,
  197
imagery   27, 30, 154–5, 159, 191
individual differences   4, 7, 47–60,
  94, 96

Korsakoffs disease   248, 249

lexical agraphia   6, 139–49, 175
limbic system   247, 248
lip-reading   55–6, 57–8, 204, 223

lobectomy   162, 249
logogen model   132–3, 224
logographic phase   38, 39, 40, 113,
  114

Marr's theory, visual
  perception   27, 165, 204, 207,
    220
mental rotation   174, 207, 208,
  220
metamemory   247
mind-blindness   21–3
models
  auditory comprehension   122–4
  face recognition   204–6, 221–3
  graphic processing   179–80
  logogen model   132–3, 224
  spelling   140–1
  visual object recognition   27–8
  word retrieval   137
modular view   3–4, 5, 154, 165–6,
  167
morphemes   47, 102

naming disorders   *see* anomic
  aphasia

object-centred description   166,
  204, 207, 221, 226, 229, 235
occipital lobe   8, 150, 162, 163
oral dyspraxia   86
orthographic phase   39, 113, 114
orthographies   38, 56

person identity node   205, 206,
  209–10, 213, 224–5, 226, 235
phonemes   38, 40, 101
phonological agraphia   142
plasticity   199, 234, 235
plurality   52, 63–7, 71, 73–5, 87
primal sketch   204
progressive aspect   68–9, 71
prosopagnosia   200, 204, 205–6,
  217–18, 234

reading
  context-dependent rules   41

model of 38–9, 113
by sight 38, 39, 113
by sound 38, 40–2, 57, 101–2,
  104, 109, 113
and speech-programming 89,
  90, 91, 95
reading by Braille 36–42
  Braille system 36–8
  letter recognition 39–40
  alphabetic phase 40–1
  and spelling 41
  and semantics 41–2
remote memory 151, 267–8
  see also retrograde amnesia
repetition
  of non-words 7, 138, 147
  in word comprehension 124,
    128–30
  in word-retrieval 138, 146
retrograde amnesia
  autobiographical memory 240,
    241–2, 246, 250
  remote memory 240, 242,
    244–6, 248–9, 250, 251
rule abstraction 52, 57, 63–72

schemata 58, 179, 180
semantic knowledge
  and faces 205, 206, 209–10,
    213, 224–5, 226, 235
  functional properties 166–7
  hemispheric asymmetry 256,
    265–72
  modality-specificity 127–8,
    132–3
  organization of 153
  and sensory knowledge 153–60,
    166–7, 171–2
  see also categories
sign languages 47–8, 52, 53, 55,
  58
  v. spoken language 56–7
single case studies 2–3
  and controls 6–8
spatial agnosia 263
spatial frequency 219
spatial memory 26, 32, 34, 243, 244

spelling
  lexical strategy 41, 106
  model of 140–1
  by sound 57, 102–3, 104–6,
    109–11, 112, 114–15, 140–8
  and speech programming 7–8,
    89, 90, 91, 95
  and spoken naming 142–8
split-brain 5, 9, 255–75
  and dreaming 262
  dual semantic system 256,
    265–72
  and memory 262, 263–4
  strange hand syndrome 264–5
structural descriptions 27, 29, 33,
  166, 167
structural encoding 204, 205,
  207–9, 210, 223, 224, 226,
  228–9, 235
subject-pronoun omission 69, 71
surface dysgraphia *see* lexical
  agraphia
surface dyslexia 2, 175
sylvian fissure 180
syntax 69–70, 81, 87, 89, 94, 107

tactual object recognition 28–34,
  265–6
task difficulty 7, 156–7
temporal lobe 134, 247, 248, 249
tense, grammatical 67–8, 71, 73,
  75–7
topographical memory 200, 211,
  217, 263–4
Transient Global Amnesia 6, 9,
  237–54
  anterograde amnesia 242–4,
    247–8
  preserved abilities 247
  recovery phase 251
  retrograde amnesia 244–6,
    247–51
  theories of 249–51

viewer-centred descriptions 204,
  207, 229, 235
visual agnosia 8, 161–77, 179,

180, 187, 191, 200, 204
category-specificity   170–1, 172
and remediation   173–4
and visual impairment   163–4,
   167
visual object knowledge   150–60,
   161–77, 178–98
and functional knowledge
   153–60, 166–7, 171–2
visual object recognition   33–4,
   161–77, 178–98, 220–1
model of   27–8

word-class effects
in reading   41, 104, 109, 175
in spelling   41, 110, 142, 143–6,
   175

word-form deafness   118, 123
word-form systems   132–3
word-frequency effects   136, 137,
   138, 143, 146
word-meaning deafness   118–33
category-specificity   125–7
covert comprehension   130–1
modality-specificity   127–8,
   132–3
Word-retrieval   27, 133, 134–49,
   181–3
frequency effects   136, 137, 138,
   143, 146
model of   137
repetition   138
Word-sound deafness   118, 123,
   124–5